"An excellent coverage of the theory and practice of the economic, social and environmental dimensions of sustainable development, aiming ultimately at improving happiness and wellbeing, characterizes this book. Peter Bartelmus helps us identify balanced inclusive green growth (BIGG) pathways to achieve sustainability in the twenty-first century. The book is a must-read for decision-makers, researchers and the concerned public."

Mohan Munasinghe, Munasinghe Institute for Development (MIND), shared the 2007 Nobel Prize for Peace (Vice Chair IPCC-AR4), Sri Lanka

"Peter Bartelmus is one of the most eminent global environmental scholars and his new book is proof of his status. His extraordinary experience and deep knowledge brings a very necessary insight into the complex issue of economic and social development constrained by planetary environmental processes. Is there any progress? Can we reliably assess it? These are the questions for which the book gives clear answers – answers that are the more useful today when we have the Global Sustainable Development Goals and badly need a good measuring stick to fathom their effectiveness."

Bedrich Moldan, Director of the Charles University Environment Center, Prague, First Minister of the Environment of the Czech Republic

"I recommend this book to all scientists, who see long-run environmental sustainability as the essential human project of our times. Peter Bartelmus is one of the leaders of the team that created the first 'Green Accounting' framework for the UN Statistical Office. Now he brings all of that background into a single *magnum opus*. Recognizing that policy without science and science without quantification are useless, Bartelmus asks 'are we better off today than we were 50 or 100 years ago?' and 'can we expect to be better off in the future?'"

Robert U. Ayres, Emeritus Professor of Economics, Political Science, Technology Management, INSEAD, France

"*Sustaining Prosperity, Nature and Wellbeing* is a pragmatic, hard-nosed overview of how our understanding of sustainability squares off with the notions of economic growth and the broader concepts of prosperity and wellbeing from the point of view of measurement. Peter's book is informed by his nearly unparalleled, decades-long scholarship in a perennially important field and a timely reminder that we still have much to do to make sure we apply what we already know about accounting for sustainability consistently in policy and practice."

László Pintér, Department of Environmental Sciences and Policy, Central European University (CEU), Hungary

"Peter Bartelmus' new book is a historic, contemporary and future oriented work on sustainable growth and development. It looks for objective answers, using well-defined concepts and indicators of economic prosperity, environmental quality, and 'greened' economic activity. The indicators tell that we know a great deal about economic prosperity, environmental integrity and damage, about green and dirty technology, while other aspects of wellbeing and policy making still lack systemic frameworks of measurement and evaluation. The author tries to open a thorough discourse between politicians, civil society and researchers who want to make us better off."

Udo E. Simonis, Professor of Environmental Policy at the Berlin Social Science Center (WZB), Germany

"Few people have a command of economic and environmental data and their integration equal to that of Peter Bartelmus. In this important new book, he draws on his extensive knowledge to assess the data on prosperity, nature and wellbeing, and its reliability as a foundation for policy."

Peter A. Victor, Professor Emeritus, York University, UK

"This comprehensive assessment of economic, environmental and wellbeing indicators provides an excellent basis for measuring how well present economic developments make us feel better off or not. The author concludes that the best way forward is internalizing measures of environmental damage and wellbeing into economic frameworks such as national accounting."

Jan W. van Tongeren, Ex-Chief National Accounting UNSD and Ex-Researcher Tilburg University, the Netherlands

SUSTAINING PROSPERITY, NATURE AND WELLBEING

This book explores what is needed for an overall evaluation of the prosperity and wellbeing of people within a framework of sustaining the economy, environment and development.

The book begins by assessing the validity of available data, indicators and indices in decision and policy making. It describes what the data tell us about the effects of economic activity on the quality of life and prosperity of people and nations, now and in the future, and highlights how a reliance on partial and distorted information can thwart rational policies. It also examines whether less tangible notions of wellbeing and happiness lend themselves to quantification and prediction. Overall, Bartelmus demonstrates the need for integrated accounting and analysis to revise policy priorities around environmental, social, economic and sustainability concerns.

Confronting the persisting polarization of environmentalists and economists, this book will be of great relevance to students, scholars and professionals with an interest in environmental and ecological economics, sustainability indicators and their use in integrative policy.

Peter Bartelmus is an honorary professor at the Bergische Universität Wuppertal, Germany. After his work in the United Nations, he taught economics of sustainable development at Wuppertal and Columbia (USA) universities.

SUSTAINING PROSPERITY, NATURE AND WELLBEING

What Do the Indicators Tell Us?

Peter Bartelmus

First published 2018
by Routledge
2 Park Square, Milton Park, Abingdon, Oxon OX14 4RN

and by Routledge
711 Third Avenue, New York, NY 10017

Routledge is an imprint of the Taylor & Francis Group, an informa business

© 2018 Peter Bartelmus

The right of Peter Bartelmus to be identified as author of this work has
been asserted by him in accordance with sections 77 and 78 of the
Copyright, Designs and Patents Act 1988.

All rights reserved. No part of this book may be reprinted or reproduced or
utilized in any form or by any electronic, mechanical, or other means, now
known or hereafter invented, including photocopying and recording, or in
any information storage or retrieval system, without permission in writing
from the publishers.

Trademark notice: Product or corporate names may be trademarks or
registered trademarks, and are used only for identification and explanation
without intent to infringe.

British Library Cataloguing-in-Publication Data
A catalogue record for this book is available from the British Library

Library of Congress Cataloging-in- Publication Data
Names: Bartelmus, Peter, author.
Title: Sustaining prosperity, nature and wellbeing : what do the indicators
tell us? / Peter Bartelmus.
Description: Abingdon, Oxon ; New York, NY : Routledge, 2018. |
Includes bibliographical references and index.
Identifiers: LCCN 2017060836| ISBN 9780815351702 (hbk) |
ISBN 9780815351740 (pbk) | ISBN 9781351140607 (ebk)
Subjects: LCSH: Environmental economics. | Sustainable development–
Economic aspects. | Economic development–Environmental aspects.
Classification: LCC HC79.E5 B3684 2018 | DDC 338.9/27–dc23
LC record available at https://lccn.loc.gov/2017060836

ISBN: 978-0-8153-5170-2 (hbk)
ISBN: 978-0-8153-5174-0 (pbk)
ISBN: 978-1-351-14060-7 (ebk)

Typeset in Bembo
by Wearset Ltd, Boldon, Tyne and Wear

CONTENTS

Lists of figures	*x*
List of tables	*xii*
List of boxes	*xiv*
Preface	*xv*
Acknowledgments	*xvii*

PART I

What should we sustain?   **1**

1 Environmental impacts: triggering sustainability concerns   3

    1.1 What on earth is wrong? 3
    1.2 Non-sustainability from environmental impacts 6

2 A framework for concepts and measures of sustainability   10

    2.1 Categories of sustainability 10
    2.2 Schools of thought 12
    2.3 An operational framework 15

viii Contents

PART II
Economic sustainability: getting richer? 19

3 We, the people: are we better off? 21

   3.1 Personal wealth and income 21
   3.2 Who owns the wealth, who gets the income? 23
   3.3 Sustainability 28

4 We, the nation: towards a sustainable economy 34

   4.1 National welfare and wealth 34
   4.2 Greening the national accounts 40
   4.3 Has economic growth been sustainable? 47

5 Modeling economic sustainability: will we be better off? 53

   5.1 Business as usual: what can we expect? 53
   5.2 Constraints for optimality and sustainability 58

PART III
Ecological sustainability: how much nature do we need? 65

6 How much nature do we use? 67

   6.1 Natural wealth 67
   6.2 Environmental pressure 75
   6.3 Environmental impact 80

7 Sustainability: reaching the limits? 95

   7.1 Transgression of biocapacity 96
   7.2 Standards and targets of ecological sustainability 99
   7.3 The cost of maintaining nature's services 103

PART IV
Cornucopia from sustainable development? 111

8 What do we want: happiness, wellbeing, the good life? 113

   8.1 Beyond prosperity – the quality of life 113
   8.2 Combining subjective and objective indicators 119

Contents **ix**

9 What can we get? 124

    9.1 Development: improving living standards 124
    9.2 Measuring development 128

10 Sustainable development: blueprint or fig leaf? 141

    10.1 A murky concept 141
    10.2 Measuring sustainable development 144
    10.3 Has it run its course? 152

PART V
What should we do about it? **157**

11 What do the indicators tell us? 159

    11.1 Accounting for prosperity 159
    11.2 Beyond prosperity: are we really better off? 166
    11.3 Summary and evaluation 175

12 Strategies, policies, politics 181

    12.1 From vision to mission 181
    12.2 Muddling through: piecemeal solutions 184
    12.3 Integrative policy 189
    12.4 Global governance 194

13 Bridging the environmental–economic polarization 203

    13.1 The nature of polarization 203
    13.2 Overcoming the polarization 205

14 Conclusions 212

Annex: a brief history of sustainability science and thought *216*
Index *221*

FIGURES

1.1	Environment–economy interaction	6
3.1	Global personal wealth, 2000–2016	24
3.2	Regional distribution of global personal wealth, 2016	25
3.3	Income and wealth shares of the top decile and top percentile, USA 1910–2013	26
4.1	GPI, GDP and personal consumption per capita, USA 1950–2004	35
4.2	SEEA	43
4.3	ECF in world regions	48
5.1	EKC confirmed and rejected	54
5.2	LTG model – components and interactions	56
5.3	Linear programming of ecologically sustainable and optimal economic activities	59
6.1	Cascade of ecosystem stocks, services and benefits	70
6.2	Global land cover shares	71
6.3	Shares of global wealth	73
6.4	Material flow accounts of the European Union	76
6.5	Shares of global resource extraction by world region, 1980–2013	78
6.6	Average Ecological Footprint and deficit or reserve, 2012	83
7.1	Ecological Footprint trend	96
7.2	CO_2 emission and projected global warming by 2100	104
9.1	Meeting the SDG and achieving human development	133
9.2	Subjective wellbeing and human development	134
9.3	GCI profile of China	137
10.1	Growth in average happiness, human development and GDP per capita, 2005–2015	146

10.2	Regional changes in HDI levels	147
11.1	Comparing indicators for the USA	164
11.2	Will we be better off?	177
13.1	Environmental–economic polarization	204
13.2	Bridging the polarization	206
A.1	Historical sketch of environmental–economic thought	217

TABLES

1.1	Environmental indicators for selected countries	5
2.1	Micro- and macro-concepts of sustainability	11
2.2	Schools of environmental–economic thought	14
2.3	Operational framework of sustainability	15
3.1	Distribution of income between labor and capital, Europe and USA	28
4.1	Global inclusive and comprehensive wealth, 1995 and 2005	40
4.2	External effects of/on economic activity	41
4.3	Simplified structure of a hybrid environmental–economic accounting system	46
6.1	Biocapacity of world regions, 2012	72
6.2	Shares of global energy stores	72
6.3	Countries with high damage value of CO_2 accumulation	74
6.4	Material Footprint and domestic extraction per capita, 2008	79
6.5	Physical input–output table, Germany 1990	81
6.6	Ecological Footprint 2012, selected country rankings and ecological deficits/reserves	84
6.7	Global status of ecosystem services	85
6.8	Carbon Footprint, 2012	89
7.1	Sustainability of global land use	97
7.2	Projections of resource capacity and consumption, 2000–2050	100
7.3	Global cost of climate change	105
7.4	The cost of natural capital maintenance	105
7.5	Natural wealth per person in world regions, 1995 and 2005	106
8.1	Happiness surveys	116
8.2	Happiness ranking of countries	117
8.3	Welfare ranking for OECD member states	121

9.1	From MDG to SDG	127
9.2	Development indices, purpose and methods	129
9.3	Development ranks compared	131
9.4	Ranking of world regions by wellbeing, development and economic performance	134
9.5	Poverty in world regions	136
10.1	Changes in country ranks	145
10.2	Selected indicators of MDG achievements, 1990–2015	149
10.3	MDG evaluation, 1990–2015	151
11.1	Global environmental impact and sustainability	168
11.2	Regional distribution of environmental impacts	171
11.3	Global and regional development	173
11.4	Indicators and indices – summary results	176
12.1	Policy responses to selected indicators	185
12.2	Measurement and evaluation – score of discrepancy	189
12.3	Environmental–economic policy tools	191
12.4	Globalization effects	195

BOXES

3.1	Accounting and analysis of income and wealth	30
3.2	Inequality in the USA	31
4.1	World Bank estimation of comprehensive wealth	37
4.2	Adjusting the accounting indicators	44
8.1	The rights to happiness and wellbeing	114
8.2	Better Life Index: topics and indicators	119
9.1	International development strategies	125
12.1	Costing climate change	192
12.2	Earth Summits	197

PREFACE

What do we want, will it last?

Are we better off? Those living in developed post-industrial nations probably are, or at least a major part of their population is. The rich enjoy high standards of living, expect to live long, are in relatively good health and are well educated. Comparing their situation to the less privileged should make us pause: are national and international inequalities turning into inequity? Moreover, the lives of both the rich and the poor are threatened by crime, war, terrorism and environmental disaster. Is current progress unsustainable in the long run?

This book avoids the visions and rhetoric that obscure what we want and can achieve. It looks for objective answers using well-defined concepts of prosperity, environmental quality and "greened" economic activity that lend themselves to measurement and evaluation. The book is forward-looking, but remains grounded in past trends of quantifiable indicators. The purpose is to avoid being drawn into the speculative assumptions of many models of economic growth and development.

The book is organized around different notions of the sustainability of economic growth, environmental quality and development. For each of these concepts it raises basic questions of

- *what* is the meaning of "better off?"
- *how* can it be measured?
- *who* is better off, and by *how much*?
- *can* we attain and sustain desirable standards of living?

The colloquial term "better off" can refer to a materialistic view of being more prosperous and to more emotional feelings of wellbeing or happiness. Our needs and wants affect, and are affected by, both. Some of these needs are basic such as food and shelter, others are more ambitious like tasty food, comfortable housing or higher education, and still others may come close to philosophy or religion by wondering about the purpose of life. An integrative data analysis brings together the determinants of and obstacles to our wellbeing.

Economic analysis condenses information about myriads of economic activities into manageable measures and models. It looks for optimality, or at least efficiency, in using scarce resources. Economic optimality relies, however, on questionable theories about the preferences and behavior of producers and consumers seeking to maximize profits and benefits. This is the reason why the book remains close to the data rather than moving on to highly assumptive modeling.

The crucial question is whether the indicators can represent overall wealth and wellbeing and can be used to predict future developments. Doubtful data are treated with doubt since they can distort decision making. The established data systems tend to ignore, though, many non-economic – social, cultural, political and institutional – objectives that do contribute to a satisfactory life or even happiness. Do past trends in available data show that we really are or will be better off? Can we ignore the risks of future decline? And how can we sustain positive trends and reverse negative ones? To provide some answers within the constraints of one book the focus is more on regional and global assessments than on the situation in individual countries.

Part I presents a framework, which organizes the book around what should be sustained – economic prosperity, the natural environment and all-encompassing development. Parts II, III and IV elaborate our needs and wants in these areas and their measurement. Part V summarizes what the indicators tell us about our striving for wealth, health and happiness, and what we could and should do about it.

The conclusion is that we know a good deal about economic prosperity and its lack. The national accounts focus on assessing economic activity, and market prices make it possible to aggregate detailed indicators into comprehensive indices of economic performance and growth. Economic indicators provide a significant base for assessing and addressing human wellbeing and policy making. These indicators can and should be extended, notably into environmental fields where economic valuation can reflect the increasing scarcity of nature's services.

Other areas of wellbeing and policy making lack a systemic framework. They can be assessed in part but should not be ignored, despite the dominant role of economic measures. Many social, cultural and political objectives may have to yield to political negotiation. This is why we still believe more than we believe. This book aims to promote a better understanding and open dialogue between politicians, members of civil society and researchers who want to make us better off.

Peter Bartelmus

ACKNOWLEDGMENTS

This book set out from two previous publications on "Quantitative *Eco*-nomics" (Springer) and "Sustainability Economics" (Routledge). I am grateful to the publishers for their permission to reproduce text and figures from these publications. My thanks also go to the editorial staff of Routledge, to Hannah Riley, Matthew Shobbrook and Sally Quinn, who showed great patience with my queries and supported untiringly the publication process.

Permission to reproduce tables and figures from other publications are also gratefully acknowledged. They include Elsevier, the Encyclopedia of Life Support Systems and the World Economic Forum, as well as the authors of working papers, S. Bringezu, and J.B. Sachs et al.

I also drew on publications, which did not require a permission to reproduce, or where I modified the material considerably. They were of great help to present summary tables and figures where cumbersome explanations would otherwise be needed. They include material of the Environment Programme, the Food and Agriculture Organization, the Development Programme and the Statistical Division of the United Nations. Further material was found in the publications of Crédit Suisse, Gallup, Redefining Progress, the Sustainable Europe Research Institute et al., the Intergovernmental Panel on Climate Change, Elsevier and Harvard University Press.

PART I

What should we sustain?

… the people, the environment, economic development? Who does not want a good thing to last? Unfortunately there are many obstacles that lie in the way of improving wellbeing and socioeconomic progress. Besides war and other political upheavals, environmental degradation has been *the* major concern that triggered doubts about the sustainability of our lifestyles. This part categorizes the different sustainability of economic activity, the environment and all-encompassing development. The categorization serves to develop a framework that can assess and improve sustainability. The framework also provides the basic structure of this book.

1

ENVIRONMENTAL IMPACTS

Triggering sustainability concerns

1.1 What on earth is wrong?

The biblical call to "subdue the earth" (Gen 1: 28) set off a heated debate about Christian arrogance towards nature and resulting environmental decline (White 1967). Most religions, including Christian ones, accept now the obligation of environmental stewardship for the sustainable use of nature. The overuse of natural resources contributed to the downfall of ancient cultures and empires like Mesopotamia, and the Mayan and Roman empires. In the eighteenth and nineteenth century resource-exploiting colonization helped Europe to escape the fates of ancient civilizations (Tainter 2001). More recently, securing energy sources drove the war in Iraq. The use of nuclear power and genetic resources might now pose a threat to human survival.

Is apocalypse the consequence of subduing the planet? Or are environmental concerns just another bug in our search for prosperity? Conspicuous environmental pollution and natural resource depletion brought about the environmental movement and doomsday literature; both predict the collapse of society unless we change our destructive ways. Titles like *The Death of Tomorrow* (Loraine 1972), *Silent Spring* (Carson 1965), "A Blueprint for Survival" (Goldsmith and Prescott-Allen 1972) or *Conservation for Survival* (Curry-Lindahl 1972) indicate the environmental mood in the late 1960s and early 1970s. A seemingly objective computerized global model of the *Limits to Growth* gained widespread attention: it warned of "a rather sudden and uncontrollable decline in both population and industrial capacity" within a century if growth trends remained unchanged (Meadows et al. 1972, p. 29).

Activist individuals, environmental protection agencies and non-governmental organizations like Greenpeace, the Worldwatch Institute or the Club of Rome keep the environmental movement alive. They warn us about overtaxing the earth's carrying capacity:

4 What should we sustain?

- The world is in an "overshoot-and-collapse mode" (Brown 2006, p. 5).
- "The impacts of climate change ... threaten our health by affecting the food we eat, the water we drink, the air we breathe, and the weather we experience" (US EPA 2017).
- "Our planet is poised at the brink of a severe environmental crisis" (Conserve Energy Future 2017).

Population growth and economic preferences of profit- and utility-maximizing economic agents can be blamed for the overuse of nature's source and sink functions. The depletion of natural resources of forests, fish, soils, land, minerals, metals and water undermines economic activity. Discharges of wastes and pollutants into the atmosphere, water and land impair human health and wellbeing. The IPAT equation (Ehrlich and Holdren 1971) decomposes environmental impacts of depletion and degradation into population growth and concentration, affluence and damaging technologies. The latter include the use of nuclear energy and genetically modified natural resources:

$$EI = P \times A \times T = P \times GDP/P \times EI/GDP = EI$$

where EI is environmental impact, P is population size, GDP is gross domestic product, $A = GDP/P$ is affluence and $T = EI/GDP$ is technological impact of economic activity.

Exponential population growth could bring about a Malthusian decline in social welfare. According to Daly (1996), a leading "green" economist, a world full with buildings, infrastructure, and people and their wastes is overloading the planet's carrying capacity. Such a world is likely to collapse unless we find ways of drastically reducing the use of the natural environment. Mainstream economists, on the other hand, doubt that the end is near. One "skeptical environmentalist" even claims that we have mostly experienced an improvement rather than a decline in environmental and economic conditions (Lomborg 2001). The ensuing debate is at least an eye-opener on widely different conclusions, often from the same data.[1]

Environmental indicators, compiled by the Statistics Division of the United Nations, illustrate the difficulty of assessing trends of environmental quality and their effects on standards of living (Table 1.1). Politicians, researchers, the media and the general public face an abundance of data that are not comparable within and across countries as the data differ in concepts, coverage, time of data collection and units of measurement. Different indicators alert to increasing emissions and decreasing natural resources but do not provide an overall assessment of environmental change, let alone socioeconomic progress. Previous attempts at evaluating this information by face icons (Bartelmus 2013, Table 2.1) are judgmental and were abandoned by the Statistics Division of the United Nations.

The information overload of large sets of indicators needs to be reduced. A review of international environmental reports points to key measures that are

Environmental impacts **5**

TABLE 1.1 Environmental indicators for selected countries

	Australia	*China*	*Germany*	*South Africa*	*USA*
Water					
Renewable freshwater resources per capita (m³)	–	1514 (2012)	2247 (2013)	–	–
Air pollution					
SO_2 emission per capita (kg) (2012)	35	–	5	–	15
Climate change					
Greenhouse gas emission per capita (tons CO_2-equivalent)	24 (2012)	6 (2005)	12 (2012)	9 (1994)	21 (2012)
Waste					
Municipal collection per capita (kg)	628 (2011)	126 (2012)	624 (2014)	–	1000 (2012)
thereof: recycled (%)	45 (2011)	–	47 (2013)	–	26 (2012)
Hazardous waste per capita (kg)	–	739 (2012)	1983 (2014)	641 (2011)	–
thereof: treated or disposed (%)	–	78 (2011)	94 (2014)	–	–
Land use					
Change in forest area 1990–2014 (%)	1	3	0	0	0
Biodiversity					
Threatened species (number) (2015)	931	1080	116	570	1514

Source: UNSD (2017).

Note
Year of compilation in parentheses.

typically cited as evidence for the non-sustainability of human activity. They include, in particular,

- *global warming*, which for most atmospheric greenhouse gas concentrations is likely to exceed 2 °C by 2100 (IPCC 2014, p. 72);
- a loss of three million ha per year of *forest* since the 1990s to between 2000 and 2011 (UNEP 2012, p. 72);
- a loss of 68 *species* since 1970 (UNEP 2002, p. 122); in contrast, between 200 and 2000 species are lost annually according to a low estimate by the WWF (2017a);
- degradation of 23 percent of usable *land* area (UNEP 2002, p. 64);
- unsustainable overexploitation of 29 percent of *fish* stocks in 2011 (FAO 2014, p. 7);

6 What should we sustain?

- lack access to safe drinking *water* by 15 percent of the world population (WWF 2017b);
- return to 1980 levels in 20–40 years of the total *ozone* column (WMO et al. 2014, p. 10).

1.2 Non-sustainability from environmental impacts

The above selection of indicators cannot generate an overall picture of environmental deterioration and of the sustainability of the economy or society. The indicators do point, though, to the roots of potential non-sustainability and its possible underestimation.

Figure 1.1 depicts the interaction of the economy and the environment as natural resource inputs from the environment to the economy and residual output of wastes and pollutants from the economy to the environment. Economic production transforms resource inputs (together with other materials) into goods and services, and production and consumption may deplete natural resources and discharge residuals. The consumption of goods and services and the exposure to residuals create positive and negative effects on the wellbeing of people. Mainstream economists treat environmental impacts as an "externality" in the established economic measures and models. They describe externalities as unintended and unpriced effects of economic activities (see section 4.2.1). Producers and consumers of goods and services can, however, be prompted to internalize the externalities as additional costs and benefits in their budgets.

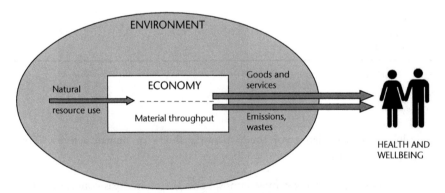

FIGURE 1.1 Environment–economy interaction. The natural environment provides source and sink services to the economy. They include natural resource supply and the absorption of wastes and pollutants. Environmentalists often treat the economy as a black box (shown white in this figure) which swallows materials and releases residuals resulting from production and consumption. The consumption of goods and services and exposure to unabsorbed residuals affect human wellbeing

Source: © UNESCO-Encyclopedia of Life Support Systems (EOLSS), from Bartelmus (2001, Fig. 1, modified), with permission from UNESCO-Encyclopedia of Life Support Systems.

Assessing the sustainability of human activity needs to account at least for economic and environmental concerns. A number of statistics and indicator frameworks seek to systematically list economic, environmental and other data to this end. As early as 1984 the author and his team at the United Nations Statistics Division advanced a Framework for the Development of Environment Statistics (FDES). The framework applied an activity–impact–response sequence to present statistical topics and corresponding environmental statistics (United Nations 1984). The loose connections of human activities with environmental conditions does not allow an overall measurement of the impacts on the state of the environment; it can facilitate, though, a better understanding of the data for reporting and evaluating environmental quality and its trends.[2]

Another indicator framework of the United Nations is even less integrative, using international political goals or otherwise determined "themes" (United Nations 2007). Indicator frameworks and lists may cover a wider range of development concerns, including economic, social, cultural and political "dimensions" of the quality of life (OECD, no date) or wellbeing (Prescott-Allen 2001). Reports of the state of the environment may cover a wide range of subjects but succeed in selective or partial measurement only (MEA 2005; UNEP 2014; EEA, no date).

A more comprehensive quantification of being better off and its sustainability requires more. The following chapter advances a simple operational framework. It will help find out what can be reasonably measured and combined, and what should be left to judgmental assessments.

Notes

1 Critique and counter-critique of Lomborg's assessment can be found on www.lomborg-errors.dk and www.lomborg.com (accessed 10 March 2017).
2 A recent revision of the FDES has given up on even this weak linkage of environmental impacts and responses with environmental assets: it just surrounds environmental conditions and quality by five other related components (UNSD 2016).

References

Bartelmus, P. (2001). Accounting for sustainability: greening the national accounts, in M.K. Tolba (ed.), *Our Fragile World: Challenges and Opportunities for Sustainable Development*, Oxford: Eolss Publishers: 1721–35.

Bartelmus, P. (2013). *Sustainability Economics: An Introduction*, London and New York: Routledge.

Brown, L.R. (2006). *Plan B: Rescuing a Planet Under Stress and a Civilization in Trouble*, New York: Norton.

Carson, R. (1965). *Silent Spring*, London: Penguin.

Conserve Energy Future (2017). Environmental problems. Online: www.conserve-energy-future.com/15-current-environmental-problems.php (accessed 8 October 2017).

Curry-Lindahl, K. (1972). *Conservation for Survival: An Ecological Strategy*, New York: Morrow.

Daly, H.E. (1996). *Beyond Growth*, Boston, MA: Beacon Press.

8 What should we sustain?

Ehrlich, P.R. and Holdren, J.P. (1971). Impact of population growth, *Science* 171: 1212–17.

European Environment Agency (EEA) (no date). SOER 2015: The European environment – state and outlook 2015. Online: www.eea.europa.eu/soer (accessed 19 July 2017).

Food and Agriculture Organization of the United Nations (FAO) (2014). *The State of World Fisheries and Aquaculture, Opportunities and Challenges*, Rome: FAO. Online: www.fao.org/3/a-i3720e.pdf (accessed 29 October 2017).

Goldsmith, E. and Prescott-Allen, R. (1972). A blueprint for survival, *Ecologist*, special edition, January.

Intergovernmental Panel on Climate Change (IPCC) (2014). *Synthesis Report*, Geneva: IPCC. Online: www.ipcc.ch/pdf/assessment-report/ar5/syr/SYR_AR5_FINAL_full_wcover.pdf (accessed 11 March 2017).

Lomborg, B. (2001). *The Skeptical Environmentalist: Measuring the Real State of the World*, Cambridge: Cambridge University Press.

Loraine, J.A.C. (1972). *The Death of Tomorrow*, London: Heinemann.

Meadows, D.H., Meadows, D.L., Randers, J. and Behrens III, W.W. (1972). *The Limits to Growth*, New York: Universe Books.

Millennium Ecosystem Assessment (MEA) (2005). *Ecosystems and Human Well-being: Synthesis*, Washington, DC: Island Press. Online: http://millenniumassessment.org/documents/document.356.aspx.pdf (accessed 29 October 2017).

Organisation for Economic Co-operation and Development (OECD) (no date). Better life index. Online: www.oecdbetterlifeindex.org (accessed 3 October 2017).

Prescott-Allen, R. (2001). *The Wellbeing of Nations: A Country-by-Country Index of Quality of Life and the Environment*, Washington, DC: Island Press.

Tainter, J.A. (2001). Complexity, collapse, and sustainable problem-solving, in M.K. Tolba (ed.). *Our Fragile World: Challenges and Opportunities for Sustainable Development*, Oxford: Eolss Publishers: 1803–26.

United Nations (1984). *A Framework for the Development of Environment Statistics*, New York: United Nations.

United Nations (2007). *Indicators of Sustainable Development: Guidelines and Methodologies*. New York: United Nations. Online: www.un.org/esa/sustdev/natlinfo/indicators/guidelines.pdf (accessed 10 July 2017).

United Nations Environment Programme (UNEP) (2002). *Global Environmental Outlook 3*, Nairobi: UNEP. Online: http://web.unep.org/geo/sites/unep.org.geo/files/documents/chapter2-4_biodiversity.pdf (accessed 3 November 2017).

United Nations Environment Programme (UNEP) (2012). *Global Environmental Outlook 5*, Nairobi: UNEP. Online: http://web.unep.org/geo/assessments/global-assessments/global-environment-outlook-5 (accessed 25 August 2017).

United Nations Environment Programme (UNEP) (2014). Global Environmental Outlook 6. Online: www.unep.org/geo/ (accessed 3 October 2017).

United Nations Statistics Division (UNSD) (2016). *Framework for the Development of Environment Statistics (FDES 2013)*, New York: United Nations. Online: http://unstats.un.org/unsd/environment/FDES/FDES-2015-supporting-tools/FDES.pdf (accessed 29 October 2017).

United Nations Statistics Division (UNSD) (2017). UNSD environmental indicators. Online: http://unstats.un.org/unsd/ENVIRONMENT/qindicators.htm (accessed 25 August 2017).

U.S. Environmental Protection Agency (US EPA) (2017). Climate change impacts. Online: www.epa.gov/climate-impacts/climate-impacts-human-health (accessed 25 August 2017; website changed by the Trump administration).

White, L. (1967). The historical roots of our ecological crisis, *Science* 155: 1203–7.

World Meteorological Organization (WMO), United Nations Environment Programme, National Oceanic and Atmospheric Administration, National Aeronautics and Space Administration and European Commission (2014). *Assessment for Decision Makers, Scientific Assessment of Ozone Depletion: 2014*, Report no. 56, Geneva. Online: www.esrl.noaa.gov/csd/assessments/ozone/2014/assessment_for_decision-makers.pdf (accessed 29 October 2017).

World Wide Fund for Nature (WWF) (2017a). How many species are we losing? Online: http://wwf.panda.org/about_our_earth/biodiversity/biodiversity/ (accessed 3 November 2017).

World Wide Fund for Nature (WWF) (2017b). Threats: water scarcity. Online: www.worldwildlife.org/threats/water-scarcity (accessed 11 March 2017).

2

A FRAMEWORK FOR CONCEPTS AND MEASURES OF SUSTAINABILITY

2.1 Categories of sustainability

Environmental impacts caused by economic production and consumption triggered concern about the sustainability of economic activity. Lists of impact indicators cannot, however, assess the sustainability of economic activity. The indicators need to be aggregated or otherwise combined to represent overall net progress that includes detractions by environmental and other hazards.

Extended coverage and aggregation of indicators is therefore a prerequisite for assessing the sustainability of people's wellbeing and socioeconomic development. The paradigm of sustainable development provides the broadest view of sustainability referring to the needs of the current and future generations (WCED 1987). Criticism of the narrow view of economic outcomes suggests a palette of human needs and wants and a search for alternative measures that look beyond gross domestic product (GDP) (European Commission 2015). Proliferation of concepts and measures of the sustainability of human and economic development, the quality of life, wellbeing and even happiness is the result.

A commonly accepted framework might bring order into the different concepts and measures. The first step would be to specify sustainability categories that define what should be sustained. Three basic categories of sustainability can be distinguished (Bartelmus 2013, p. 120):

- *Ecological sustainability* focuses on maintaining the health of ecosystems; the ecocentric view wants to maintain ecosystems in their natural state, whereas the anthropocentric view seeks to maintain the benefits people draw from ecosystem services.
- *Economic sustainability* aims to maintain economic wealth, output, income or welfare, generated by the production and consumption of goods and services;

economic indicators should be measured net of the consumption of natural and other capital used.

- *Sustainability of development* reflects a broader anthropocentric view as it seeks to meet the needs and wants of society, now and in the future.

The three sustainability categories can be defined for the activities of economic agents of government, private households, enterprises and non-governmental organizations, and for natural systems and larger territories such as the nation or the planet. Table 2.1 presents different sustainability concepts that can be applied at micro- (including local) and macro-levels of analysis.

The resistance of ecosystems to perturbations represents local-level ecological sustainability. Carrying capacity, on the other hand, refers usually to people and their activities in larger regions. Overuse and abuse of ecosystems can overcome the innate resilience of ecosystems to ward off disturbances of their equilibrium. Limits of ecosystem resilience, carrying capacity of larger regions and of the rather normative "environmental space" for the rights to environmental services (Weterings and Opschoor 1992) are key determinants of ecological sustainability. Ecological economists tend to stay in practice at the local (ecosystem) levels of measurement and analysis. For national and international policies they would have to expand their focus to larger regions. Rezai and Stagl (2016) call therefore for developing an "ecological macroeconomics."

Economic sustainability can set out from micro-economic wellbeing (utility) of individuals to define non-declining macro-economic welfare as a rather abstract aggregated sustainability concept. Alternatively a focus on the role of production

TABLE 2.1 Micro- and macro-concepts of sustainability

Sustainability categories	Micro- and local levels	Macro-level
Ecological sustainability	Resilience of local ecosystems	Maintenance of the carrying capacity of territories
Economic sustainability of wellbeing and welfare	Non-declining utility, allowing for disutility and benefits from environmental and other effects of individual economic activity	Non-declining welfare from the consumption of goods and services, allowing for external environmental and other social costs and benefits
Economic sustainability of capital maintenance	Produced and non-produced (natural) capital maintenance for sustaining the productivity of enterprises	Capital maintenance for sustaining economic growth
Sustainable development	Sustaining the needs and wants of local communities (eco-development)	Sustaining the needs and wants of society

Source: Bartelmus (2013, Table 11.1. modified), with permission from Taylor & Francis.

12 What should we sustain?

factors in the generation of capital services obtains a more practical concept of sustainability as the maintenance of produced, natural and other forms of human and social capital. The purpose is to sustain the output and consumption of goods and services of the national economy.[1]

Sustainable development encompasses all human needs and aspirations at local, national and international levels. The United Nations Environment Programme defined "eco-development" as local development, which "respect[s] the natural ecosystems and local sociocultural patterns" (UNEP 1975). The 1992 Rio Earth Summit later attempted to revive the concept in its Agenda 21 (United Nations 1994). At the macro-economic level, sustainable development refers to economic, environmental, social and institutional "pillars" or "dimensions" of development and would thus cover corresponding sustainability concerns. Broadening the concept of produced capital by including environmental and social features brings the effects of capital use close to general human welfare. Such welfare blurs the distinction between economic and developmental sustainability. Considering human "wants" beyond needs leads into the realm of life satisfaction or happiness as particularly broad notions of welfare and development.

2.2 Schools of thought

Different views of sustainability characterize different schools of thought. The eco-centric view seeks to maintain nature in its original form or at least to ensure the continuous flow of ecosystem services to humans and non-humans in physical (non-monetary) terms. On the other hand, the anthropocentric view looks into human preferences for goods and services, including those of nature. The assessment of human preferences compares economic and environmental goods and services in terms of the willingness to pay for them, or at least to cost the maintenance of their supply. These views gave rise to a distinct polarization between economists and environmentalists, and, more specifically, between environmental and ecological economists.[2]

Funtowicz and Ravetz (1991) are ecological economists, who claim that irreversible environmental impacts and externalities render mainstream economics irrelevant. As a protagonist of ecological economics puts it: "optimally overloaded boats will sink under too much weight" (of people and their goods and wastes) (Daly 1996, p. 50). Conventional economics is seen to be in denial as it clings to its formalistic axioms of rational behavior in perfectly competitive markets.

Economists defend their basic rationality axiom, suggesting that action based on an ideal situation might contribute to achieving this situation, possibly by a "sequence of policy reforms" (Dasgupta 1994, p. 42). Samuelson and Nordhaus (1992, p. 295) argue that "using economics in a vacuum" will gain insight into complicated problems. As long as nothing drastic happens, one can probably live with the "semi-fiction" (Solow 1992, p. 165) of perfect markets. Mainstream economists tend therefore to relegate environmental phenomena as "externalities" to a sideline of their domain, i.e., environmental economics.

Yet drastic things do happen in the natural environment and drastic views on tackling environment decline emerged. Deep ecologists go beyond the "shallow" (Naess 1976) anthropocentric view of nature's value for human health and well-being. They insist on the equality of all species (Sessions 1995). The ultimate step in deeply ecological thought is the near-religious appreciation of Earth as a living, self-regulating entity – the so-called *gaia* hypothesis (Lovelock 1988/1995).

Surprisingly, economists and environmentalists seem to repress their different views as they go their own separate ways. The reasons could be that they consider their differences either as insurmountable or that they skirt a debate that might threaten the tenets of their disciplines. By clinging to the rationality of perfect markets, economists seek to give their evaluative approaches – in terms of economic preferences – a touch of "scientificity." On the other hand, environmentalists doubt that economics is a science. They claim that their own approaches, based on ecology, are a part of the natural sciences. However, as discussed in section 7.2, the attempt to link this science to economics comes at the price of losing objectivity by setting goals and targets for prosperity and wellbeing.

Rather than entering a hardly productive discussion of what is science in the models and assumptions of ecological and environmental economics this book will stay close to the available database. This avoids drifting off into the norms and convictions of ethics and related philosophies. Table 2.2 describes different notions of environmental and economic thought in terms of their objectives, sustainability concepts and strategies. An annex to the book provides a historical sketch of the different approaches to dealing with the interaction of environment and economy. Early efforts to link ecology to mainstream economics and mainstream economics to the natural environment have now generated separate disciplines of ecological and environmental economics.

Utility and profit maximization are the fundamental objectives of conventional economics, expanded by environmental economists for the internalization of ignored environmental costs. Such treatment relies on human ingenuity to restore or substitute depleted and degraded natural capital in production and consumption. Assuming substitution or reuse of depleted natural capital represents a "weak" form of sustainability. If the irreplaceable nature of exhaustible natural capital prevents this approach, ecological economists call for a slower pace of the use of non-renewable resources or full preservation of "critical" natural capital (de Groot et al. 2003; Ekins et al. 2003). The preservation of natural capital represents "strong" sustainability with little concern for its economic cost. The strength of sustainability is a distinguishing characteristic of economic and environmentalist schools.

Economists believe that markets can bring about an efficient use of natural resources by putting a price on the depletion and degradation of natural capital. Where markets fail, instruments of internalizing external cost into the budgets of households and enterprises can extend efficiency into the use of non-produced natural resources. Environmental economists tend to ignore the standards and targets of physical indicators, pushing strong sustainability out of their tenets into normative disciplines of institutional economics or sustainable development. They

14 What should we sustain?

TABLE 2.2 Schools of environmental–economic thought

	Conventional (neoclassical) economics	Environmental (neoclassical) economics	Ecological economics	Deep (human) ecology
Objectives	Maximization of utility, profit and economic growth	Maximization of utility, profit and economic growth, taking externalities into account	• Protection of nature • Reduced or zero economic growth • Qualitative development	• Symbiosis with nature • Negative growth of economy and population
Sustainability concepts	Maintenance of the value of produced capital: very weak sustainability	Maintenance of the monetary value of produced and natural capital: weak sustainability	Maintenance of critical natural capital: relatively strong sustainability	Preservation of nature: strong sustainability
Strategies	Economic efficiency	Eco-efficiency by internalization of environmental externalities	• Eco-efficiency in production and sufficiency in consumption • Dematerialization of the economy	• Sufficiency in production and consumption • Consistency with natural processes • Restoration of nature

Source: Bartelmus (2008, Table 2.1, modified), with permission from Springer Nature.

assess future sustainability by putting a monetary value on the preferences of the current generation, discounting the value of uncertain consumption of future generations (see section 4.1).

Ecological economists see critical natural capital as "priceless." Biophysical indicators need therefore to monitor its depletion and degradation in non-monetary terms. Norms and standards determine the level of action necessary to preserve critical environmental assets. The approach is to supplement or even replace resource-depleting economic activities by eco-efficient production and consumption processes. Alternatives should be in harmony with nature, i.e., "consistent" with natural processes, or they should be curbed to meet requirements of environmental protection. Standards, rules, regulations and education should bring about the new production and consumption patterns. Ecological economists also give near-equal weight to the environmental needs of the current and future generations. "Deep" ecologists are more radical. They want to restore nature's pristine quality, which would require curtailing current economic activity.

Section 13.2 will look into possibilities of bridging the economic–environmental polarization. It will expand economic accounting and will introduce non-economic goals and standards into economic analysis.

2.3 An operational framework

The three categories of ecological, economic and developmental sustainability represent one dimension of a practical framework. They provide a structure for finding out what makes us better off and whether it could last. Confronting the sustainability categories with key physical, monetary and hybrid measures builds a two-dimensional framework for identifying the quantifiable aspects of sustainability. Catering to the above-mentioned polarization, Table 2.3 distinguishes physical measures of ecological sustainability from monetary aggregates mostly used for economic sustainability. A mix of physical and monetary indicators, combined in hybrid indices, seeks to cover the wide range of the components of sustainable development. Hybrid accounts and indicators also find their way into ecological and economic sustainability; their purpose is to reach out to other sustainability categories.

Table 2.3 reveals differences and connections between the sustainability concepts and aggregation methods. Ecological sustainability uses mostly commensurable indicators of mass/weight for material flows, area for footprints or joules for energy use. By themselves they do not measure sustainability. They require some kind of standard that reflects the standard setter's judgment of how much decline of indicators can be tolerated. Material flows are confronted with "factors" calling, for example, for halving resource inputs while doubling economic growth

TABLE 2.3 Operational framework of sustainability

	Physical measures	Monetary measures	Hybrid indices
Ecological sustainability	• Total Material Input and Output • Ecological Footprint • Energy accounts • Environmental theme equivalents • Sustainability gap	• Value of ecosystems and their services	• Resource productivity • Emission intensity
Economic sustainability			
• economic welfare, wealth	–	• Genuine Progress Indicator • Economic wealth and welfare	–
• output, income	–	• Green accounting aggregates • Models of sustainable economic growth	Hybrid accounts and models
Sustainable development	–	• Wealth and welfare measures • Distributional equity	Sustainable development indices

Source: Bartelmus (2017, Table 4.1), with permission from Edward Elgar Publishing.

16 What should we sustain?

(von Weizsäcker et al. 1997). Ecological Footprints face limits of "biocapacity" (Borucke et al. 2013), and theme equivalents and the sustainability gap face policy targets (Adriaanse 1993; Ekins 2011).

Economic sustainability addresses economic wealth, welfare, income and output. Accounting systems and models of economic growth use prices for the valuation of physical indicators. As far as monetary indicators represent long-term economic goals, sustainability can simply be defined as the non-decline of the indicators. Of course, the validity of monetary measures depends not only on the underlying physical data but also on the methods of "pricing the priceless" to determine the value of natural capital assets and their services. The problem is that these assets and services are normally not traded in markets.

Recent attempts to measure the costs and benefits of ecosystems services still have to prove their validity beyond local areas. So far they did not come up with a definite comprehensive measure of ecological sustainability. Environmental economists prefer monetizing environmental services that have become scarce and are thus subject to scarcity pricing. Environmentalists, on the other hand favor physical indicators that measure the "real" pressure of the economy on ecosystems. Hybrid ratios of resource productivity (GDP per resource input) and emission intensity (emission per GDP) connect ecological concerns with economic analysis.

Indicators and indices of sustainable development build upon physical and monetary measures. Like the physical indicators of ecological sustainability their assessment depends on setting goals and targets such as the recently approved Sustainable Development Goals (United Nations, no date). Some monetary wealth and welfare indicators claim, however, to be measures of non-declining human welfare when they cover all goals of sustainable development (World Bank 2011; UNEP and UNU-IHDP 2014). The distribution of wealth, income and wellbeing is an often-neglected part of the relationships between micro- and macro-economics at national and international levels. Distribution is normally expressed in monetary terms of wealth owned and income gained. Other distributional concerns of health, education, land ownership and the marginalization of social groups use non-monetary units and are therefore more difficult to combine. They could be considered as a part of the social dimension of sustainable development.

The following parts of the book will examine in detail the use and usefulness of all these measures for assessing past sustainability and predicting its fate. Here we note that sustainability is in principle a forward-looking notion, wondering whether past trends of non-sustainability will continue in the future and what should and could be done about it. Modeling the future is of course less certain than observing the past. Any conclusions about the sustainability of environmental quality, economic outcomes and broad-based development should therefore make clear whether they are based on *ex-post* observation or models of the future.

Notes

1 This book makes a clear distinction between "ecological sustainability" of nature's (ecosystem) quality and parts of nature's sustainability that serve as natural capital to support economic activity. The latter is therefore included in "economic sustainability." The ecological and economic functions of the natural environment are often combined in the popular term of "environmental sustainability"; this term is used in the book when both functions of nature are referred to as for instance in the sustainable development goals (cf. section 9.1).
2 Distinguishing between environmental and ecological economists is a simplification of the differences between environmental–economic schools of thought. Related schools such as "industrial ecology" (Ayres and Ayres 2002) or "co-evolutionary economics" (Norgaard 1994) modify and sometimes combine concepts and methods of greening economics. Chapter 13 describes the environmental–economic polarization and discusses ways of overcoming it.

References

Adriaanse, A. (1993). *Environmental Policy Performance Indicators*, Koninginnegracht: Sdu Uitgeverij.

Ayres, R.U. and Ayres, L.W. (eds.) (2002). *A Handbook of Industrial Ecology*, Cheltenham, UK: Edward Elgar.

Bartelmus, P. (2008). *Quantitative Eco-nomics: How Sustainable are Our Economies?* Dordrecht: Springer.

Bartelmus, P. (2013). *Sustainability Economics: An Introduction*, London and New York: Routledge.

Bartelmus, P. (2017). Sustainability metrics and their use, in P.A. Victor and B. Dolter (eds.), *Handbook on Growth and Sustainability*, Cheltenham, UK and Northampton, MA: Edward Elgar: 59–84.

Borucke, M., Moore, D., Cranston, G., Gracey, K., Iha, K., Larson, J., Lazarus, E., Morales, J.C., Wackernagel, M. and Galli, A. (2013). Accounting for demand and supply of the biosphere's regenerative capacity: the national footprint accounts, *Ecological Indicators* 24: 518–33.

Daly, H.E. (1996). *Beyond Growth*, Boston, MA: Beacon Press.

Dasgupta, P. (1994). Optimal versus sustainable development, in I. Serageldin and A. Steer (eds.), *Valuing the Environment: Proceedings of the First Annual International Conference on Environmentally Sustainable Development*, Washington, DC: World Bank.

De Groot, R., van der Park, J., Chiesura, A. and van Vliet, A. (2003). Importance and threat as determining factors of criticality of natural capital, *Ecological Economics* 44: 187–204.

Ekins, P. (2011). Environmental sustainability: from environmental valuation to the sustainability gap, *Progress in Physical Geography* 35 (5): 629–51. Online: http://journals.sagepub.com/doi/pdf/10.1177/0309133311423186 (accessed 16 January 2017).

Ekins, P., Simon, S., Deutsch, L., Folke, C. and de Groot, R. (2003). A framework for the practical application of the concepts of critical natural capital and strong sustainability, *Ecological Economics* 44: 165–85.

European Commission (2015). Beyond GDP, measuring progress, true wealth, and the well-being of nations. Online: http://ec.europa.eu/environment/beyond_gdp/index_en.html (accessed 4 October 2017).

Funtowicz, S.O. and Ravetz, J.R. (1991). A new scientific methodology for global environmental issues, in R. Costanza (ed.), *Ecological Economics: The Science and Management of Sustainability*, New York: Columbia University Press: 137–52.

18 What should we sustain?

Lovelock, J.E. (1988/1995). *The Ages of Gaia: A Biography of Our Living Earth*, New York: Norton.

Naess, A. (1976). The shallow and the deep, long-range ecology movement, a summary, *Inquiry* 16: 95–100.

Norgaard, R.B. (1994). *Development Betrayed: The End of Progress and a Coevolutionary Revisioning of the Future*, London: Routledge.

Rezai, A. and Stagl, S. (2016). Ecological macroeconomics: introduction and review, *Ecological Economics* 121: 181–5.

Samuelson, P.A. and Nordhaus, W.D. (1992, 14th ed.). *Economics*, New York: McGraw-Hill.

Sessions, G. (ed.) (1995). *Deep Ecology for the 21st Century: Readings on the Philosophy and Practice of the New Environmentalism*, Boston, MA: Shambhala (distributed by Random House).

Solow, R. (1992). *An Almost Practical Step Toward Sustainability*, Washington, DC: Resources for the Future. Online: http://web.stanford.edu/class/econ155/coursework/Course Materials/Readings/Solow-Sustainability.pdf (accessed 8 October 2017).

United Nations (1994). *Earth Summit, Agenda 21: The United Nations Programme of Action from Rio*, New York: United Nations.

United Nations (no date). Sustainable development goals. Online: www.un.org/sustainable development/sustainable-development-goals/ (accessed 27 August 2017).

United Nations Environment Programme (UNEP) (1975). The proposed programme, (UNEP/GC/30), Nairobi.

United Nations Environment Programme (UNEP) and United Nations University-International Human Dimensions Programme (UNU-IHDP) (2014). *Inclusive Wealth Report 2014: Measuring Progress Toward Sustainability*, Cambridge: Cambridge University Press.

von Weizsäcker, E.U., Lovins, A. and Lovins, H. (1997). *Factor Four: Doubling Wealth, Halving Resource Use*, London: Earthscan.

Weterings, R. and Opschoor, P.H. (1992). *The Ecocapacity as a Challenge to Sustainable Development*, Rijkswijk: Netherlands Advisory Council for Research on Nature and Environment.

World Bank (2011). *The Changing Wealth of Nations: Measuring Sustainable Development in the New Millennium*, Washington, DC: World Bank. Online: http://siteresources.worldbank.org/ENVIRONMENT/Resources/ChangingWealthNations.pdf (accessed 1 September 2017).

World Commission on Environment and Development (WCED) (1987). *Our Common Future*, Oxford: Oxford University Press.

PART II

Economic sustainability
Getting richer?

Economic sustainability refers to the maintenance of economic wealth, income and wellbeing. More specifically, it addresses the underlying economic activities of accumulation, production and consumption of goods and services. People and countries can be rich or poor in owning "real" and financial wealth and producing and consuming economic products. This part explores personal wealth and income and their distribution (Chapter 3). It also looks into the role of wealth as produced and natural capital in the generation of national income and economic growth (Chapters 4 and 5). Judgment about distributional "fairness" is left to the social goal of sustainable development (Part IV). A common feature of measuring economic performance and its sustainability is the use of monetary values to reflect economic preferences and to obtain commensurability.

3

WE, THE PEOPLE

Are we better off?

Micro-economic analysis explores what makes people feel better off in a materialistic sense. Being better off is thus a matter of greater wealth owned and income received. Economic wealth increases by accumulating long-lasting goods of "real" assets and financial resources. Besides returns of income from using wealth in production or holding it for future returns, owning financial and non-financial wealth provides status, independence and power in society. Supplying skills and knowledge, i.e., human capital, to production earns the bulk of national income. Income can be used for the current consumption of goods and services or can be saved for future consumption, creating financial wealth. Current consumption per capita determines our standards of living. It might be closer to human wellbeing than income but does not reflect the potential for future consumption and security provided by personal wealth. Still, income and wealth serve similar purposes of improving our economic situation.

Are we richer? How does it compare to other people within and among countries? Can we sustain prosperity threatened by non-market effects? Is inequality in the distribution of income and wealth a sign of non-sustainability? These are the questions this chapter will address.

3.1 Personal wealth and income

Prosperity is the materialistic side of being better off. Ownership of long-lasting non-financial assets, consumer durables and financial resources make up personal wealth. Besides potential income and consumption, wealth conveys status in society and reduces economic vulnerability. Income generated by produced and human capital makes it possible to acquire goods and services in markets. Government and non-profit institutions can add free or subsidized goods and services for education and material aid as non-market transfers.

22 Economic sustainability

The availability of wealth and income to people is not only the result of supplying labor and capital to production but also of distribution. The national accounts recommend measuring the flows of income to labor, capital (owners) and government as the primary distribution of income (European Commission et al. 2009, paras. 2.91, 2.92). They do not show, though, how income and wealth are distributed among individuals and social groups (ibid., paras. 24.4, 24.69), focusing narrowly on market transactions. As discussed in Chapter 8, non-market processes and activities can also have significant effects on individual prosperity and wellbeing.

There are doubts whether being rich can make us better or happier. Religious sentiment expresses these doubts when comparing a rich man's access to God's kingdom to a camel passing through the eye of a needle. Maybe a socialist playwright's view is more realistic: "on happiness this I can tell: it is your wealth that makes you living well."[1] At any rate, prosperity and its causes are easier to measure than heavenly bliss, and more objectively at that. Chapter 8 will examine if measurability is a good enough argument for rejecting happiness as a realistic social goal of "development."

The measurement of wealth as an indicator of prosperity might be easier, but it is not easy. The System of National Accounts (SNA) defines wealth owned by individuals as "net worth," i.e., the difference between their assets and liabilities (European Commission et al. 2009, paras. 2.122, 3.109). Assets yield benefits whereas liabilities need to be paid back to the creditor with interest. The SNA is less clear about the nature of a benefit − "a gain or positive utility arising from an action" (ibid., para. 3.19) − and about "disbenefits" stemming from a liability.

Benefits would include the rewards of income for providing labor and capital to production. Such income can be spent on goods and services after maintaining net worth, i.e., accounting for capital consumption and meeting liabilities. The widely used measure of income has, however, its own difficulties of definition and measurement. It can be viewed as a flow of revenue that accounts for (deducts) expected wealth losses. It can also be considered as a measure that accounts for both expected and unexpected losses and "windfalls" from resource depletion, discovery, and human-made and natural disasters (see Box 3.1 in section 3.3.1 below).

There are good reasons therefore to look first into what can be measured and hence rationally managed. We will not obtain in this case what we might ultimately look for, i.e., the effects of income and wealth on utility or feelings of wellbeing. The established indicators of wealth, income and consumption can, however, set benchmarks, validated by accounting checks and balances. From here one could venture into more evaluative analyses of wellbeing and happiness.

Wealth is a matter of holding and using assets. Economic agents of enterprises, households, government and non-profit organizations can own financial assets of cash, deposits or shares and non-financial assets such as buildings, equipment, natural resources and durable goods in inventories. As mentioned, debts and other liabilities detract from personal wealth because of commitments made to pay off creditors. The accounting measure of net worth is therefore a better indicator of personal wealth than the gross value of assets and resources owned.

Capital used as a factor of production is a narrower concept of "productive" wealth as it excludes inventories of short-lived goods and financial resources. Contrary to personal wealth owned by people, non-financial capital focuses on its use in production and its maintenance for generating future output and income, i.e., the sustainability of economic growth. Chapters 4 and 5 deal with the macro-economic concern of sustainable growth. Here the focus is on personal wealth and income. But there is of course a connection between micro-economic prosperity and macro-economic sustainability that is fluid because the former contributes to the latter, which is based on the total of individual incomes used and assets owned.

This interface becomes a problem when the national accounts exclude human capital and consumer durables from productive capital. For human capital the reason is that the notion of ownership of humans and the evaluation of their health and skills is uncomfortably close to slavery. Consequently, and because of their contribution to wellbeing, the accounts treat increases in human capital through health services, education and training as personal consumption rather than productive investment. Similarly, the repeated use of long-lasting consumption goods is deemed to be a one-time consumption expenditure rather than a capital investment; these goods are not used in production like capital inputs and are therefore assumed to be part of household consumption. Alternative (satellite) accounts (ibid., paras. 29.45, 29.152) could, however, be more experimental in treating labor and consumer durables as capital.

3.2 Who owns the wealth, who gets the income?

Average per-capita wealth and income can compare the prosperity of people in countries and regions, but averages can hide large inequalities. Most national offices shy away from assessing the distribution of wealth and income because of the difficulty in getting access to individual balance sheets of households. Moreover, distributional concerns cannot be directly combined with the levels of income generated or wealth owned. This section deals with the distribution of income and wealth in some detail because personal prosperity is a question of income and wealth available to individuals or individual households.

3.2.1 Distribution of personal wealth and income

Less hampered by qualms about estimating the value and distribution of personal wealth, non-governmental organizations and scholars present data on the level, distribution and trend of personal wealth in and among countries and major world regions.[2] The personal wealth data compiled by the Credit Suisse Research Institute (2016) exclude governmental assets and debts, which could not be assigned to individual owners. They also ignore human capital for the reasons discussed in section 3.1. Figure 3.1 shows that *total* personal wealth doubled globally since 2000 in current exchange rates to reach US$256 trillion in 2016. The decline in 2008 reflects the financial crisis that was overcome just a few years later. However, the

24 Economic sustainability

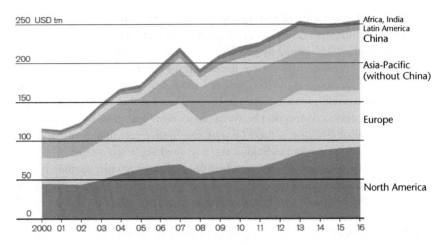

FIGURE 3.1 Global personal wealth, 2000–2016 (by region, current US$ exchange rates). Wealth increased in all regions of the world. North America and Europe hold most of the world's wealth, but wealth increased most rapidly in China

Source: Credit Suisse Research Institute (2016, p. 14, Fig. 1).

increase slowed down in recent years. North American and Western European residents and those of rich Asia-Pacific and Middle Eastern countries hold most of total wealth, but China shows the fastest (fivefold) increase of personal wealth.[3]

According to the Credit Suisse Research Institute (2016, Table 1), global wealth per adult increased during 2000–2016 from US$31,600 to US$52,800. In 2016, North America and Europe were the richest regions with wealth per adult of US$337,000 and US$125,000, respectively. Africa and India were the poorest with wealth per adult of about US$4000. Figure 3.2 gives a first impression how this wealth is distributed among the people of the world's regions. It shows the shares of the number of individuals in the different deciles of the distribution of wealth. The figure does not show, though, the large variations within and among different countries. Still, it reveals:

- a distinct concentration of people with low wealth (in the first four deciles) in Africa and India;
- mid-to-high wealth ownership concentrated in the fifth to ninth deciles for China;
- concentration of Europe's and North America's wealth in the highest deciles; and
- a rather equal spread of wealth in Asia and Latin America over the different wealth brackets.

Note the distinct contrast in the distribution of wealth between China and India in the higher and lower deciles, respectively.

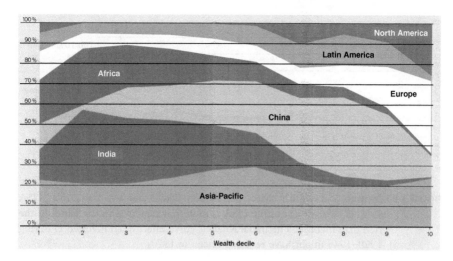

FIGURE 3.2 Regional distribution of global personal wealth, 2016. Most wealth is concentrated in the hands of the rich in North America and Europe. In contrast, in India and Africa the poor hold most of the wealth at low per-capita levels. Latin America shows a relatively equal distribution over its wealth strata

Source: Credit Suisse Research Institute (2016, p. 11, Fig. 8).

Average (median) wealth increased in all regions during 2000–2016, but showed different trends after the financial crisis: it increased in North America and China and decreased in Europe and the world (ibid., p. 19, Fig. 9). Current global personal wealth is over three times the value of global gross domestic product (GDP) (ibid., p. 39, Fig. 1), which is often used as a proxy for (gross) national income. Wealth is generally more heavily concentrated in the hands of the rich than income. For instance, in the USA, the concentration is about 20–30 percent higher for wealth than for income – a pattern that has been quite stable for the last 100 years (Figure 3.3). This pattern would make either wealth or income suitable for assessing the distributional trends in countries like the USA. At least there, the trends in the earlier 1900s of decreasing concentration of income and wealth for the rich seem to be in reverse now. Since the 1970s the top 10 percent of income earners in the USA increased their share of total income from about 30 percent to nearly 50 percent.

Piketty (2014, Fig. 9.8) finds a similar increase for the USA. He sees a much lower increase for the share of income of the top 10 percent in European countries: since 1970 their share rose from 30 to 35 percent by 2010. Selected developing countries (Indonesia, South Africa, Argentina) show rising income inequality in terms of increasing shares of the top 10 percent (ibid., Fig. 9.9), but at much lower overall income levels than those of industrialized nations. Income inequality also increased in the emerging economies of China and India from 4 percent to about 10 percent since the 1980s. A lack of data does not allow, though, a comprehensive assessment of inequality in developing countries.

26 Economic sustainability

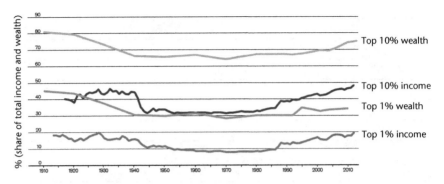

FIGURE 3.3 Income and wealth shares of the top decile and top percentile, USA 1910–2013. Wealth in the USA is more concentrated in the hands of the rich than income. The initial Kuznets curve effect of an inverted U during 1920–1945 might have reversed since the 1970s

Source: Credit Suisse Research Institute (2014, p. 29, Fig. 1).

Disdaining the "scientificity" of theoretical economic models, Piketty relies on historical trends – like those of Figure 3.3 – to explain increasing inequality in rich countries. He rejects the deterministic hypothesis of Kuznets (1955), according to which income inequality first increases with initial industrialization and then declines with further economic development in capitalist economies. Figure 3.3 indicates that this movement of an inverted U holds until the 1940s in the USA, but might have reversed since the 1970s. Piketty (2014, pp. 13, 237) holds that the Great Depression and the World Wars created "accidental shocks" that reduced inequality temporarily only in 1914 and 1945.

Piketty (2014, pp. 20, 21) concludes therefore that all we can do is observe the "deeply political" forces of "convergence" to and "divergence" from equality. In rich countries, the spread of knowledge and skills has been a factor in convergence to income equality, whereas weak economic growth and high returns to capital caused divergence in wealth ownership. The forces of divergence tend now to overwhelm those of convergence. The author believes to have found a widening global gap between the return to capital and economic growth and a corresponding increase in the concentration of wealth owned by the rich. The future, notably of technological effects, is of course hardly possible to predict.

Developing countries, which are about to take off, should be aware that an increase in inequality of their people might be in the cards. For those developing countries, for which total income distribution could be estimated, Piketty predicts a rapid convergence towards US levels of inequality as these countries already surpassed Europe's levels. A recent study (Pressman and Scott III 2017, p. 362) found that Piketty overlooked that rising inequality might cause environmental decline affecting economic growth when scarce resources are used to "save the planet."

The few examples do not confirm, though, the more comprehensive regional findings of the Credit Suisse Research Institute. Piketty (2014, pp. 436, 437) is quite skeptical about the validity of these estimates because of the absence of data available from taxation for most countries. A United Nations (2013, p. 25) report comes yet to another conclusion, claiming that "inequalities have declined somewhat across countries in recent years, but they have risen within many countries." All these estimates are highly uncertain as they are based on trends for different time periods in selected countries. Changes in technology, attitudes towards holding and increasing property, and distributive policies might bring about unexpected changes in the future.

3.2.2 Labor vs. capital

A closer look at the distribution of income and wealth would allocate the indicators to different social groups in society. The United Nations (2013) report describes the disadvantages faced by social groups characterized by age, ethnicity, disability and migration. All groups share some of the disadvantages in income, education, employment and health. As these effects may go beyond economic wellbeing they are discussed as part of broader development and its sustainability (see Part IV). The following addresses therefore briefly only the historical confrontation of labor and capital in society.

Marx (1894) considered this confrontation as the root cause of class struggle where capital owners exploit wage earners. In contrast, mainstream economists tend to tone down this division as a matter of different marginal productivities of production factors in models of perfect competition. In these models, everyone gets the income he/she deserves according to the respective contribution to production and demand. The real world is not perfect, however, giving rise to glaring inequalities in the distribution of income between labor inputs and capital services. The question is, how imperfect is it? The economic theory of marginal productivity claims to provide the benchmark from which to determine and evaluate actual inequalities in income distribution.

Piketty (2014, p. 330) sees an "illusion" of the theory of marginal productivity. He finds high inequality in income and wealth in Europe and especially the USA, which cannot be explained by theoretical analysis. He considers such inequality "less apocalyptic" than Marx's view of unlimited accumulation of capital in the hands of the few, but still deems recent developments to be "quite disturbing" (ibid., p. 10). At least in OECD countries the share of labor income in total national income dropped to about 62 percent from 66 percent in the 1990s (OECD 2012, p. 110). Stiglitz (2013) describes vividly the growth of inequality in the USA, brought about by government policy, monopolies and the power of interest groups favoring the "one percent" at the top. At the same time their growing income remains hidden from the other "ninety-nine percent."

Piketty deserves credit for exploring the differences in income generated by labor and capital and their distribution among "classes" of high-, middle- and low-income earners. For those countries where sufficient data were available (Europe and USA), Table 3.1 compares the distribution of these incomes. The table shows

28 Economic sustainability

TABLE 3.1 Distribution of income between labor and capital, Europe and USA[a]

	Labor		Capital	
	Europe	*USA*	*Europe*	*USA*
Top 10% (upper class)	25%	35%	60%	70%
Middle 40% (middle class)	45%	40%	35%	25%
Bottom 50% (lower class)	30%	25%	5%	5%
Gini coefficient	0.26	0.36	0.67	0.73

Source: based on Piketty (2014, Tables 7.1 and 7.2).

Note
a At around 2010.

that labor income is fairly well distributed, but capital incomes (returns) are highly concentrated in the hands of the rich (upper 10 percent) who earn 60–70 percent of total income. The author claims that this unequal split between labor and capital can be found in all countries where data are available. The Gini coefficient for labor and capital income confirms these results: the coefficient for capital income is more than double the income coefficient for labor. The USA generally shows higher inequality in capital and labor income than Europe. The bottom capital income earners in the table are the exception; they do not own a significant portion of financial and non-financial wealth.

3.3 Sustainability

Personal prosperity is measured as an average of income and wealth. Only their distribution can indicate who, i.e., which stratum of the population, might actually have enough income and wealth to enjoy their fruits. The ultimate evaluation of a particular distribution is a question of determining its fairness or equity, which is treated in section 10.1 as the social dimension of rather normative sustainable development. The maintenance of average per-capita income and wealth is a matter of economic sustainability. It should tell us if, when and for whom prosperity can be expected to increase.

3.3.1 Sustainable income and wealth

Section 2.3 reminds us to distinguish between *ex-ante* analysis of expected sustainability and statistical observation of past sustainability. This is particularly relevant for the assessment of a theoretical income concept. Hicks (1946, p. 172) can be credited with introducing sustainability into personal income, defining it as "the maximum value ... [a man] can consume during a week, and still *expect* [own emphasis] to be as well off at the end of the week as he was at the beginning." He also claimed that the conventional measurement of individual incomes and their aggregation into social income has little meaning; the reason is unexpected windfalls and losses that should not be ignored in the "prudent" management of income and wealth (ibid., p. 178).

Unexpected windfalls and losses are the result of non-market activities and events which are not part of the regular plans and budgets of economic agents. They can, however, drastically affect their activities and wellbeing and could render conventional income accounts unsuitable for the analysis of future sustainability. The SNA (European Commission et al. 2009, para. 8.25) acknowledges the discrepancy between a theoretical and an accounting concept of income, but does not explain what using the *ex-post* accounting measure would do to economic analysis. Essentially the descriptive accounts of the SNA leave the evaluation of future events to assumptive modeling of the growth of wealth and income. Such models might have some influence on the expectations of economic agents, their market negotiations and the resulting prices of goods and services. Where such market valuation does not regularly take place – as in the case of rarely traded natural resource deposits – the discounting of expected changes in the value of wealth could provide an estimate of the present value of wealth (see section 4.2).

Box 3.1 elaborates on the disconnect between the *ex-ante* and *ex-post* income concepts caused by unexpected changes in wealth that affect the sustainability of future income flows. Hicksian income seeks to maintain people's ability to spend their income "without impoverishing themselves" (Hicks 1946, p. 172). The sustained ability to spend makes people at least as well off at the end of an accounting period as at the beginning. We are offered here one of the first definitions of – economic – sustainability in terms of maintaining the capital value of income generation. Hicks is of course aware of the problems facing the definition and measurement of "true" income, including changing interest (discount) rates and prices, and the existence of consumer durables and windfalls. True income is therefore not directly measurable. Hicks suggests, though, exploring ways of adjusting income to obtain an improved "statistical estimate" of social income (ibid., pp. 179–80). This is the approach taken in the next chapter for improving the *ex-post* sustainability of *national* income.

Rough estimates of the net wealth of private households, narrowly defined in section 3.2.1, is predicted to grow "roughly in line with nominal GDP" (Credit Suisse Research Institute 2016, p. 39). This assumption would indicate sustained growth of wealth in the future. Per-capita wealth might rise by 21 percent by 2021, with Switzerland, Australia and the USA maintaining their highest ranks over the near future. China may not reach this height but is predicted to show a dynamic leap-frogging in country ranks.

3.3.2 Towards greater equality?

Unexpected gains and losses affect the maintenance of stocks of wealth owned and income flows received, and, hence, the ability to avoid impoverishment. They are hard to assess. Measuring deviation from equality in personal wealth and income might be a more objective way to measure trends in *relative* prosperity, i.e.,

30 Economic sustainability

BOX 3.1 ACCOUNTING AND ANALYSIS OF INCOME AND WEALTH

Adjusting national income for taxes, subsidies and transfers obtains disposable income that can be used for consumption and saving. Controversy sets in when economic agents are not content with using current income for their purchases, financing further acquisitions by credit. The income accounts do not enter this controversy about income overuse but switch to another set of "capital accounts," where post-consumption savings, a residual of disposable income use, provide just one source of finance for capital formation.

Not so economists à la Hicks, who interpret income as a measure that maintains the net worth (commonly called "wealth") of an economic agent. Debt incurred to finance asset acquisition beyond savings would detract from the agent being as well off as before since his/her net worth (the difference between assets and liabilities) is reduced. Sustainability is thus part of an analytical income concept which allows maximum consumption for economic agents while maintaining their wealth. Unexpected positive and negative windfalls are part of the analysis of maximum feasible consumption.

In contrast, the national accounts allow only actual or at least expected changes in wealth – notably of the depreciation of fixed assets – into their income concepts. Any other changes in wealth such as unrequited capital transfers, discovery and depletion of natural resources, impacts of natural disasters and wars, and price changes are pushed into separate balance sheets and asset accounts (European Commission et al. 2009, para. 16.38). Sustainability in terms of maintaining net worth does not, or at least not fully (beyond capital depreciation), feature in the accounting concept of disposable income.

---

inequality. Section 3.2 gave some impression of increasing inequality. The question is when inequality affects the sustainability of generating and receiving personal income and enjoying wellbeing therefrom. Unhappiness with falling behind society's trend in prosperity is a detractor from wellbeing. It is difficult to measure as it refers to some kind of jealousy popularly expressed as "keeping up with the Joneses."

Rather than dealing with feelings of unhappiness, Piketty (2014, p. 15) seeks to integrate distributional concerns into "the heart of economic analysis." He compares trends in the return to produced capital to the returns of all factors of production, as a measure of change in the inequality of income distribution. Historically he finds at least for a few rich countries for which data are available that taxation pushed the rate of capital return below the rate of economic growth. This would indicate a successful reduction of inequality during 1913–2012. However, the recent explosion of income absorption by the top 10 percent of rich countries, notably in the USA (Box 3.2), might indicate a reversal of the trend of declining

BOX 3.2 INEQUALITY IN THE USA

Inequality in the USA stands out. Stiglitz (2013) blames government policies. Deregulated financial markets and low progressivity of the tax system encourage "rent seeking," i.e., the exploitation of the poor and uninformed. Some of the consequences of glaring inequality in incomes are unmanageable student loans, lack of opportunity because of a skewed educational system and low life expectancy, notably for women. Stiglitz also argues that the excessive inequality in the USA might undermine the sustainability of economic growth.

Piketty (2014) also finds extreme inequality in the USA, effectively turning the Kuznets Curve hypothesis on its head for the twentieth century. He predicts extremely high inequality of about 60 percent of total income in the hands of the top 10 percent (25 percent held by the top 1 percent).

Extreme inequality in the next decades would bring about "horrors" and "nightmares" (Shiller 2016). Such anxiety is symptomatic of a growing fear of unsustainable extremes in the country's distribution of income and wealth.

inequality. By the end of the twenty-first century the returns to capital might exceed the economic growth rate by 3 percent (ibid., p. 356, Fig. 10.10). Increased possession of income and wealth by the wealthy would be the result.

If the increase in inequality reaches 50 percent of income absorption by the top decile of income earners, "a revolution will likely occur" (Piketty 2014, p. 263). In other words, income distribution would be non-sustainable. Setting such a standard of non-sustainability is of course judgmental and lower or higher thresholds could be imagined. Any development towards these standards is also highly uncertain since no natural path of a balanced (*à la* Kuznets, see section 5.1.1) or imbalanced growth and a corresponding societal response can be anticipated. Moreover, the estimates for just a few industrialized countries cannot reflect global outcomes. The more comprehensive analyses of the Credit Suisse Research Institute (2016, p. 42, Fig. 5) predict that the low segment of wealth owners will expand slowly by about 2 percent only, whereas the middle class will see a growth rate of wealth of over 20 percent by 2021.

It is another question whether such increase in inequality could be tolerated or not, in other words, whether it is sustainable or unsustainable from a normative point of view. Intuitively one would believe that high inequality is not a good thing, and we would be better off if income and wealth were more equally distributed. Behind this objective is a notion of equity that needs to be more clearly specified. The above-mentioned 50 percent-of-income absorption by the top 10 percent is judgmental. Other settings of quantifiable targets for the Gini coefficient, which measure income and wealth in top and bottom quantiles, or a poverty line are of course also a rather subjective assessment of inequality in the distribution of income and wealth. The latest Earth Summit addresses such "inequity" by calling for the

32 Economic sustainability

mitigation of poverty at particular poverty lines, and as part of the goals of sustainable development (United Nations, no date). Chapter 10 will address distributional goals and targets of the social dimension of sustainable development.

Notes

1 Own translation of "Mir löst sich ganz von selbst das Glücksproblem, nur wer im Wohlstand lebt, lebt angenehm" (Brecht, B., Threepenny Opera: "The ballad of good living").
2 Note in particular the "Standardized world income inequality database" (Solt 2016), the United Nations (2013) *Report on the World Social Situation* and the *Global Wealth Report* (Credit Suisse Research Institute 2016).
3 In current US$ exchange rates reflecting the current distributions of personal wealth among countries and regions; using constant rates China's dominant growth in wealth is surpassed by Latin America and about equalized by India and Africa (Credit Suisse Research Institute 2016, pp. 16, 17).

References

Credit Suisse Research Institute (2014). *Global Wealth Report 2014*. Online: http://economics.uwo.ca/people/davies_docs/credit-suisse-global-wealth-report-2014.pdf (accessed 30 August 2017).

Credit Suisse Research Institute (2016). *Global Wealth Report 2016*. Online: www.credit-suisse.com/corporate/en/articles/news-and-expertise/the-global-wealth-report-2016-201611.html (accessed 4 October 2017).

European Commission, International Monetary Fund, Organisation for Economic Co-operation and Development, United Nations and World Bank (2009). *System of National Accounts 2008*. Online: http://unstats.un.org/unsd/nationalaccount/docs/SNA2008.pdf (accessed 29 October 2017).

Hicks, J.R. (1946, 2nd ed.). *Value and Capital: An Inquiry into Some Fundamental Principles of Economic Theory*. Oxford: Oxford University Press.

Kuznets, S. (1955). Economic growth and income inequality, *American Economic Review* 45: 1–28.

Marx, K. (1894). *Das Kapital*, reprint 1981: *Capital*, Harmondsworth, UK: Penguin.

Organisation for Economic Co-operation and Development (OECD) (2012). *Employment Outlook 2012*, Paris: OECD. Online: www.oecd-ilibrary.org/employment/oecd-employment-outlook-2012_empl_outlook-2012-en (accessed 6 August 2017).

Piketty, T. (2014). *Capital in the Twenty-first Century*, Cambridge, MA and London: Belknap Press of Harvard University Press.

Pressman, S. and Scott III, R.H. (2017). Thomas Piketty, growth, distribution and the environment, in P.A. Victor and B. Dolter (eds.), *Handbook on Growth and Sustainability*, Cheltenham, UK and Northampton, MA: Edward Elgar: 356–71.

Shiller, R.J. (2016). Inequality today, catastrophe tomorrow, *New York Times*, 28 August 2016, Sunday Business. Online: www.nytimes.com/2016/08/28/upshot/todays-inequality-could-easily-become-tomorrows-catastrophe.html?_r=0 (accessed 29 October 2017).

Solt, F. (2016). The standardized world income inequality database, *Social Science Quarterly* 97 (5): 1267–81. Online: http://onlinelibrary.wiley.com/doi/10.1111/ssqu.12295/abstract (accessed 11 May 2017).

Stiglitz, J.E. (2013). *The Price of Inequality: How Today's Divided Society Endangers Our Future*, New York and London: Norton.

United Nations (2013). *Inequality Matters: Report of the World Social Situation 2013*, New York: United Nations. Online: www.un.org/esa/socdev/documents/reports/Inequality Matters.pdf (accessed 1 October 2017).

United Nations (no date). Sustainable development goals. Online: www.un.org/sustainable development/sustainable-development-goals/ (accessed 27 August 2017).

4

WE, THE NATION

Towards a sustainable economy

Chapter 3 describes sustainability as a feature of personal income and wealth. Hicks' (1946) income concept advises people to maintain their net worth when embarking on consumption. This notion of sustainability is often called upon for measuring sustainability collectively at the national level as non-declining wealth or capital. The purpose is to maintain national income, product or economic welfare. This chapter examines the meaning and measurability of these concepts and indicators. Chapter 5 explores the future sustainability of national income and wealth.

4.1 National welfare and wealth

4.1.1 Economic welfare

Direct measures of national welfare add positive and deduct negative welfare effects to/from economic indicators. Reacting to the critique of using national income, product or consumption as indicators of economic welfare, Nordhaus and Tobin (1973) were among the first to compile a Measure of Economic Welfare (MEW). Their measure adds the monetary benefits of "desirables" of leisure and non-market output and deducts "regrettables" of environmental and other social costs to and from gross national product.

Still, environmentalists criticized the MEW for its preconceived faith in economic growth. Large positive imputations for leisure and non-market subsistence and relatively low deductions for environmental and social deterioration understated in their opinion the social cost of economic growth. They advanced therefore their own Index of Sustainable Economic Welfare (Daly and Cobb 1989), which included a broader list of regrettable expenditures and environmental damages. After some modification for leisure and work, the index was later promoted as a Genuine Progress Indicator (GPI) (Cobb et al. 1995).

The GPI deducts the "cost" of defensive expenditures, unequal income distribution, pollution damage and underemployment from, and adds benefits of volunteering, household work, leisure and durable goods to, personal consumption. Further adding net capital investment turns adjusted consumption into an adjusted income measure. Expenditures for defending society against crime, accidents, preventable disasters and environmental deterioration are considered "needless" (Talberth et al. 2007, p. 2) because they serve only to maintain rather than increase welfare.

Unsurprisingly, the GPI leans heavily towards the negative side of welfare losses. The intention might be to prove a "threshold hypothesis" (Max-Neef 1995), according to which welfare reaches a turning point because of the damaging effects of high-level economic growth. First estimates of the GPI seemed to confirm the hypothesis for the USA (Cobb et al. 1995). Revised calculations, shown in Figure 4.1, dilute the hypothesis: they indicate stagnating welfare since the 1970s, with gross domestic production (GDP) continuing to increase (at least until the 2008 recession). The GPI for the USA was not extended beyond the year 2003. A revised version was recently launched for 2012–2014, whose greater coverage of non-market effects and other methodological changes increases the GPI/GDP ratio to over 50 percent (Talberth and Weisdorf 2017). Extending the GPI of 17 rich (non-US) countries (representing almost 60 percent of world GDP) to global levels

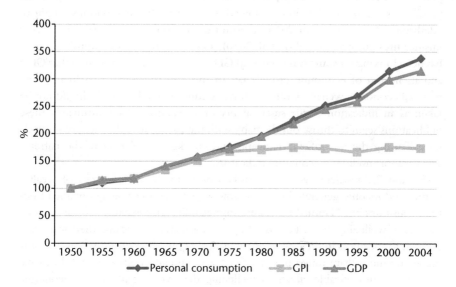

FIGURE 4.1 GPI, GDP and personal consumption per capita, USA 1950–2004 (in constant prices, 1950 = 100). GDP and personal consumption moved in tandem with the GPI until the 1970s. Since then they separated in a scissor movement: economic welfare (GPI) stagnated while the economy showed steady growth

Source: based on data from Talberth et al. (2007).

36 Economic sustainability

(Kubiszewski et al. 2013)[1] indicates stagnation of average global GPI with GDP nearly doubling – similarly to the trends observed in the USA.

Major flaws impair the validity of the GPI as a measure of sustainable welfare; they include the

- judgmental distinction and selection of regrettable and desirable expenditures: should we really count expenses for environmental protection, natural disasters, defense, security and accidents as regrettable? In most cases these expenses might actually improve our less than perfect real-life conditions. How about unhealthy food and drink, tasteless entertainment and useless defense? Who is to judge?
- opaque valuation mix of market values for natural resource use with controversial welfare/damage values for ecosystem services and environmental externalities;
- mixing of non-comparable and possibly overlapping sustainability concepts of non-declining welfare and capital maintenance.[2]

The merit of the GPI is to draw attention to the misuse of GDP as a welfare measure. The authors seem to be blinded, though, by their antagonism to mainstream economics, proclaiming that the GPI "would blast away the obfuscatory polemics of growth – and the devious politics that goes with it" (Cobb et al. 1995, p. 72). A wave of GDP bashing followed: US non-profit organizations sought to "dethrone" GDP (Talberth 2010), a group of economists explained why "GDP mismeasures our lives" (Stiglitz et al. 2010), and the European Commission (2015) has been looking for some time "beyond GDP." The general argument is that GDP and its notion of economic growth fail to measure the sum of wellbeing, i.e., national economic welfare. Consequently, continuing GDP growth should not be taken as an indication of the sustainability of an economy.[3] Unfortunately these publications seem to throw out the baby with the bath water; they ignore possibilities of using the quantifiable concepts and checks and balances of the national accounts for modifying economic indicators.

Section 2.1 restricted economic sustainability to the maintenance of wealth, output and income generated by economic activity, and wellbeing obtained from final consumption. National economic sustainability thus excludes non-economic sources of wellbeing either because they are not scarce or because their scarcity is difficult to specify as in the case of distributional equity or altruistic action. Extending economic welfare into a notion of general "human" welfare would thus have to add non-monetizable effects of wellbeing that would have a zero economic value. They would have to be assessed by indicator averages of development, quality of life or even happiness (see Part IV).

4.1.2 Economic wealth

Boulding (1966) famously asked: "Is it ... eating that is a good thing, or is it being well fed?" In his view the "spaceman economy" with limited stocks of natural assets makes minimizing production and consumption flows, while maximizing the state of wellbeing, a much better option for generating human welfare than maximizing consumption. Boulding also complained that "the economics profession has neglected with astonishing singlemindedness" the state and stocks aspects of human welfare.

His assertion that wellbeing is more in the nature of a state than a continuous flow, created and changed by consumption, can, however, be questioned. Three decades after Boulding's complaint, the World Bank (1997) advanced a broader Measure of Comprehensive Wealth. The reason for shifting the focus from flow indicators of national output and income to the "portfolio management" of stocks of wealth differs from Boulding's call for limiting the consumption of goods and services: wealth is seen as an easier-to-measure proxy for generating economic welfare, the ultimate objective of economic activity.

Economic theory provides the justification for using the value of wealth as a measure of national welfare. Box 4.1 describes the assumptions necessary for estimating comprehensive wealth and welfare of an economy. The "trick" is to assume that the current value of total wealth equals the present (discounted) value of future

---

BOX 4.1 WORLD BANK (2011) ESTIMATION OF COMPREHENSIVE WEALTH

Assumptive steps:

1 National income is seen as the return to using comprehensive wealth in production. Contrary to the balance sheets of the national accounts, which cover produced and non-produced natural capital, comprehensive wealth includes also human, social and institutional capital.

2 Income is considered as the level of actual and deferred (through saving) consumption, generating economic welfare. Discounting future consumption, assumed to be constant over the average lifetime of assets, allows interpretation of the present value of wealth as the present value of welfare it generates.

3 The assumption of constant consumption "in a competitive economy" facilitates the calculation of comprehensive wealth, as a measure of sustainable (non-declining) welfare.

4 Separate estimates of produced and natural capital (and their depreciation) can be subtracted from total (comprehensive) wealth to obtain "intangible" (human, social and institutional capital) wealth as a residual value.

38 Economic sustainability

consumption generated by existing assets. Current wealth, measured as the present value of consumption is then assumed to equal the welfare generated by the use of comprehensive wealth in production during an accounting period.

The Comprehensive Wealth Measure (CWM) thus reflects only *economic* welfare obtained from the consumption of produced goods and services. The comprehensiveness of capital categories covered seems to have lured World Bank economists into treating the maintenance of capital used in production as a criterion of broad sustainable development (World Bank 2011, p. 3) rather than sustainable economic growth. Even the broadest notion of people's willingness to *pay* for their wellbeing keeps them in the realm of economics and economic sustainability. Any payment is obviously restricted by the ability to pay either from income or by incurring an – eventually to be paid off – debt. Development in monetary terms (beyond economic growth) is difficult to imagine.

There is no evidence that the basic assumption of an optimal (competitive) path of economic growth (see Box 4.1) has been realized or will be reached in the future. Other rather judgmental assumptions admittedly affect the validity of the estimates. They include the reinvestment of economic rent from exhaustible natural resources according to the Hartwick (1977) rule,[4] the setting of the discount rate, the validity of the implied welfare function and the scope and contents of residual "intangible" wealth. The value of using abstract economic theory seems to be more in the conceptualization of wealth, welfare and sustainability than in realistic measurement.

More recently, United Nations organizations advanced an Inclusive Wealth Index (IWI) (UNEP and UNU-IHDP 2012). The index also refers to non-declining welfare, but does not make sustainability a condition for measurement. Rather, it applies directly "shadow prices" of the contribution of a marginal unit of a capital asset to current and (discounted) future welfare (ibid., Annex 1). In practice, it replaces the contribution to welfare by (net) income obtained from using produced, human and natural capital in production. The IWI also treats remaining effects of "social capital" as a residual. This residual supposedly represents the "enabling functions" of knowledge, institutions, culture and religion. This would obviously go well beyond economic welfare and wealth. An adjustment for "total factor productivity" corrects the index for social capital use in the creation of wealth and welfare. Total factor productivity thus seeks to cover all "missing factors" in economic growth.

The CWM and IWI acknowledge both the outstanding role of climate change in future welfare losses; they actually treat CO_2 emission as a surrogate for environmental degradation. The two indices differ, however, in attributing the damage of carbon emissions. The IWI distributes global damage according to the "potential effect of global warming in ... economies" (ibid., p. 215). Global damage is valued as a kind of capital consumption at a rather arbitrary value of US$50 per ton of carbon. The CWM, on the other hand, estimates a value for the carbon stock as the social cost that would have avoided climate change damage if no CO_2 had been emitted. It shows this value as a share of the CWM but does not include it in the total CWM value. To do so would have to treat the carbon stock as a rather unusual counterproductive negative form of capital, i.e., an environmental debt for dealing with this damage. Such a debt would be owed to nature rather than economic agents. It is therefore treated as a detraction from natural wealth in section 6.3.4.

Both indices come with questionable assumptions. For one, they take discounted income or consumption obtained from capital use over the lifetime of an asset as a measure of the welfare it generates. There is, however, no clear measurable connection between economic indicators and the welfare they might generate for and among a country's inhabitants, unless one takes the discounting of the future as a valid estimate of potential welfare effects. Also, the indices consider the difference between market-priced assets and total wealth/welfare (discounted income or consumption) as the value of residual assets used in production. Moreover, the mix of market prices, discounted rents and damage values used in the wealth/welfare estimates makes the total a rather murky aggregate.

A largely ignored issue is the role of financial wealth in the assessment of economic sustainability. Chapter 3 treated the sustainability of non-financial and financial *personal* (net) wealth as a matter of its distribution among people. At the macro-economic level domestic claims and liabilities cancel out, leaving only foreign debts and loans as the "international investment position" (IIP) (European Commission et al. 2009, paras. 13.2, 26.12). Reflecting financial claims of one economy on other economies of the "rest of the world," the IIP can be seen as an indicator of international liquidity and vulnerability. The question is how to translate such vulnerability into a macro-economic sustainability measure. The two wealth indices give different answers.

The World Bank includes the IIP as a further type of productive capital in its CWM. It assumes that net claims on foreign financial assets contribute to national wealth, economic growth and welfare. The IWI omits financial assets in both the regular and adjusted version of the index. The recessions of debtor nations such as Greece suggest, however, that excessive foreign debt can indeed be the cause of non-sustainability of an economy.

The question is how to translate "excessive" foreign and national, notably governmental, debt into a non-sustainable economic performance. Governmental debt or surplus is a valid tool or source of having invested or planning to invest in public goods and services. It is also a policy instrument of counteracting cyclical ups and downs of the economy, providing stability to economic growth. Non-sustainability is caused when public debt or surplus exceed the level of "normal" spending and efforts of growth stabilization. Any normality standard would be rather arbitrary. At any rate, anti-cyclical public spending is more in the nature of conventional economic policy; it is therefore not further pursued here.[5]

Differing concepts and methods create different results. Both, the CWM and IWI, claim to cover most of the world's wealth, despite introducing a different number of countries. The comparison of 1995 and 2005 global wealth indicates that the value of the IWI is 93 percent of the CWM value in 1995 and about 80 percent in 2005 (Table 4.1). Global wealth thus grew at different rates from 1995 to 2005: about 15 percent for the IWI and 25 percent for the CWM. Table 4.1 also

40 Economic sustainability

TABLE 4.1 Global inclusive and comprehensive wealth, 1995 and 2005

	Inclusive wealth[a]				Comprehensive wealth[b]			
	1995		2005		1995		2005	
	US$ '000 billion	%	US$ '000 billion	%	US$ '000 billion	%	US$ '000 billion	%)
Low-income countries	4.1	0.9	4.6	0.9	2.4	0.5	3.6	0.5
Lower-middle-income countries	29.9	6.4	35.1	6.4	34.0	6.7	58.0	8.6
Upper-middle-income countries	94.6	20.2	108.6	20.1	36.8	7.3	47.2	7.0
High-income countries	339.7	72.5	392.2	72.6	421.6	83.6	552.0	81.9
TOTAL	468.3	100	540.5	100	504.5	98.1	673.6	98.0

Sources: UNEP and UNU-IHDP (2014), World Bank (2011).

Notes

a Human, produced and natural capital of 140 countries.

b Produced, natural and intangible capital of 120 countries; income groups exclude oil exporting countries.

shows that the concentration of wealth in countries with different levels of income differs notably for high- and upper-middle-income countries. For the latter, wealth is almost three times higher in the IWI than the CWM.

4.2 Greening the national accounts

4.2.1 Ignored non-market effects

The above-described estimates of the value of wealth and welfare and their sustainability are questionable because of the use of assumptive utility/welfare valuations. The indices may be derived from the national accounts conventions of economic (capital) assets but their extended wealth measures go beyond a realistic measurement when they include intangible wealth of human and social capital.

The national accounts, on the other hand, seek objectivity by using observable data.[6] They reject the measurement of welfare and focus on assets that are traded and valued by markets, or for which market values can be plausibly estimated. Rather than incorporating a wide range of opaque social concerns, the standard System of National Accounts (SNA) cuts through the fog of an overload of information about people and their activities by "condensing" the data according to "universally valid" economic principles and accounting rules (European Commission et al. 2009, paras. 1.1, 1.4).

We, the nation: towards a sustainable economy **41**

One could argue, though, that the SNA takes the condensation of information too far when it ignores the measurement and use of scarce non-market types of capital. The use of scarce assets that are not traded in markets can affect the values of economic production, consumption and capital formation. In particular, there is a risk of undermining economic growth by over-mining natural capital. The problem is how to deal with non-market impacts of economic activities and with the effects of natural events on economic activities. The national accounts and conventional economic analysis generally ignore these impacts and effects as "external."

Table 4.2 categorizes these impacts as the results of economic activities of production and consumption on other economic activities ("genuine" externalities) and of non-economic activities and events on economic activities. Externalities of economic activities are the effects of unintended interdependent economic activities. They remain therefore uncontrolled, unpriced and uncompensated (Das Gupta and Pearce 1972; Mishan 1973). In particular, they include environmental effects of natural resource depletion[7] and environmental degradation from wastes and pollutants. Effects of predominantly non-economic activities and events such as war, terrorism or natural disaster are not the results of a joint economic activity but can have significant impacts on production and consumption. In a broader sense they can be also be considered as external effects on economic activity.

The SNA excludes explicitly external effects, insisting that its input and output indicators represent consensual market transactions and values only. It also leaves the depletion of natural resources as an "economic disappearance" to its asset accounts, thus avoiding its costing in the production accounts. It does consider

TABLE 4.2 External effects of/on economic activity

To/from	P_E	P_G	C
P_E	• Pollution • Natural resource depletion	–	• Pollution (health effects) • Loss of environmental services
P_G	Policy failure (errors, inefficiency)	–	Policy failure (errors, inefficiency)
C	• Pollution • Degradation of natural resources	–	• Pollution • Degradation of natural resources
NAE	Damage to produced capital	Damage to governmental infrastructure and capital	Damage to human capital and consumption goods

Source: Bartelmus (2008, Annex I, modified).

Note

P_E = production of private enterprises; P_G = production of government; C = personal consumption; NAE = non-economic activities and events.

42 Economic sustainability

external effects as a "major cause of concern" for measuring welfare and economic growth; they should therefore be dealt with in "satellite" accounts (European Commission et al. 2009, para. 1.82).

4.2.2 Integrating environmental and economic accounts

The author and his team at the United Nations Statistical Office extended the national accounts system as a satellite account of the SNA (Bartelmus et al. 1991). They included environmental externalities and natural resource depletion as additional costs of production. Aware of environmental concerns that threaten the sustainability of economic activity, but also aware of considerable progress made in measuring these concerns, they advanced the System for integrated Environmental and Economic Accounting (SEEA). This approach makes use of input–output tables, which connect physical and monetary indicators that flow through the economy. Extended input–output tables thus allow the consistent introduction of environmental depletion and degradation into the national accounts.

The United Nations (1993) later published the system, albeit as an "interim version."[8] The SEEA included, in particular,

- the value of nature's resource stocks and sinks for wastes and pollutants as natural capital, and
- natural capital consumption as the costs of observed depletion and degradation of natural capital.

Figure 4.2 illustrates this approach. The shaded areas show the stocks and changes in stock of non-produced environmental assets in addition to produced economic ones. Stock and flow accounts overlap, where flows of capital formation and produced and natural capital consumption represent stock changes. Produced and natural capital consumption is also recorded as costs of production.

The SEEA measures the measurable features of natural capital in addition to produced capital. Rather than welfare effects of environmental decline it records the market value of natural resources and the costs of natural resource depletion and environmental degradation. "Maintenance costs" of avoiding or reducing environmental impacts assess environmental degradation. The idea is to measure potential expenditure that should have been made to avoid environmental damage.[9] The depletion of a natural resource is costed as a change in the economic value of the stock of exhaustible natural resources. In practice, lack of data on ownership and the value of natural capital hamper the regular collection of a nation's stock of natural capital. They restrict the accounts, at least for now, to the measurement of expected depletion and degradation flows.

It is a "prudent"[10] step to extend the concepts of capital consumption and maintenance from produced to natural capital. Making an allowance for reinvestment in, and hence the maintenance of, produced and natural capital is an operational concept of economic sustainability. As such investment assumes that the loss of

OPENING STOCKS	Produced assets	Environmental assets

+

	PRODUCTION (industries)	FINAL CONSUMPTION	CHANGES IN CAPITAL STOCKS	CHANGES IN NATURAL CAPITAL	REST OF THE WORLD
SUPPLY OF PRODUCTS	Outputs (O)				Imports (M)
USE OF PRODUCTS	Inputs (I)	Final consumption (C)	Gross capital formation (GCF)		Exports (X)
PRODUCED CAPITAL USE	Capital consumption (CC_p)		Capital consumption (CC_p)		
NATURAL CAPITAL USE	Environmental cost (EC) (natural capital consumption)			Natural capital consumption (CC_n)	

+

Other asset changes	Other asset changes

=

CLOSING STOCKS	Produced assets	Environmental assets

FIGURE 4.2 SEEA. The SEEA incorporates natural capital and its depletion and degradation as capital consumption into the national accounts. Environmentally adjusted indicators of net capital formation and of net domestic product are the result when the cost of natural capital consumption is deducted from the conventional net indicators

Source: © UNESCO-Encyclopedia of Life Support Systems (EOLSS), from Bartelmus (2001) with permission from UNESCO-Encyclopedia of Life Support Systems.

44 Economic sustainability

exhaustible natural capital can be compensated by investing in reproducible capital, this valuation represents a "weak" sustainability concept (see section 2.2). The objective of such investment is to ensure the combined economic–environmental sustainability of economic growth. The value of natural capital consumption can be seen as the cost that society should have shouldered to avoid or mitigate environmental decline. Investment in the maintenance of natural capital is an indicator of concern about nature's contribution to long-term prosperity.

Deducting the costs of produced and natural capital consumption from economic indicators obtains Environmentally adjusted net Domestic Product (EDP) and Environmentally adjusted net Capital Formation (ECF). Box 4.2 shows the accounting equations for calculating the "greened" indicators of the SEEA.[11] Growing, or at least non-declining, EDP would indicate that the economy performed sustainably in the past. This is, however, just a starting point for assessing future performance. For this, one would need long time series to model future trends of EDP to reduce the usual uncertainties in projections of economic growth and its environmental impacts (see Chapter 5). Lacking these time series for the EDP, an alternative way of looking at economic sustainability is using the ECF. Positive ECF indicates that investment in produced and natural capital increased the net value of capital. The economy performs sustainably when it keeps intact or even increases the value of its productive capital base.

The World Bank (2003) advanced Adjusted Net Saving as a measure of increasing human wellbeing. The measure deducts the value of depletion of some natural resources and the emission of CO_2 from national income while adding investment in education to final consumption. However, the mix of finance for financial and non-financial capital and educational investment obscures the meaning of this indicator for measuring the sustainability of wealth, welfare or income. The SEEA's ECF is more consistent with the accounting conventions of consumption and capital formation; it is also clearer in its interpretation of the sustainability of economic growth as real (non-financial, produced and natural) capital maintenance.

BOX 4.2 ADJUSTING THE ACCOUNTING INDICATORS

The 1993 SEEA modifies national accounts indicators, deducting the consumption of natural capital (CC_n) as environmental cost (EC) from net domestic product (NDP) and net capital formation. The following equations show how this turns GDP and Gross Capital Formation (GCF) into the environmentally adjusted indicators of EDP and ECF (for other acronyms – see Figure 4.2):

(1) $GDP = O - I = C + GCF + X - M$

(2) $GDP - CC_p = NDP$

(3) $NDP - EC = \mathbf{EDP} = C + (GCF - CC_p - CC_n) + X - M$

(4) $\mathbf{ECF} = GCF - CC_p - CC_n$

Much of the critique of changing the conventional economic indicators is about the valuation of non-market processes and effects. National accountants took heed of this critique and issued a revised "central framework" of the SEEA (United Nations et al. 2014a). This framework remains in the realm of "market transactions" and a range of physical (non-monetary) statistics (Bartelmus 2013). The revised SEEA adjusts the SNA indicators therefore only for natural resource depletion, which is actually accounted for as "disappearance" in the SNA asset accounts (European Commission et al. 2009, Table 12.2). Environmental degradation, notably from pollution, is deemed to be the task of "experimental" ecosystem accounts (United Nations et al., 2014a, Preface, para. 8).

The ecosystem accounts seem to reject, however, the monetary valuation of ecosystems (United Nations et al. 2014b, paras. 5.2, 5.12). They consider a cost allowance for replacing capital consumed, whether produced or natural as "hypothetical," because the actual wear and tear is not necessarily prevented or mitigated; however, capital wear and tear did occur, even if enterprises did not account for their replacement. Natural capital consumption can thus be seen as society's evaluation of environmental deterioration in terms of the expenditures that could and should have been made to prevent environmental depletion and degradation. Section 12.3 will discuss how such costing can provide the information for a rational setting of environmental market instruments. The revised 2012 SEEA is thus basically still part of the conventional accounts. It records actual environmental protection expenditure and rearranges natural resource depletion from asset accounts to production accounts to calculate depletion-adjusted economic indicators (United Nations et al., 2014a, para. 2.63).

4.2.3 Hybrid accounts

A large part of the central framework of the revised SEEA is devoted to physical data. They could extend the physical production boundary to include environmental sink services that are rejected for the monetary accounts. However, the SEEA keeps the physical production boundary identical with the monetary SNA boundary of supply and use of produced goods and services.

Physical data expressed in different units of measurement are difficult to aggregate and are probably better organized in frameworks of environment statistics (UNSD 2016). Physical accounts might help though to identify and measure critical (non-substitutable) capital and corresponding "strong" sustainability. Hybrid (combined physical and monetary) accounts could trace the use of physical critical capital down to production and consumption processes to identify their roots of destruction.

The 2012 SEEA (United Nations et al. 2014a, para. 6.54) considers its combination of physical and monetary data as "one of the strongest features." Its companion volume on "Applications and Extensions" (FAO et al. 2014) presents an environmentally extended hybrid (physical and monetary) input–output table. Table 4.3 is a simplified format of such a table, showing physical material flows of natural resource use and emissions of residuals next to monetary flows that are the cause of

TABLE 4.3 Simplified structure of a hybrid environmental–economic accounting system

SUPPLY (of)	USE (by)				
	Industries 1, 2, …	Final demand			PHYSICAL material flows (natural resources, residuals)
		Households	Capital formation and accumulation	Rest of the world (ROW)	
Outputs	Intermediate consumption	Final consumption	Capital formation	Exports	Emissions from industries and households
Income	Value added, NDP	–	–	–	–
Rest of the world (ROW)	Imports	–	Capital transfer to ROW	Balance of payments	Imports of natural resources and residuals
PHYSICAL material flows (natural resources, residuals)	Natural resource inputs, residuals received	Natural resource use, "consumption" of residuals	Net accumulation of materials and substances	Exports of natural resources and residuals	Physical balances

Source: Bartelmus (2004, p. 49, Table II), with permission from Elsevier.

environmental impacts. The physical part of the table could be used as an accounting framework for material flows, linking its national aggregates to their origins and destinations of industries and households.

The revised SEEA could use this framework to compensate for rejecting the costing of environmental degradation. The integration of hybrid accounts, beyond the "linkage" of physical and monetary data, for a comprehensive analysis is a costly exercise, though, and is not further pursued by the SEEA. Cost might also be the reason why the SEEA relegates the costing of environmental degradation to its experimental ecosystem accounts, which, however, consider such costing to be hypothetical (see section 4.2.2). Section 13.2 will explore the possibility of using hybrid accounts and analysis to overcome – at least in theory – the prevailing polarization between environmentalists and economists.

A review of hybrid accounts describes case studies for a few European countries (Constantini et al. 2012). The authors focus on the physical side of hybrid accounts and input–output tables; they do not provide a common view of sustainability or policy use.[12] Welfens et al. (2016) advance a "global sustainability indicator," which would overcome the hybrid split by combining energy use with monetary measures of genuine savings and green exports.

4.3 Has economic growth been sustainable?

International organizations called for greening the economy (UNEP 2011) and economic growth (OECD 2011) in preparation for the United Nations Conference on Sustainable Development in 2012. Twenty years earlier the first United Nations Conference on Environment and Development recommended implementing the SEEA as a satellite of the conventional accounts in its Agenda 21 (United Nations 1994, paras. 8.41, 8.42). Except for a few early pilot projects (Bartelmus 2008, pp. 155–9), national statistical services have not so far implemented either the comprehensive 1993 SEEA or the truncated 2012 SEEA. The reason could be the wavering of national accountants between wanting to manage any change in the national accounts but at the same time fearing that such change might impair the validity and use of the conventional accounts.

For now, a rough first global study by the author has to do (Bartelmus 2009). The study reveals an increase of hitherto ignored environmental cost during the 1990–2006 period: global depletion and degradation costs more than quadrupled from US\$661 billion to almost US\$3 trillion or from 3.2 percent to 6.1 percent of world GDP. There are of course considerable differences in these costs caused by regions and countries. European Union (EU) member states and the USA decreased their share of world environmental cost. The EU actually gave the best environmental performance, reducing an already low share of 6.5 percent of the global environmental cost in 1990 to 4 percent in 2006. The most conspicuous increase in environmental cost took place in China, whose share grew from 6 to 11 percent.

The above-described environmentally adjusted economic indicators combine negative environmental trends with positive economic ones. The ECF, in particular, shows if countries, regions and the world were able to offset increasing environmental costs by capital formation, in other words if their economies performed sustainably. Worldwide, ECF remained close to stagnation, while the conventional indicator (GCF) increased. Still, non-negative ECF indicates sustainable economic growth of the world economy during the 1990–2006 period.

Figure 4.3 shows the share of ECF over EDP in world regions. Industrialized countries (EU, USA) and China maintained positive net capital formation and hence economic sustainability throughout 1990–2006. China's share of ECF in its EDP is three to four times the share of industrialized countries reflecting the country's accelerated economic efforts, even after taking environmental depletion and degradation into account. In contrast, the situation is clearly non-sustainable in Africa and is beginning to look so in other developing countries. Negative ECF in Africa, Latin America and Asia's developing countries in 2006 indicates that in these regions actual consumption drowned out saving and reinvestment if both economic and environmental depreciation costs are taken into account.

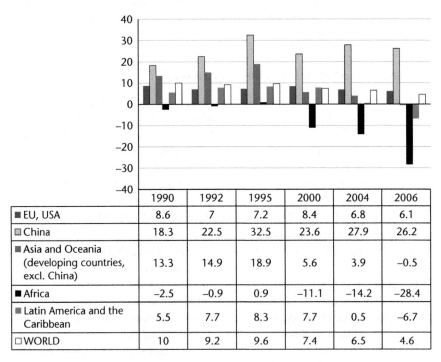

FIGURE 4.3 ECF in world regions (percent of EDP). Positive ECF in industrialized countries (EU, USA) and China indicates (weakly) sustainable economic growth. Negative ECF of developing countries of Africa and Latin America presents a non-sustainable economic performance that diminishes capital for consumption purposes. GDP growth in these countries presents a misleading picture of the sustainability of economic growth and development

Source: Bartelmus (2009, Fig. 4, modified).

The relatively rosy picture of rich nations' sustainability can be deceptive. It ignores dependence of these countries on natural resource imports and outsourcing of hazardous industrial processes. Such "burden shifting" has been observed in particular for EU countries (Bringezu et al. 2004); it can be seen as an import of sustainability by rich nations from poor (but resource-rich) ones.

All in all, the green accounting indicators present a weakly sustainable world, with persisting non-sustainability in the poorest countries of Africa, Latin America and Asia. Undercoverage and comparability problems of the environmental data sources and the assumption of weak sustainability of substitutable capital inputs make this first assessment rather tentative. There is no reason why these questions should not be addressed in future applications of the SEEA. As satellites of the SNA these studies would leave the conventional accounts undisturbed while providing useful data for integrative environmental and economic policies.

A review of country efforts in implementing the SEEA and related approaches (Fenton et al. 2015) found most progress in Europe and Canada. However, even these applications omit significant parts of environmental depletion and degradation. This might be the result of curtailing the 2012 SEEA and slow acceptance of new approaches by official statistics. It comes as no surprise that in the meantime non-governmental organizations, and especially those that disdain monetary evaluation, look for and aggregate selected indicators to measure the environmental and economic performance of nations. The Global Green Economy Index (Tamanini and Valenciano 2016) thus combines 32 indicators in hardly comparable fields of leadership and climate, selected economic sectors, markets and investment, and environmental impacts, generating difficult-to-interpret ranks of country performance.

Notes

1 Using the ratio of GPI over world GDP for those countries for which GPI is available with some adjustment for population growth.
2 Kubiszewski et al. (2013, p. 58) claim first that there is a need for estimating the cost of the permanent loss of natural capital, which seems to refer to strong sustainability; then they argue for the short-term compensation of environmental degradation by welfare gains from economic benefits, i.e., weak sustainability, "since the GPI was never designed to be a strict measure of sustainability."
3 GDP was, however, not designed as a welfare measure. It is simply the sum total of the economic value (added) of economic activities, defined and measured without duplications in the worldwide adopted System of National Accounts (European Commission et al. 2009). Still, GDP or personal consumption, notably in per-capita terms, often serve as proxy measures of wellbeing, despite national accountants arguing "against the welfare interpretations of the accounts" (ibid., p. 12).
4 The Hartwick rule calls for investing the value of used-up exhaustible natural resources in the generation of produced capital; the purpose is to maintain consumption and welfare.
5 The effects of excessive deficit spending or curtailing expenditure could of course be explored as a matter of economic policy failure that increases the vulnerability of countries.

50 Economic sustainability

6 Inaccuracies in the compilation of the underlying statistics are of course unavoidable. They are not discussed here where the focus is on conceptual flaws of economic indicators.

7 The depletion of natural resources is sometimes intentional and would then not be a true externality of economic production. However, in most cases, running down natural resources is probably not the intention of economic plans that care about maintaining future production and consumption.

8 A later version of the SEEA (United Nations et al. 2014a) omits environmental degradation and can thus not really claim to be an integrated environmental–economic accounting system (see below).

9 Critique of this valuation argues that actual damage affecting production and the well-being of people should be measured as the cost of "internalizing" external effects. However such measurement would face the problems of predicting hardly measurable effects on social welfare.

10 For maintaining the flow of income (à la Hicks 1946, p. 172).

11 Note that EDP defines a green *net* domestic product, rather than the generally advocated "green GDP." Accounting only for natural capital consumption, but ignoring the consumption of produced capital by the green GDP does not make much sense. Both produced and natural capital needs to be maintained for sustaining economic performance and growth. Crumbling infrastructure in the USA and many developing countries reminds us of the consequences of neglecting the wear and tear of produced capital goods.

12 The review is based on the Dutch NAMEA accounts (Keuning and de Haan 1998); however, the SEEA does not credit NAMEA as the original version of hybrid accounting.

References

Bartelmus, P. (2001). Accounting for sustainability: greening the national accounts, in M.K. Tolba (ed.), *Our Fragile World: Challenges and Opportunities for Sustainable Development*, Oxford: Eolss Publishers: 1721–35.

Bartelmus, P. (2004). Green accounting and energy (reference module in earth systems and environmental sciences, 2013). Online: www.sciencedirect.com/science/article/pii/B012176480X002448 (accessed 6 August 2017).

Bartelmus, P. (2008). *Quantitative Eco-nomics: How Sustainable are Our Economies?* Dordrecht: Springer.

Bartelmus, P. (2009). The cost of natural capital consumption: accounting for a sustainable world economy, *Ecological Economics*, 68: 1850–7.

Bartelmus, P. (2013). Environmental–economic accounting: progress and regression in the SEEA revisions, *Review of Income and Wealth* 60 (4): 887–904.

Bartelmus, P., Stahmer, C. and van Tongeren, J. (1991). Integrated environmental and economic accounting: framework for a SNA satellite system, *Review of Income and Wealth* 37: 111–48.

Boulding, K.E. (1966). The economics of the coming spaceship earth, in H. Jarret (ed.), *Environmental Quality in a Growing Economy*, Baltimore, MD: Johns Hopkins Press for Resources for the Future: 3–14. Online: http://arachnid.biosci.utexas.edu/courses/THOC/Readings/Boulding_SpaceshipEarth.pdf (accessed 29 October 2017).

Bringezu, S., Schütz, H., Steger, S. and Baudisch, J. (2004). International comparison of resource use and its relation to economic growth, *Ecological Economics* 51: 97–124.

Cobb, C., Halstead, T. and Rowe, J. (1995). If the GDP is up, why is America down? *Atlantic Monthly*, October: 59–78.

Constantini, V., Mazzantani, M. and Montini, A. (eds.) (2012). *Hybrid Economic–Environmental Accounts*, Abingdon, UK and New York: Routledge.

Daly, H.E. and Cobb, Jr., J.B. (1989). *For the Common Good: Redirecting the Economy Towards Community, the Environment, and a Sustainable Future*, Boston, MA: Beacon Press.

Das Gupta, A.K. and Pearce, D.W. (1972). *Cost Benefit Analysis: Theory and Practice*, London: Macmillan.

European Commission (2015). Beyond GDP, measuring progress, true wealth, and the well-being of nations. Online: http://ec.europa.eu/environment/beyond_gdp/index_en.html (accessed 4 October 2017).

European Commission, International Monetary Fund, Organisation for Economic Co-operation and Development, United Nations and World Bank (2009). *System of National Accounts 2008*. Online: http://unstats.un.org/unsd/nationalaccount/docs/SNA2008.pdf (accessed 5 November 2017).

Fenton, I.E., Andersen, L.E. and Li, T. (eds.) (2015). *Global Green Accounting 2015*, La Paz: Fundación INESAD. Online: www.nas.gov.ua/text/pdfNews/Fundacion_INESAD_Global_Green_Accounting_2015.pdf (accessed 5 November 2017).

Food and Agriculture Organisation of the United Nations, European Commission, Organisation for Economic Co-operation and Development, United Nations and World Bank (2014). *System of Environmental–Economic Accounting 2012: Applications and Extensions* (white cover publication). Online: http://documents.worldbank.org/curated/en/893701468198001180/pdf/103742-WP-PUBLIC-applications-and-extensions.pdf (accessed 20 March 2017).

Hartwick, J.M. (1977). Intergenerational equity and the investing of rents from exhaustible resources, *American Economic Review* 67 (3): 972–4.

Hicks, J.R. (1946, 2nd ed.). *Value and Capital: An Inquiry into Some Fundamental Principles of Economic Theory*, Oxford: Oxford University Press.

Keuning, S.J. and de Haan, M. (1998). Netherlands: what's in a NAMEA? Recent results, in K. Uno and P. Bartelmus (eds.), *Environmental Accounting in Theory and Practice*, Dordrecht: Kluwer: 143–56.

Kubiszewski, I., Costanza, R., Franco, C., Lawn, P., Talberth, J., Jackson, T. and Aylmer, C. (2013). Beyond GDP: measuring and achieving global genuine progress, *Ecological Economics* 93: 57–68.

Max-Neef, M. (1995). Economic growth and quality of life: a threshold hypothesis, *Ecological Economics* 15: 115–18.

Mishan, E.J. (1973). *Elements of Cost–Benefit Analysis*, New York: Praeger.

Nordhaus, W.D. and Tobin, J. (1973). Is growth obsolete? *Studies in Income and Wealth* 38: 509–64. Online: www.nber.org/chapters/c3621.pdf (accessed 21 March 2017).

Organisation for Economic Co-operation and Development (OECD) (2011). *OECD Better Life Initiative: Compendium of OECD Well-being Indicators*, Paris: OECD. Online: www.oecd.org/std/47917288.pdf (accessed 24 January 2017).

Stiglitz, J.E., Sen, A. and Fitoussi, J.P. (2010). *Report by the Commission on the Measurement of Economic Performance and Social Progress*. Online: http://library.bsl.org.au/jspui/bitstream/1/1267/1/Measurement_of_economic_performance_and_social_progress.pdf (accessed 4 June 2017).

Talberth, J. (2010). Measuring what matters: GDP, ecosystems and the environment. Online: www.wri.org/blog/2010/04/measuring-what-matters-gdp-ecosystems-and-environment (accessed 5 November 2017).

Talberth, J. and Weisdorf, M. (2017). Genuine progress indicator 2.0: pilot accounts for the US, Maryland, and City of Baltimore 2012–2014, *Ecological Economics* 142: 1–11.

Talberth, J., Cobb, C. and Slattery, N. (2007). *The Genuine Progress Indicator 2006: A Tool for Sustainable Development*, Oakland, CA: Redefining Progress. Online: www.scribd.com/doc/3061355/Genuine-Progress-Indicator-2006 (accessed 6 October 2017).

Tamanini, J. and Valenciano, J. (2016). *The Global Green Economy index, GGEI 2016.* Online: http://dualcitizeninc.com/GGEI-2016.pdf (accessed 4 October 2017).

United Nations (1993). *Integrated Environmental and Economic Accounting*, New York: United Nations.

United Nations (1994). *Earth Summit, Agenda 21: The United Nations Programme of Action from Rio*, New York: United Nations.

United Nations, European Commission, Food and Agriculture Organization of the United Nations, International Monetary Fund, Organisation for Economic Co-operation and Development and World Bank Group (2014a). *System of Environmental–Economic Accounting 2012: Central Framework.* New York: United Nations. Online: http://unstats.un.org/unsd/envaccounting/seeaRev/SEEA_CF_Final_en.pdf (accessed 19 March 2017).

United Nations, European Commission, Food and Agriculture Organization of the United Nations, International Monetary Fund, Organisation for Economic Co-operation and Development and World Bank Group (2014b). *System of Environmental–Economic Accounting 2012: Experimental Ecosystem Accounting*, New York: United Nations. Online: http://unstats.un.org/unsd/envaccounting/eea_white_cover.pdf (accessed 19 March 2017).

United Nations Environment Programme (UNEP) (2011). *Towards a Green Economy, Pathways to Sustainable Development and Poverty Eradication*, UNEP. Online: http://web.unep.org/greeneconomy/sites/unep.org.greeneconomy/files/field/image/green_economy report_final_dec2011.pdf (accessed 5 November 2017).

United Nations Environment Programme (UNEP) and UNU-IHDP (2012). *Inclusive Wealth Report 2012: Measuring Progress Toward Sustainability*, Cambridge: Cambridge University Press.

United Nations Environment Programme (UNEP) and UNU-IHDP (2014). *Inclusive Wealth Report 2014: Measuring Progress Toward Sustainability*, Cambridge: Cambridge University Press.

United Nations Statistics Division (UNSD) (2016). *Framework for the Development of Environment Statistics (FDES 2013)*, New York: United Nations. Online: http://unstats.un.org/unsd/environment/FDES/FDES-2015-supporting-tools/FDES.pdf (accessed 9 October 2017).

Welfens, P.J.J., Perret, J.K., Irawan, T. and Yushkova, E. (2016). *Towards Global Sustainability*, Heidelberg, New York, Dordrecht and London: Springer.

World Bank (1997). *Expanding the Measure of Wealth: Indicators of Environmentally Sustainable Development.* Washington, DC: World Bank.

World Bank (2003). *World Development Report 2003: Sustainable Development in a Dynamic World, Transforming Institutions, Growth, and Quality of Life*, New York: Oxford University Press.

World Bank (2011). *The Changing Wealth of Nations: Measuring Sustainable Development in the New Millennium*, Washington, DC: World Bank. Online: http://siteresources.worldbank.org/ENVIRONMENT/Resources/ChangingWealthNations.pdf (accessed 5 November 2017).

5

MODELING ECONOMIC SUSTAINABILITY

Will we be better off?

Sustainability is really a question for the future. The reason for looking into the past in Chapters 3 and 4 is to define quantifiable concepts of sustainability for finding trends that can be extended into the future. Of course, observations of past developments are more realistic than modeling the uncertain future. This chapter looks at tools of extrapolating trends and finding obstacles that might threaten our standards of living in the future. The question is what to expect when no additional corrective action is taken in "business-as-usual" scenarios. The assumption that shortsighted policy makers ignore medium- and long-term risks of non-sustainability or rely on automatic built-in responses of the economy is not altogether unrealistic. Further assumptions of optimal economic behavior might be questioned, especially when the exhaustion of production factors and pollution curtail planned activities.

5.1 Business as usual: what can we expect?

Two models can serve as an illustration of what business-as-usual scenarios might predict. They explore future economic growth if not much is done about any sustainability constraints. The environmental Kuznets curve (EKC) hypothesis claims that environmental obstacles will be overcome without further policy intervention by economic growth. The limits-to-growth (LTG) model comes to the opposite conclusion that business as usual will lead to economic and social disaster.

5.1.1 EKC – an automatic development?

Neo-liberal economists expressed their laissez-faire view of the relationship between environmental impact and economic growth in the EKC hypothesis.[1] According to this hypothesis, industrializing countries generate initially high and increasing environmental impacts. Once they reach a certain level of prosperity, greater demand for environmental quality and the transition to a dematerialized service-economy reverse the initial correlation of environmental deterioration and economic growth (Figure 5.1, part A).

The original study by Grossman and Krueger (1995) found an EKC relationship of urban air and river quality with gross domestic product (GDP). The study was later expanded to include ambient concentrations of SO_2, smoke, heavy particles, heavy metals, nitrates, biological and chemical oxygen demand, and fecal coliform. The authors rejected the hypothesis for fecal coliform only. In all other cases they found an inverted-U relationship with a turning point at less than US$8000 per-capita GDP (in 1985 US$). They explained relinkage for some of the variables at very high income levels as stemming from poor data at these levels.

The authors also referred to other studies that confirm their findings and in fact extend it to deforestation, carbon oxide and access to safe water. They cite, in particular, a World Bank (1992) report, which establishes an EKC relationship for SO_2 and suspended particulates for high-, middle- and low-income cities, but rejects the hypothesis for CO_2 and municipal waste. Summing up, Grossman and Krueger (1995, p. 370) assert that while they cover "relatively few dimensions for environmental quality" their study is "the most comprehensive possible, given the limited availability of comparable data from different countries."

Most other studies find the EKC relationship to hold only for local air pollutants, rejecting the hypothesis for global pollutants such as CO_2. Some even see a relinkage

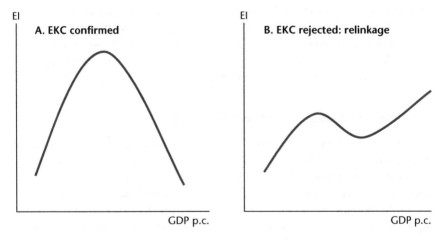

FIGURE 5.1 EKC confirmed and rejected. Part A shows the inverted-U relationship of the EKC hypothesis: environmental impact (EI) increases with economic growth at low levels of GDP per capita and decreases after the economy reaches a certain level of income and wealth. Part B illustrates a relinkage of environmental deterioration with economic growth after an initial EKC effect

Source: Bartelmus (2008, p. 199, Fig. 11.1), with permission from Springer Nature.

of environmental impact and economic growth (part B of Figure 5.1). Turning points of per-capita income also vary widely. For instance, SO_2 is found to reach the maximum at values between US\$823 and US\$10,800 (Barbier 1997).[2] Dasgupta et al. (2002, p. 158) "remain cautious optimists" about a flatter EKC with lower pollution levels and doubts about globalization impacts and the use of new toxic chemicals; they are also optimistic about the success of environmental regulation.

The relatively simple econometric analysis points to a crucial role of data. It reveals also the limits of correlational methods for explaining the causes of environmental trends. The critique of the EKC focuses therefore on its database and the interpretation of a statistical regression as a cause–effect relation. In particular, it refers to the

- application of cross-country parameters to estimate time series of individual countries;
- reduced-form analysis of associating environmental quality solely with economic growth, ignoring underlying exogenous influences such as structural change in the composition of variables, technological developments and autonomous policies;
- selectivity in choosing the environmental impact variables, covering only a few pollutants;
- cause–effect interpretations, which assume that environmental policy is brought about by economic growth.

In summary, testing the EKC remains inconclusive. Some EKC relationships seem to exist for selected pollutants. Most authors also conclude that out of the above-discussed driving forces income-induced environmental policy is the dominant force for environmental action. This does not necessarily mean automaticity in policy response, and additional policy intervention might still be warranted.

5.1.2 The LTG model: automatic disaster?

The LTG model (Meadows et al. 1972, 1992, 2004) is one of the best-known predictions of declining global economic growth and welfare. The model blames population growth and environmental impacts of economic activity for this decline. More specifically, the overuse of natural resources and environmental sinks is deemed to be the main cause of decreasing industrial capacity and food production in the business-as-usual scenario.

The first edition of the LTG report in 1972 created an uproar, with the clash of environmentalist acclamation and mainstream economists' rejection. Environmentalists embraced the model as a systemic confirmation of transgressions of environmental limits. Economists were quick to reject the Malthusian model of doom (Cole et al. 1973) because of its neglect of counteracting market forces and technological innovation. Still, the model made an important contribution to the assessment of potential long-term environmental impact by

56 Economic sustainability

- serving as an underpinning, if not *raison d'être*, of ecological economics, which otherwise relies on sets of diverse indicators of environmental impacts;
- its attempt to overcome the hardly quantifiable complexities of optimal and sustainable growth analysis (see section 5.2.2) by means of simulating "plausible" feedback loops;
- raising basic questions about the use of assumptive models in sustainability analysis and policy response.

The LTG model is a computerized dynamic simulation of the interaction among population, industrial and agricultural production, and natural resource use and pollution. Figure 5.2 describes this interaction as direct influences and feedbacks among stocks of population, natural resources and land, and flows of outputs, capital formation, consumption and pollution.[3]

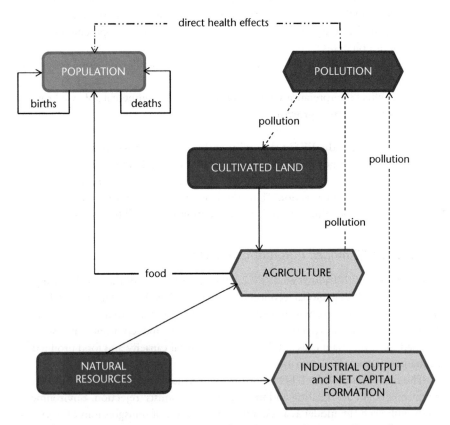

FIGURE 5.2 LTG model – components and interactions. Overuse of natural resources and pollution from economic activities bring about a decline in agricultural and industrial output, and in the health of the population

Source: Bartelmus (2008, Fig. 11.3), with permission from Springer Nature.

The model employs the Ecological Footprint measure to represent overall environmental impact and the Human Development Index to reflect human welfare (cf. sections 6.3.1 and 9.2.1). Different scenarios show the development of economic welfare and environmental change for 1990–2100:

- *Business as usual* (scenario 1) leads to the collapse of society and economy, famously described in the first LTG report (Meadows et al., 1972, p. 29):

  > If the present trends in world population, industrialization, pollution, food production and resource depletion continue unchanged, the limits to growth on this planet will be reached sometime within the next one hundred years. The most probable result will be a rather sudden and uncontrollable decline in both population and industrial capacity.

  Continuing exponential growth in the model variables might diminish our standards of living (welfare) within the next decade, down to year-1900 levels in 2100. Environmental impact decreases correspondingly with reduced economic activity. The latest report (Meadows et al., 2004) confirms this prediction. The other scenarios show the progressive introduction of positive factors that could delay or prevent socioeconomic collapse.
- *Doubling resource availability* (scenario 2) delays collapse by a decade or two. It generates, however, a "global pollution crisis" reflected in a steep increase of the Ecological Footprint. As a consequence, land fertility declines and mortality increases due to the decrease in food production.
- Further introduction of *resource-saving and environmental protection technology* (scenario 6) generates a more positive picture of human welfare oscillating around current standards of living. However, the authors believe decline to begin in the later part of the twenty-first century.
- Introducing *zero-growth in population and industrial output* (scenario 9) generates the most optimistic result and a most unrealistic "no-problem" scenario. This scenario would lead to a steady-state economy with welfare slightly above year-2000 levels and no indication of decline. Environmental impact stabilizes at a low level.

Economists see most of their own analyses, notably of adaptive behavior ignored. They also criticize the lack of empirical validation of functional relationships, dubbed by Nordhaus (1973) as "measurement without data." In response, the LTG authors point out (in Cole et al. 1973) that their intention is not to predict any precise catastrophic development. Rather, they want to show potential scenarios that may occur if there are no radical changes in social values and choices. Nevertheless, they deem the more optimistic scenarios unlikely and reject faith in the ability of markets and human ingenuity to prevent the collapse of society. The "most likely" mode of behavior of the model is thus "overshoot and collapse." The model is in their opinion less a prediction than a warning about imminent disaster.

58 Economic sustainability

5.2 Constraints for optimality and sustainability

The Credit Suisse Research Institute (2014, pp. 38, 40) predicts that global personal economic wealth will increase by 40 percent by 2019, two-thirds of which will be generated by emerging markets, notably China and India. The USA will remain the richest country in owning economic wealth, followed by China, whose wealth per adult will, however, be only a fraction of US per-capita wealth. But this rosy picture is more and more challenged by psychological, demographic, environmental and political constraints to the maintenance and creation of economic and non-economic wealth and prosperity.[4]

5.2.1 Sustaining economic output

Net output – taking capital depreciation into account – and corresponding national income are generated by the use of produced and non-produced capital in the production of goods and services. Redistribution of income could subsidize others who did not or could not contribute. This is well documented and measured by the national accounts that are unrivaled by any other data system in the economic domain. The accounts shy wisely away from exploring what drives income and utility maximization by enterprises and households. Rather, they leave assumptions about optimal behavior to economic theory whose core principles of competitive market equilibrium and optimal growth seek to justify their tenets. Even mainstream economists express, however, doubts about competitive market behavior. In the end, they still seem to prefer living with the "semi-fiction" of competitive markets (Solow 1992), which ensures the working of their abstract models.

New obstacles emerged to challenge the economic semi-fiction, turning it potentially into full-fledged fiction. Disappointment in past economic growth, caused by financial and economic downturns, might curtail future investments at least in the short and medium term. Low real GDP growth of about 1 percent in industrialized countries seems to reflect pessimistic expectations. Besides monopolistic market control, new scarcities of environmental services could prevent the attainment of general equilibrium and its maximum levels of utility and economic welfare. Different approaches by those who still believe in the power of modifying markets to tackle market and policy failure, and those who would like to replace this fuzzy vision by radical control of market behavior, created a distinct polarization of environmental and ecological economists (see sections 2.2 and 13.1). It remains to be seen if the publicity around the Nobel-prize winning argument of irrational economic behavior will significantly affect conventional economic modeling (Thaler and Sunstein 2008, 2009); it might just push their arguments of irrationality deeper into non-economic analysis of health, wealth and nature.

Nature seems to have run out of its hitherto freely available natural resource and sink services for wastes and pollutants. There is therefore no way around seriously addressing environmental constraints that might prevent sustaining general equilibrium and optimal growth. One can conceive impacts on sustainability as inner and outer limits of a feasibility framework for an economy of interdependent industries (Bartelmus 1979, 2008). Introducing explicitly social and environmental constraints into input–output analysis and maximizing the feasible output in monetary terms turns the input–output model into a linear programming problem of economic activity. Figure 5.3 illustrates this approach for a two-commodity economy with maximum limits of natural resource availability and sinks for pollution, and minimum (basic) human needs.

Socioeconomic and environmental constraints define the borders of the feasibility space. Within this space, economic activities can be played out sustainably, catering to the carrying capacities of a region or nation. Actual net output, exceeding maximum feasible output $Z^\star$ or violating the feasibility constraints, would indicate non-sustainable behavior of economic agents. Such a result provides a warning that the economy performed unsustainably. However, to determine the level of the

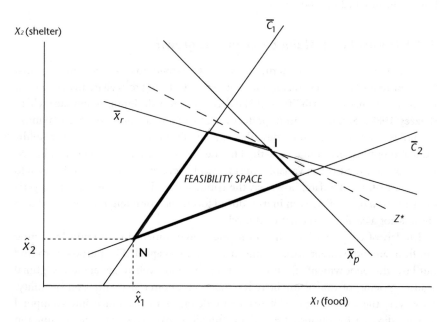

FIGURE 5.3 Linear programming of ecologically sustainable and optimal economic activities. Food and shelter production and consumption represent the economy in this illustrative presentation. Minimum requirements for food $\bar{c}_1$ and shelter $\bar{c}_2$, and standards for maximum use of a natural resource $\bar{x}_r$ and maximum emission of a pollutant $\bar{x}_p$ define the (bold-bordered) feasibility space for economic outputs x_1 and x_2. $\hat{x}_1$ and $\hat{x}_2$ (at point N) are the feasible outputs that meet minimum standards of living represented by $\bar{c}_1$ and $\bar{c}_2$ constraints. The tangent value $Z^\star$ (dashed line) represents the highest net value for the feasible combinations of food and shelter (weighted by monetary unit values) at the tangent point I

Source: Bartelmus (2008, Fig. 12.3), based on Bartelmus (1979), with permission from Springer Nature.

60 Economic sustainability

social cost of setting environmental constraints for the assessment of feasibility and sustainability is difficult. The simple deduction of produced and natural capital consumption from standard economic indicators by the System for integrated Environmental and Economic Accounting (SEEA) is more realistic and consistent with business and national accounting practices. It does not require the modeling of optimal performance in a fully competitive economy.

Most empirical applications of linear programming deal with local ecosystems and corporate management rather than national policies. The reason could be that the rather rigid assumption of fixed production coefficients and corresponding technologies in input–output analysis and linear programming hold, if at all, only in the short term and can more easily be monitored at local levels. This applies especially to exhausted sinks of wastes and pollutants. Linear programming appears to be indeed more useful for short-term managerial action at ecosystem levels than for long-term sustainability policies.

5.2.2 Optimal vs. sustainable economic growth

For the medium and long term, economists extend micro-economic optimal behavior to analyze macro-economic outcomes. Catering to welfare maximization macro-economic sustainability could be defined as non–declining economic welfare (Pezzey 1989). Setting out from perfect micro-economic conditions for maximizing utility, welfare economics describes the conditions for overall market equilibrium and optimal economic growth. The use of the new environmentally adjusted indicators of the SEEA as variables in sustainable "greened" growth models would be more realistic. To date, however, the national statistical services have not (yet?) implemented the SEEA, even in its reduced form, and comprehensive greened data are just not available at the national level.

Models of economic growth can include environmental constraints by setting out from an endowment with produced and natural capital. The purpose is to find out how this endowment affects long-term maximum welfare generation. Optimal shadow pricing of capital might reflect micro-economic maximization of utility. However, the main purpose of macro-modeling is to maximize inter-temporal welfare directly by means of a welfare function. An extended welfare function might include final consumption, labor, produced and natural capital, and environmental damages (e.g. Solow 1974a, b; Dasgupta and Mäler 1991). For attaining sustainable economic growth the models typically claim that

- non-declining welfare is ensured only if the value of the total capital stock (valued in constant shadow prices) does not decrease (Mäler 1991), and
- reinvestment of the rent, i.e., profit from the use from exhaustible resources, into reproducible capital secures at least constant consumption (Hartwick 1977).

Modeling for optimality depends, apart from assuming perfect markets, on the substitutability of production factors and on what is packed into the welfare function. In particular, there is a wide variety of different and differently categorized primary production factors that are included or ignored. Moreover, the production factors can interact in many ways in generating widely differing welfare effects. As Arrow et al. (2004, p. 155) point out: "no one can seriously claim to pinpoint the optimal level of current consumption for an actual economy."

Aware of the rather unrealistic assumption of perfect market conditions, Arrow et al. (2003) show that sustainability could replace optimality for modeling the growth of imperfect economies. They still remain, however, in the realm of conceptualizing theory. For his own climate model, Nordhaus (2008, p. 80) observes that the results of such models "convey a spurious precision" only, but are at least "internally consistent." Mathematical elegance may mask data gaps and thus trump realistic measurement. A case in point is the prediction of CO_2 emission representing environmental impact (see section 6.3.4).

As expected, optimal growth analyses come to different conclusions about the relevance of environmental limits, depending on their assumptions. To illustrate the range of arguments about optimality, sustainability and technological progress in optimal growth models it may suffice here to summarize the increasingly pessimistic conclusions of models presented in a reader on environmental macroeconomics (Munasinghe 2002):

- Technological progress can overcome environmental scarcities through the reduction of extraction cost, substitution, discovery and environmental protection. The "huge reserve of detailed physical, chemical, geological and physiological relationships" just needs to be unveiled by natural scientists and engineers. There is no "clear and present case" of a non-substitutable resource "in limited supply, essential to life and welfare" (Koopmans 1973, pp. 249, 250).
- Technological progress, substitution of natural capital by produced capital and increasing returns to scale make sustainable growth of per-capita consumption feasible, with optimal rates of natural resource use "of the order of magnitude observed for many natural resources" (Stiglitz 1974, p. 136).
- With relative scarcity of natural capital and diminishing returns to technological progress, a global steady-state economy can be reached during a transitional period of slowing increase of labor productivity and per-capita income (England 2000).
- Model runs show that an optimal growth trajectory and a transition to a steady-state economy may not exist. In the absence of governmental intervention, the ecosystem collapses, and optimization and forecasting do not produce a feasible solution. "An ecological economy cannot grow limitlessly" (Islam 2001, p. 261).

Technological progress plays a crucial role in arguing the sustainability of economic growth and its welfare effects. Most economists rely on human knowledge and inventiveness as the savior from environmental and related economic collapse.

62 Economic sustainability

Environmentalists, on the other hand, point to the physical laws of entropy and complementarity in the use of energy and materials: critical natural capital (see sections 2.2 and 7.3) is bound to run out eventually if current demographic and economic growth patterns continue.

Empirical evidence seems to be on the side of the economists, at least as far as natural resource depletion is concerned. Decreasing natural resource prices reflect reduced resource scarcity for many natural resources. As a result, we could expect an increase in effective natural resource stocks. Barnett and Morse (1963) are among the first to find a long-term decrease in real extraction cost of most minerals. According to Baumol (1986, p. 168), the "effective quantity" of natural resources (even of non-renewable resources) might increase when technological innovation leads to a revision of usable resource stock at a rate that exceeds resource use. However, the view of pending environmental disaster from climate change seems now to prevail, even among economists (see section 6.3.4). All depends, of course, on our ingenuity. Will technology be the savior? Possibly.

It is not clear to what extent the models reflect policy intervention. In other words: are the resulting predictions of output truly in the nature of business as usual or do they contain implicit elements of responsive policies, advocated by a "social planner"? Section 13.2 will at least examine to what extent modeling could help overcome the environmental–economic polarization by integrating the underlying analyses.

Notes

1 The name stems from a similar inverted-U relationship between the level and distribution of income found by Kuznets (1955).
2 Two journals happen to devote a special issue to the topic: *Environment and Development Economics* 2 (1997) and *Ecological Economics* 25 (2) (1998) examine the correlation of environment and economic growth. The authors of *Ecological Economics* mostly reject the EKC hypothesis.
3 The figure is a simplification of the many feedback loops used in the model; it also distinguishes more clearly between stocks (rounded rectangles) and flows (hexagons) and omits non-material "knowledge" flows. This is to help understand the model's stock and flow variables in more conventional economic terms. The model uses differential and difference equations to reflect the time paths and interactions of its variables.
4 Many measures include non-economic gains and losses; they are treated in Chapter 8 as part of a broad development concept.

References

Arrow, K.J., Dasgupta, P. and Mäler, K.-G. (2003). Evaluating projects and assessing sustainable development in imperfect economies, *Environmental and Resource Economics* 26: 647–85.
Arrow, K., Dasgupta, P., Goulder, L., Daily, G., Ehrlich, P., Heal, G., Levin, S., Mäler, K-G., Schneider, S., Starrett, D. and Walker, B. (2004). Are we consuming too much? *Journal of Economic Perspectives* 18: 147–72.
Barbier, E.B. (1997). Introduction to the environmental Kuznets curve, special issue, *Environment and Development Economics* 2: 357–81.

Barnett, H. and Morse, C. (1963). *Scarcity and Growth: The Economics of Natural Resource Availability*, Baltimore, MD: Johns Hopkins University Press.

Bartelmus, P. (1979). Limits to development: environmental constraints of human needs satisfaction, *Journal of Environmental Management* 9: 255–69.

Bartelmus, P. (2008). *Quantitative Eco-nomics: How Sustainable are Our Economies?* Dordrecht: Springer.

Baumol, W.J. (1986). On the possibility of continuing expansion of finite resources, *Kyklos* 39 (2): 167–79.

Cole, H.S.D., Freeman, C., Jahoda, M. and Pavitt, K.L.R. (1973). *Models of Doom: A Critique of the Limits to Growth*, New York: Universe Books.

Credit Suisse Research Institute (2014). *Global Wealth Report 2014*. Online: http://economics.uwo.ca/people/davies_docs/credit-suisse-global-wealth-report-2014.pdf (accessed 30 August 2017).

Dasgupta, P. and Mäler, K.-G. (1991). The environment and emerging development issues, in *Proceedings of the World Bank Annual Conference on Development Economics 1990*, Washington, DC: World Bank: 101–31.

Dasgupta, S., Laplante, B., Wang, H. and Wheeler, D. (2002). Confronting the environmental Kuznets curve, *Journal of Economic Perspectives* 16 (1): 147–68. Online: http://siteresources.worldbank.org/DEC/Resources/Confronting.pdf (accessed 21 March 2017).

England, R.W. (2000). Natural capital and the theory of economic growth, *Ecological Economics* 34 (3): 425–31.

Grossman, G.M. and Krueger, A.B. (1995). Economic growth and the environment, *Quarterly Journal of Economics* CX: 353–77. Online: www.econ.ku.dk/nguyen/teaching/Grossman%20and%20Krueger%201995.pdf (accessed 21 March 2017).

Hartwick, J.M. (1977). Intergenerational equity and the investing of rents from exhaustible resources, *American Economic Review* 67 (3): 972–4.

Islam, S.M.N. (2001). Ecology and optimal economic growth: an optimal ecological economic growth model and its sustainability implications, in M. Munasinghe, O. Sunkel and C. de Miguel (eds.), *The Sustainability of Long-term Growth: Socioeconomic and Ecological Perspectives*, Cheltenham, UK: Edward Elgar: 227–3.

Koopmans, T.C. (1973). Some observations on "optimal" economic growth and exhaustible resources, in H.C. Bos, H. Linnemann and P. de Wolff (eds.), *Economic Structure and Development: Essays in Honour of Jan Tinbergen*, Amsterdam: North Holland: 239–56.

Kuznets, S. (1955). Economic growth and income inequality, *American Economic Review* 45 (1): 1–28.

Mäler, K.-G. (1991). National accounts and environmental resources, *Environmental and Resource Economics* 1: 1–15.

Meadows, D.H., Meadows, D.L. and Randers, J. (1992). *Beyond the Limits*, Post Mills, VT: Chelsea Green Publishing.

Meadows, D.H., Meadows, D.L., Randers, J. and Behrens III, W.W. (1972). *The Limits to Growth*, New York: Universe Books.

Meadows, D., Randers, J. and Meadows, D. (2004). *Limits to Growth: The 30-years Update*, White River Junction, VT: Chelsea Green Publishing.

Munasinghe, M. (ed.) (2002). *Macroeconomics and the Environment*, Cheltenham, UK: Edward Elgar.

Nordhaus, W.D. (1973). World dynamics: measurement without data, *Economic Journal* 83: 1156–83.

Nordhaus, W.D. (2008). *A Question of Balance: Weighing the Options on Global Warming Policies*, New Haven, CT: Yale University Press.

64 Economic sustainability

Pezzey, J. (1989). Economic analysis of sustainable growth and sustainable development, Environment Department Working Paper No. 15, Washington, DC: World Bank.

Solow, R.M. (1974a). Intergenerational equity and exhaustible resources, *Review of Economic Studies* 41: 29–45.

Solow, R.M. (1974b). The economics of resources or the resources of economics, *American Economic Review* 64: 1–14.

Solow, R.M. (1992). An almost practical step toward sustainability, Washington, DC: Resources for the Future. Online: http://web.stanford.edu/class/econ155/coursework/CourseMaterials/Readings/Solow-Sustainability.pdf (accessed 8 October 2017).

Stiglitz, J.E. (1974). Growth with exhaustible natural resources: efficient and optimal growth paths, *Review of Economic Studies* 41 (special symposium issue): 123–37.

Thaler, R.H. and Sunstein, C.R. (2008, 2009). *Nudge: Improving Decisions about Health, Wealth, and Happiness*, New York: Penguin Group.

World Bank (1992). *World Development Report 1992: Development and the Environment*, Washington, DC: World Bank.

PART III

Ecological sustainability

How much nature do we need?

Part II looked into the obstacles that may lie in the path towards economic prosperity. A major constraint is the deterioration of the natural environment. It may have triggered the sustainability discussion, but it is only one of other factors of limited produced, human and social inputs that affect the sustainability of economic activity. Economic growth made most countries more prosperous even when taking environmental constraints into account; it eluded, however, poor African and war-torn nations.

Environmentalists and ecological economists look beyond economic growth and the capital functions of nature. They consider environmental problems as a threat to human survival and not just a trigger for discussing the potential non-sustainability of the economy. In their view, the economy is fully embedded in nature and is only a small part of human activity and natural processes. However, nature does not have a natural *numéraire* like the economy, except for proxies such as "embodied" energy.

Chapter 6 examines first how much nature is available for human and non-human uses. Then, it discusses pressures and impacts from the economy that may threaten nature's sustained use in the future. Chapter 7 discusses the measures and targets of ecological sustainability and the costs of attaining it.

6

HOW MUCH NATURE DO WE USE?

Environmentalists see impacts on nature not only as the cause of non-sustainability of economic activity but also as an attack on the ultimate sources of life. Depending on the ecocentric or anthropocentric view of ecological sustainability, the objective could be either the conservation of nature for all living beings, or only as far as nature provides "services" to humanity. Both cases reject the narrow economic view of sustainability, which is content to maintain capital for economic growth. Human impacts on nature may now have reached a level where our needs for its services cannot be satisfied anymore. But do the data confirm this view?

6.1 Natural wealth

6.1.1 On the value of nature

How much nature do we have? For what? The answer of "deep ecologists" (Naess 1976) might be: we do not "have" any; rather, we are guests on a planet, which we should leave untarnished to the next generation. Quite a number of environmentalists and ecological economists subscribe to this ecocentric view. To them, the real question is: what have we done to nature? They see the real world vandalized and on the edge of disaster. Human, notably economic, values and preferences do not count much in this situation and may even impede saving the planet (see section 12.1). The economy is seen as a black box that gobbles up nature's goods and services and spews out wastes and pollutants into the environment (cf. Figure 1.1). *Gaia* adherents go even farther: they see all of the earth as a living organism (Lovelock 2009). In these cases there is no need for assessing the value of nature, as it is truly "invaluable." All we can do is to adapt to an evolving earth to increase our chances for survival.

68 Ecological sustainability

Some ecological economists take a more realistic approach to assessing the value and availability of nature's services. They use energy flows as a common unit of measurement, claiming that "practically everything on the earth can be considered to be the direct or indirect product of past and present solar energy" (Costanza 1980, p. 1219). Looking back far enough into the past and standing back far enough for a global view of our planet, the argument is certainly valid. Solar energy generated fossil fuels over millions of years; it is also the only exogenous energy input into an otherwise closed planetary system. Energy is therefore not only the ultimate non-substitutable source of life but presents also a limit to meeting ever-increasing human needs and wants. The reason is the second thermodynamic law, which reduces the availability of useful energy, in particular through dissipation by economic production and consumption. The exclusive focus on energy flows implies that in principle all matter can be recycled or converted into energy. As a consequence the energy theory of value claims that all product, resource and waste flows can be accounted for in terms of their "natural" and "scientific" energy value.[1]

Expressing the value of goods and services in energy terms rejects human utility in favor of a "valuation system free of human bias" (Brown and Ulgiati 1999, pp. 491, 492). From this point of view "emergy," i.e., the energy embodied in a product, reflects the true value of the economy and the biosphere. Emergy is the energy the biosphere invests in all produced and natural goods and services. Science should overrule shortsighted human preferences when its findings indicate that the ultimate limits of energy supply are about to be reached. This ecocentric reasoning assumes that the biosphere's "priority" is its own preservation; human health and wellbeing are of lower priority. Nature possesses an "intrinsic" value for what it is, rather than for what it can do for people.[2]

Most ecological economists recognize, however, the need for convincing an anthropocentric society of the significance of a deteriorating environment. Since they disdain economic preferences they look in principle for non-monetary (biophysical) indicators to demonstrate environmental impacts from the overuse and abuse of the natural environment. To obtain an impression of the overall value of nature they resort to goals or standards and combine environmental impacts in indices that can be compared to environmental goals.

Recent attempts at monetary valuation of ecosystems and their services might hope for gaining popularity similar to that of the national accounts when treating ecosystems as natural capital (Guerry et al. 2015; Bateman and Nunes 2016). Others see ecosystem valuation more as a starting point for building scenarios that compare economic growth with its impacts on the contribution of ecosystems to human wellbeing (Kubiszewski et al. 2017). A more skeptical viewpoint stresses that such valuation is at best "complementary to conventional decision-making frameworks" (de Groot et al. 2012, p. 57). In fact, the large variety of ecosystems and valuations make it difficult to "integrate" these valuations for the use of natural resources (Sander et al. 2016).

Neoclassical environmental economists, on the other hand, set out from economic preferences for using environmental source and sink services in economic production and consumption. They focus on the "instrumental" rather than intrinsic value of nature. In their view, environmental benefits and damages can be aggregated in money terms by asking people about their willingness to pay for the benefits of nature or to be compensated for benefit losses.

The importance of nature can therefore either be evaluated in non-monetary terms with reference to normative goals, or it can be valued by ascribing an economic price or cost to nature's services and impacts. Non-monetary evaluations would have to find commensurability of indicators by a common unit of measurement or, if necessary, for a surrogate concern of environmental change. Monetary valuations can use prices for developing adjusted indices of economic performance and growth. Chapter 13 will examine whether these approaches reflect a persistent polarization of assessing the importance of the natural environment (and other sources of human wellbeing) in economic and non-economic terms.

Nature is valuable, but its use has been to a great extent free for all. In the absence of scarcity measures like the market price we might have overused and abused nature's source and sink services. A first step towards finding out is to measure the availability and capacity of environmental assets to generate benefits, and then confront the assets with the pressures and impacts of human use.

6.1.2 How much nature do we have?

Access to natural systems and their conditions determine the availability of nature's services to the inhabitants of a country or region. Gaining access raises questions of institutional arrangements and distribution. Measuring the condition of nature requires defining, classifying and evaluating ecosystems and their services. The equity of access and hence distributional questions are a concern of development and its sustainability, addressed in Part IV.

Frameworks such as the "cascades" of ecosystem services into human wellbeing (Figure 6.1) can bring some order into the flows and effects of using nature's assets. The elusive notion of wellbeing weakens, however, attempts at evaluating ecosystem services in monetary terms as shown in the figure by a dotted ellipse and arrow. Following the sequence of Figure 6.1, this section discusses first nature's assets, followed by pressures and impacts on ecosystem functions and services. Chapter 7 will then explore the evaluation of their sustainability in non-monetary and monetary terms.

A practical overall assessment of the availability and significance of natural assets needs to use a common unit of measurement; such units include

- the area, from which environmental services are "harvested";
- energy values, based on the above described energy theory of value;
- monetary values of natural capital used in production and consumption.

The physical accounts of the System of Environmental-Economic Accounting (SEEA) present land and inland water areas and their location as providers of space

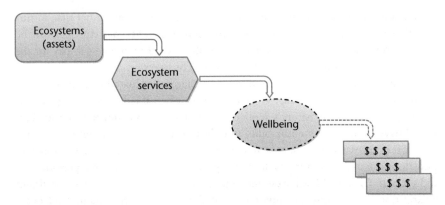

FIGURE 6.1 Cascade of ecosystem stocks, services and benefits. Ecosystems provide services that increase human wellbeing. However, the value of these services is difficult to measure

Source: based on La Notte et al. (2017, Fig. 1 and Table 2).

for economic activities and environmental processes (United Nations et al. 2014a, para. 5.239). This suggests using land and its characteristics as a surrogate for measuring the availability of nature's assets. The Food and Agriculture Organisation of the United Nations (FAO) developed a standard land cover classification of 11 primary categories. The classification seeks to "synthesize" the "best available" databases for creating "a model of the real world" (Latham et al. 2014, p. 22). Figure 6.2 shows that tree-covered areas count for the largest (28 percent) type of the 12 billion ha of global land cover, followed by land without natural vegetation (bare soil) and grass- and croplands.

On their own, land cover statistics do not assess the quality and stability of the underlying ecosystems. The SEEA (United Nations et al. 2014a) excludes the comprehensive assessment of the value of environmental services from its central framework. The intention is to include environmental services in experimental ecosystem accounts (EEA) by some "meaningful grouping" of land areas (ibid., para. 5.317). However, the EEA do not come to clear recommendations. Rather, they seem to return to the land cover accounts of the central SEEA framework, deemed to be "the type of accounting that is possible" at the ecosystem level (United Nations et al. 2014b, para. 4.57). Apparently the SEEA is more interested in the economic aspects of land accounting, i.e., land ownership and land use, than in their effects on biophysical characteristics of ecosystems and their sustainability.

Ecological economists place the economy into the wider natural world. Natural resources and environmental sinks can, however, only be exploited up to nature's carrying capacities of particular territories. Importing environmental services from other regions or leaving the territory in a more or less fallow state could mitigate any overuse of environmental capacities of the territory.

The Ecological Footprint (Borucke et al. 2013) measures the available "biocapacity" of a region by applying global area equivalents of the potential use of

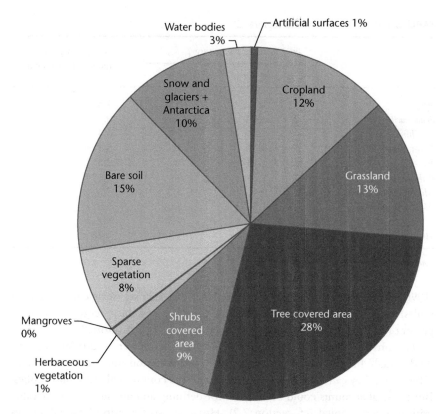

FIGURE 6.2 Global land cover shares.[a] Land covered by trees, crops and grass is more than half of the earth's land area; in contrast, areas with no or little vegetation amount to about one-third of the total

Source: Latham et al. (2014, Fig. 5).

Note
a The shares reflect the dominant characteristics of the FAO land cover classification.

environmental source and sink services.[3] The bio-productive area thus determined consists of the area available for food and wood production, urbanization and the absorption of carbon from CO_2 emissions. The footprint measure avoids a monetary valuation of nature and can therefore not assess the severity of total environmental impact. The global biocapacity of 12.6 billion ha is unevenly distributed over world regions (Table 6.1). Over two-thirds of this capacity can be found in Asia, Latin America and Europe. The USA offers the largest amount of biocapacity to its people (8.2 ha per capita), followed by European countries (7.4 ha per capita). It is of course another matter how these capacities are actually used or overused, affecting the ecological sustainability of a region (see section 7.1.1).

Brown and Ulgiati (1999) set out from the energy theory of nature's value. They estimate the total energy embodied (emergy) in the global stocks of natural resources, applying the methods of "emergy accounting" developed by Odum

72 Ecological sustainability

TABLE 6.1 Biocapacity of world regions, 2012

	Area of biocapacity		Biocapacity per person (global ha per capita)
	(bn ha)	*(%)*	
Africa	1.35	*10.7*	1.3
Asia-Pacific	3.49	*27.7*	0.9
China	1.27	*10.1*	3.4
Latin America	3.21	*25.5*	5.3
EU-27	1.16	*9.2*	2.3
Other European countries	1.21	*9.6*	5.1
Middle East/Central Asia	0.40	*3.2*	1.0
North America	1.76	*14.0*	5.0
USA	1.21	*9.6*	8.2
WORLD	12.58	*100*	1.73

Source: Global Footprint Network (2003–2017).

(1996). The breakdown of global emergy of 739.8 E25 sej (solar energy units of joules) by types of energy indicates a large share of renewable energy of almost 80 percent (Table 6.2). A lot of such energy seems to be still "in store."

The physical accounts of the SEEA (United Nations et al. 2014a) focus on "individual" biophysical assets, which possess a common unit of measurement. Obviously, they can only be aggregated as far as the common physical unit applies. But physical accounts could be the tool for defining and measuring irreplaceable critical natural capital (cf. section 2.2). However, so far, critical capital and its restrictions for economic growth, development and human wellbeing have not been assessed, neither in physical nor in monetary terms. The monetary accounts of the SEEA suggest assessing the monetary value of natural assets for which market prices can be observed or estimated. Monetary values of total wealth

TABLE 6.2 Shares of global energy stores

	Emergy stores (1995, sej, %)
Fresh water	40.4
Other renewables	37.2[a]
Coal	11.7
Crude oil	4.2
Natural gas	3.4
Uranium	0.0
Phosphate rock	0.6
TOTAL	97.5

Source: Brown and Ulgiati (1999, Table 2).

Note

a Soil organic matter, plant and animal biomass.

that include human social and other forms of capital contributing to economic growth are, at least for now, compiled outside the national accounts system. Assessing the total value of wealth assumes that any depleted or degraded asset can be replaced by other factors of production, catering to weak sustainability (cf. section 4.2.2).

Figure 6.3 shows the shares of different types of capital measured by the comprehensive wealth and the inclusive wealth indices of the World Bank (2011) and United Nations organizations (UNEP and UNU-IHDP 2014). The two indices present the same share of produced capital (18 percent), as they use the established data of the national accounts. They differ, however, in the shares of the other capital categories, due to the different amounts of capital considered to be "residual" (intangible vs. human capital).

Both indices show relatively high levels of natural capital for low-income countries and low levels for high-income countries. The inclusive wealth report finds an overall decline of the share of natural capital over the 1992–2010 period, whereas the Comprehensive Wealth Measure shows a rather stable distribution of its components during 1995–2005.

Measures of the *net* worth in wealth accounts deduct the value of people's and countries' obligation to pay off creditors (cf. sections 3.1 and 4.1). One could make a similar argument from an ecocentric viewpoint for a country's or the planet's

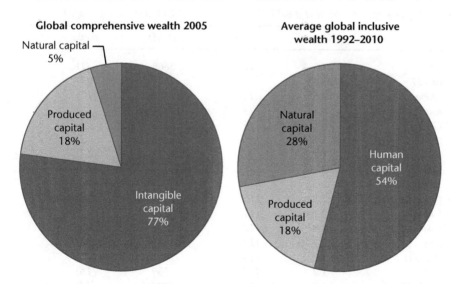

FIGURE 6.3 Shares of global wealth. The World Bank and United Nations organizations come to different results about the amount of natural capital used, albeit for different time periods. The large, but different, amount of residual capital in total discounted welfare is one reason for this difference

Sources: Global comprehensive wealth: World Bank (2011, Table 2.1); global inclusive wealth: UNEP and UNU-IHDP (2014, Table 2).

74 Ecological sustainability

"environmental debt," even if we do not own nature but should have left it intact for future generations. The World Bank (2011, Ch. 4) calculates a value of such obligation as the social cost of damage from building up the stock of CO_2 in the atmosphere since pre-industrial times. It does not invoke any country's liability for damages to other countries from CO_2 emission because of the difficulty of assigning responsibilities in the absence of a legal framework.[4]

The World Bank values the stock of accumulated CO_2 in terms of social avoidance cost at over US$3000 per capita for high-income countries and US$80 per capita for low-income ones. Such figures might indicate the origins of environmental damage, notably by comparing country ranks of causing the build-up of CO_2 stocks (Table 6.3). These ranks could be taken as measures of the origin of climate change, but with the caveat of not assigning responsibility since the effects of CO_2 emission were largely unknown at the time. Table 6.3 also indicates the ranks for per-capita stock value. However these ranks do not show who ultimately bears the damage within and among countries. For instance, China's and India's population sizes drop the overall country rankings for per-capita CO_2 accumulation from number 3 and 8 to 17 and 18, respectively.

TABLE 6.3 Countries with high damage value of CO_2 accumulation

Emitting country[a]	Share of global CO_2 stock		CO_2 stock value per capita	
	(%)	(rank)	(US$)	(rank)
USA	27.3	(1)	3865	(1)
EU-27	23.8	(2)	2079	(9)
China	10.5	(3)	377	(17)
Russia	8.1	(4)	2684	(6)
Germany	6.1	(5)	3535	(3)
United Kingdom	4.7	(6)	3808	(2)
Japan	4.2	(7)	1617	(11)
India	2.8	(8)	125	(18)
France	2.5	(9)	1984	(10)
Canada	2.2	(10)	3347	(4)
Ukraine	2.1	(11)	2223	(8)
Poland	1.8	(12)	2335	(7)
Italy	1.7	(13)	1385	(12)
Australia	1.2	(14)	2875	(5)
Mexico	1.2	(15)	559	(16)
South Africa	1.2	(16)	1229	(13)
Korea, Republic	1.1	(17)	1105	(15)
Spain	1.0	(18)	1146	(14)

Source: World Bank (2011, Table 4.2).

Note
a Countries exceeding 1% of total anthropogenic CO_2 stock in 2005.

The difficulty of applying benefit and damage valuations to nature's systems prevented comprehensive assessments of nature's assets in terms of – discounted – human welfare obtained from the use of nature's services. Assessing sink services, in particular, requires measuring the full physical emission–concentration–absorption–exposure–morbidity–mortality chain for the emissions of harmful products and substances and their impacts on human health. Omission of any component of this chain can lead to distorted evaluations.

Stock estimates, whether in money or physical units, of nature's assets provide a confusing and even contradictory picture of the availability and accessibility of nature's services to human and non-human biota. The reasons are the use of different units of measurement and differing methods of finding and applying common physical and monetary values for the assets and their services. Turning from measuring nature's stocks to stock changes, i.e., to the measurement of pressures and impacts on environmental assets, could provide better indicators of the significance of nature for human wellbeing or at least for economic activity.

6.2 Environmental pressure

6.2.1 Material flow accounts

Material flow accounts (MFA) measure the mass of material inputs and outputs. They are derived from thermodynamic laws of energy conservation and dissipation, extended to flows of materials through the economy (Georgescu-Roegen 1979). The assumption is that the use of matter follows similar laws of conservation and dispersal as those of energy. The accounts thus treat the mass of material inputs into the economy as equal to the mass of materials staying in the economy, exported to other economies as natural resources and materials contained in commodities, and released as wastes and pollutants into the environment.

The weight of different flows of raw materials, products and pollutants cannot reflect their significance for human wellbeing and nature. This is actually seen as an advantage because it "minimizes value judgments" (Fischer-Kowalski et al. 2011, p. 8). Of course, this would also mean abandoning any evaluation of nature's ability to generate services for human use. Inputs of materials and outputs of residuals measure therefore *pressure* only on the natural environment. Potentially such pressure could cause a decline in environmental quality and stability. Ecological economists take environmental pressure as an indicator of impact that disturbs the "social metabolism" of material flows through the economy (Fisher-Kowalski 2002).[5] The question is where and when pressure translates into actual environmental depletion and degradation, threatening the sustainability of economic activity and nature itself.

Figure 6.4 shows a material flow account for the European Union (EU). The account records in principle all natural resource flows in and out of the economy of the EU, including those contained in imports, their storage in the economy and their final discharges as residuals into the natural environment. The key measure of

76 Ecological sustainability

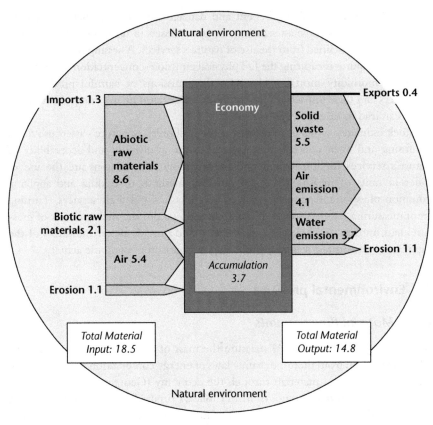

FIGURE 6.4 Material flow accounts of the European Union (EU-15, 1996, billion tons). The total mass of primary material inputs equals the mass of accumulation of materials in the economy plus total material outputs of wastes and emissions. Material flow accounts treat the economy as a black box, except for the accumulation of materials

Source: Bringezu (2002), with permission from the copyright holder S. Bringezu.

Total Material Input is also called Total Material Requirement when it includes unused materials of earth and biomass moved and disposed of in construction, mining and agriculture. Water use is generally excluded because of its relative magnitude which would "drown out" all other material flows.

The EU accounts of Figure 6.4 show that Total Material Input of 18.5 billion tons exceeds Total Material Output by 3.7 billion tons, i.e., by the accumulation of materials in the region. The aggregate flows reveal the mass of inputs of non-renewable raw materials to be four times the flow of renewable biotic materials. Net accumulation of materials is about 20 percent of total material input. Ecological economists interpret both the increase of material throughput and the accumulation of materials as "physical growth" of the economy (Bringezu and Moriguchi 2002, p. 89; Daly 1996, p. 31). Once physical growth reaches a certain level it is deemed to be responsible for non-sustainable environmental deterioration. Lacking, however, a clear connection between material flows with environmental damage, material input of natural resources remains a measure of environmental pressure rather than environmental impact.

In general, material flow accountants deal only with material inputs, ignoring outputs of residuals. The reason could be the difficulty of linking material inputs to wastes and pollutants. A global database (SERI et al. 2016/2017) compiles therefore only material inputs and some flows of unused materials. Global material extraction of natural resources amounted to almost 85 billion tons in 2013. "Overburden" of unused but moved material increases the pressure on the environment to over 100 billion tons.[6]

Figure 6.5 shows trends in the share of resource extraction in world regions. It indicates the origins of pressure as a response to international demand for natural resources. The bulk of extraction takes place in Asia, increasing distinctly since the 1990s when China entered the picture. In contrast Europe and North America decreased their extraction, possibly shifting the depletion and pollution burden of resource extraction to other regions.

Average global material consumption per person increased from about 8 tons to 10 tons from 1980 to 2009. Industrial nations bear most of the blame of high material consumption per person. China's big population makes it responsible for about a fifth of global consumption in 2009, but its average per person is still below that of the USA and Oceania.[7] Direct natural resource extraction and consumption ignore considerable burden shifting of resource use by rich countries on to less developed ones from which they import final or semi-final products. These products can contain a long chain of material inputs, for whose use the end users can be held responsible.

Wiedmann et al. (2015, p. 6272) calculate a "Material Footprint,"[8] which adds the weight of a "raw material equivalent" contained in imports to domestic extraction and deducts the equivalent from exports. It is an indicator of materials required by a country's final demand; supposedly "it is a good proxy for the material standard of living" (UNEP 2016, p. 16), even if it stays in the realm of environmental pressure from the use of materials rather than the consumption of final products.

Table 6.4 shows that a high per-capita Material Footprint can reflect a responsibility for natural resource use. Small or city-like nations like Hong Kong, Singapore or Luxembourg could thus be held responsible for resource extraction in other countries. These nations obviously need to import most of the natural resource contents of products. On the other hand, some rich, resource-exporting countries may have low domestic resource use compared to their high extraction level. This is the case of Russia and Australia and some oil-rich Arabic countries. Most of the developing countries (including China) are still close to a balance of resource extraction and use, matching responsibility for extraction of natural resources with responsibility for their own use.

The main problem of the material flow accounts is that the weight of material flows cannot assess the significance of natural resource depletion and environmental

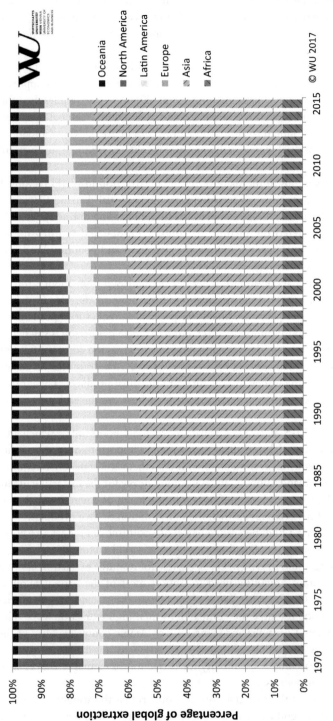

FIGURE 6.5 Shares of global resource extraction by world region, 1980–2013. North America and Europe decreased resource extraction since the beginning of the century. This could indicate a shifting of extraction to other regions, in particular Asia, by importing natural resources directly or as part of semi-finished or finished products

Source: SERI et al. 2016/2017 Global Material Flow Database, version 2017, with permission from the Research group "Sustainable Resource Use," Institute for Ecological Economics Vienna University of Economics and Business.

How much nature do we use? **79**

TABLE 6.4 Material Footprint and domestic extraction per capita, 2008

Countries[a]	(1) Material Footprint (tons per capita)	(2) Domestic extraction (tons per capita)
1 Hong Kong	155.6	3.4
2 Luxembourg	100.1	2.9
3 United Arab Emirates	83.0	75.6
4 Singapore	70.0	9.6
5 Kuwait	57.7	74.3
6 Cyprus	53.9	26.2
7 Qatar	51.1	139.1
8 Macao, SAR	49.8	10.4
9 Iceland	43.0	8.8
10 Montenegro	42.1	15.2
14 Australia	34.5	76.8
23 USA	27.2	15.8
60 Brazil	14.2	17.1
67 China	12.3	16.6
91 Russia	8.0	20.4
155 Afghanistan	1.7	1.7
156 Ivory Coast	1.5	3.1
157 Tanzania	1.5	3.1
158 Eritrea	1.3	1.1
159 Ethiopia	1.3	2.6
160 Malawi	1.3	2.7
161 Zimbabwe	1.1	2.7
162 Myanmar	0.9	3.3
163 Madagascar	0.9	2.8
164 Liberia	0.6	2.5

Source: Wiedmann et al. (2015).

Note

a Countries exceeding population size of 300,000; ranks by Material Footprint per capita.

degradation. The relation of environmental pressures to impacts might be based on "well-known processes and pathways" (Schandl et al. 2017, in prep.), but its actual measurement at national and international levels remains elusive. The weighting of measures by the weight of materials and substances ignores different impact potentials and excludes other environmental functions and effects such as those on land use, biodiversity, human health and wellbeing, as well as the ethical and aesthetic appreciation of nature. At best we obtain some impressions of environmental pressure, at worst this impression can be misleading when attempting to set policy priorities for tackling environmental impacts.[9]

80 Ecological sustainability

6.2.2 Physical input–output table

The MFA treat the economy as a black box. This might reflect environmentalist lack of confidence in the ability of economic policy to modify economic growth held responsible for environmental decline. Less radical environmental economists suggested opening the black box by showing "transformations" of materials in production and consumption in material and energy balances (MEB) (Ayres 1976).

The national-accounts-based physical input-output table (PIOT) is a compromise between covering intra-economy processes in MEB and ignoring them in MFA. Greening the PIOT introduces raw materials as primary inputs into the economy and residual outputs of wastes and pollutants as final outputs; non-material flows of labor and other services are ignored. The greened PIOT resembles MEB but with reduced and hence more manageable aggregates of material input. At the same time a PIOT can provide greater detail about production and consumption processes. Such tabulations could shed light on the cause of environmental depletion and degradation by input–output and decomposition analyses.[10]

Table 6.5 presents the results of a pioneering German PIOT (Stahmer et al. 1998), whose detailed data can be aggregated into national material flows and physical "economic" indicators. But what are we to make of a physical gross domestic product (GDP) of 3.9 billion tons, consisting of the weight of final consumption, produced capital formation and net exports,[11] but omitting non-material flows of economic services?

More radically, Strassert (2000) would treat all household consumption as an input into the national ecosystem. His modified PIOT would "endogenize" all household activity into the production sector since consumption is just a transformation of material flows that end up eventually as residuals in the natural environment. Exports, capital formation and the discharges of wastes and pollutants into the environment are the true final outputs generated in this case during an accounting period. Such final output would be almost 13 times the physical GDP, but in the view of its author would genuinely reflect human impact on the environment. The assumption is that the annual domestic use of material flows from and by nature and the economy is indeed a valid indicator of environmental impact, even if it ignores the use of renewable resources and the safe absorption of pollutants by environmental sinks. On the other hand, such tabulation would permit defining system-inherent eco-prices for assessing the ecological requirements of the economy (see section 13.2).

Costly information requirements for estimating input–output coefficients are the reason that PIOTs are rarely compiled. Exceptions are the tabulations for some European countries (Hoekstra and van den Bergh 2006).

6.3 Environmental impact

Environmental pressure can cause environmental impacts of natural resource depletion and degradation of environmental sinks. Pressure does not explain where,

TABLE 6.5 Physical input–output table, Germany 1990 (billion tons)

Output (supply)	Input (use)					Total material use
	Intermediate use of materials	Final use of materials in consumption and produced and natural assets				
	Industries 1,2, …, n	Consumption	Produced capital	Wastes, pollutants	Exports	
Industries[a]	7.6	3.1	0.7	48.3	0.2	59.9
Households[a]	2.6		0.0	0.7		3.3
Raw materials[b]	49.3	0.3[c]	0.0	0.1[d]	0.0	49.7
TOTAL SUPPLY[e]	59.5	3.4	0.7	49.1	0.2	112.9

Source: Stahmer et al. (1998, Table 12).

Notes
a Outputs.
b Provision of materials from nature and abroad.
c Consumption of non-produced natural resources by households.
d Scrapped capital goods.
e Direct material input.

82 Ecological sustainability

when or how much it transforms into actual impact. Linking the outputs of the MFA to environmental impacts and organizing impact indicators in loose statistical frameworks (UNSD 2016) are only first steps towards comprehensive evaluation. To fully assess total environmental depletion and degradation the different impacts need to be aggregated or otherwise combined.

The Ecological Footprint assesses environmental impact by the net decrease of areas that generate bioproductive source and sink services. Green accounting systems like the SEEA aggregate the depletion and degradation of nature in monetary terms and, as far as different units of measurement permit, in physical terms. The central framework of the revised SEEA ignores, however, environmental degradation as a loss of ecosystem services to be dealt with in experimental ecosystem accounts. Overuse of available stores of energy and overloading of atmospheric sinks with greenhouse gas emissions are often taken as surrogates for environmental deterioration. The question is if surrogates can provide a valid picture of total environmental impact.

6.3.1 Ecological Footprints

The Ecological Footprint seeks to measure the impact on the biocapacity of nature. As biocapacity supplies source and sink services to the economy, the Ecological Footprint claims to be a measure of demand for these services (Ewing et al. 2010). Per capita the footprint can be interpreted as the inverse of carrying capacity as it measures the average use of biocapacity. When the footprint exceeds biocapacity it creates an "ecological deficit" that may "lead to" environmental depletion and degradation if it is not compensated by the import of natural resources from other regions (ibid., pp. 5, 104). At the global level the deficit creates an "overshoot," which requires more than one year of regeneration to meet the current year's demand for nature's services.

Figure 6.6 shows the footprints and resulting ecological deficits or credits (reserves) for major world regions. In 2012 an average of 1.7 ha of biocapacity was available per person on earth confronting an average footprint of 2.8 ha. The world thus faces an ecological deficit of −1.1 ha per person, exceeding the yearly available biocapacity by nearly 40 percent. Such a deficit or "overshoot" may indeed reduce the world's biocapacity by permanent depletion and degradation.

The rich regions of North America and the EU show the highest footprints and deficits that could be a sign of ecological non-sustainability of their people and economies (cf. section 7.1.1). Latin America is the only region with a significant ecological reserve and hence the potential for sustainable economic growth. Other developing regions generate a deficit, which would call for changing their production and consumption styles to reduce natural resource use and emissions.

Table 6.6 reveals that regional footprints do not necessarily correlate with national ecological deficits or reserves as their size depends on available national biocapacities. Among highest-footprint ranked countries, Canada's large biocapacity leaves a reserve of 7.8 ha per person as does Australia with 7.3 ha,

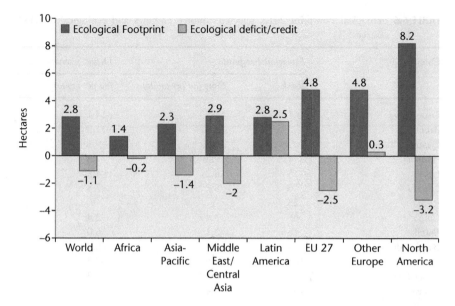

FIGURE 6.6 Average Ecological Footprint and deficit or reserve, 2012 (world regions, ha per person). A global footprint of 2.8 ha per person on available biocapacity of 1.7 ha created a global ecological deficit of −1.1 ha. North America and the European Union (EU-27) exert the highest footprints with correspondingly high deficits (except for transition economies). Only Latin America has a significant ecological reserve

Source: Bartelmus (2013, Fig. 2.2), with permission from the Taylor & Francis Group.

while the other high-ranked countries show high deficits. The lowest footprint-ranked countries are all poor nations with relatively low deficits and reserves. Industrialized countries in between show a diverse picture. Their production and consumption levels and styles require more inputs of natural resources and generate correspondingly higher wastes and pollution which meet with different amounts of biocapacities.

Measuring biocapacities and footprints faces methodological and coverage problems. Responding to criticism that the Ecological Footprint ignores the possibility of importing biocapacity from other countries, more recent calculations include the footprints of imported and exported commodities. Other improvements are an open discussion of calculation and interpretation problems (Borucke et al. 2013). However, the omission of non-renewable resources and emissions other than CO_2 limits the use of the footprint as a measure of total environmental impact.

Moreover, the conversion of biocapacities and environmental impacts into area equivalents is controversial. Equivalent factors estimate the bioproductive area required for food and wood production, urbanization and the absorption of carbon from CO_2 emissions. The weighting of different land areas by global equivalents cannot capture, however, the differing production patterns, cultures and

84 Ecological sustainability

TABLE 6.6 Ecological Footprint 2012, selected country rankings and ecological deficits/reserves

Country	Ecological Footprint		Deficit/reserve
	Rank	Score (ha per capita)	(ha per capita)
Luxembourg	1	15.8	−14.1
Aruba	2	11.9	−11.3
Qatar	3	10.8	−9.6
Australia	4	9.3	7.3
USA	5	8.2	−4.5
Canada	6	8.2	7.8
Russia	25	−	−
China	66	3.4	−2.4
Brazil	76	3.1	6.0
Bangladesh	184	0.7	−0.4
Haiti	185	0.6	−0.3
Timor-Leste	186	0.5	1.3
Eritrea	187	0.4	0.9
WORLD average	−	2.8	−1.1

Source: Global Footprint Network (2003–2017).

consumption styles of countries. Global hectares are also poor measures of the availability and needs for and uses of resources and sinks for pollution. Van den Bergh and Grazi (2013, p. 6) question therefore "whether we really need to aggregate information about different environmental problems in single indicators." They ignore though that integrative policies need to take full account of different environmental and economic problems, the purpose of overall indices that combine different and differently weighted indicators.[12]

6.3.2 Loss of ecosystem services

Ecosystem services include not only environmental source and sink functions but comprise all "benefits people obtain from ecosystems" (MEA 2005, p. v). This definition opens the door to a large variety of nature's goods and services, covering also less tangible life support and recreational, cultural and aesthetic values of nature.

The objective of the Millennium Ecosystem Assessment (MEA) report is thus "to assess the consequences of ecosystem change for human well-being" (ibid.). The report is quite comprehensive in its coverage of ecosystems, but stays mostly in the physical realm. Its generic statements about the health or quality of ecosystems are supported by different indicators that are difficult to aggregate and evaluate. One way is to use visual icons for changes in the provision of ecosystem services (Table 6.7).[13] The table appears to confirm the main conclusion of the MEA report that "approximately 60% (15 out of 24) of the ecosystem services … are being degraded or used unsustainably" (ibid., p. 6).

How much nature do we use? **85**

TABLE 6.7 Global status of ecosystem services

Provisioning services		Regulating services		Cultural services	
Food	↑↓	Air quality	↓	Spiritual, religious	↓
Fiber	↑↓	Climate, global	↑	values	
Generic resources	↓	Climate, regional	↓	Aesthetic values	↓
Biochemicals, natural	↓	and local		Recreation and	↑↓
medicines, pharmaceuticals		Water	↑↓	ecotourism	
Fresh water	↓	Erosion	↓		
		Water purification, waste treatment	↓		
		Disease	↑↓		
		Pest	↓		
		Pollination	↓		
		Natural hazard	↓		

Source: MEA (2005, Table 1).

Note
↑ enhanced, ↓ degraded, ↑↓ mixed.

Up- or down-arrows cannot provide a clear picture of the degradation or improvement of ecosystems at global, regional, national or local levels. Nor does the qualitative description of major "findings" of the MEA (ibid., p. 1), which include

- a substantial and irreversible loss in the diversity of life on earth over the past 50 years;
- net gains in human welfare during that period, offset by growing costs of ecosystem degradation;
- growing degradation of ecosystems services representing a barrier to achieving the Millennium Development Goals;
- the need for significant changes in policies, institutions and practices to conserve or enhance ecosystem services.

Perhaps setting out from physical measures of ecological processes and quantities and estimating an "inherent" eco-price for ecosystem matrices can do better. One such estimate of primary inputs into the global biosphere amounts to US$24.7 trillion for 1994 (Patterson 2002, p. 474). This is not too far from a first simple addition of monetary ecosystems services amounting to US$33 trillion per year (Costanza et al. 1997). A later estimate for 2011 (in 2007 prices) puts the value of global ecosystem services at US$125 trillion per year, which is 30 trillion above GDP (Costanza et al. 2014).

All values exceed global GDP at the time – a highly improbable result of people's willingness to pay for nature. The exceeding of the value of ecosystem services

86 Ecological sustainability

over GDP can be explained by the combination of valuations that includes non-market and non-use values; they "poorly fit" into market valuation (Kubiszewski et al. 2017, p. 292). Also system-inherent eco-prices refer usually to a fixed standard price, which would prevent determining absolute levels of ecosystem values.

Embedding the impacts on ecosystems and their services into the – greened – national accounts could be a more practical and systematic approach. The central framework of the revised SEEA avoids, though, assessing environmental degradation from the emission of wastes and pollutants; it treats environmental degradation as a change in ecosystem conditions to be measured by experimental ecosystem accounts. However, the experimental accounts still face the problem of aggregating the large number of indicators of ecosystem conditions. They reject therefore the monetary valuation of these indicators (United Nations et al. 2014b, paras. 5.2, 5.12; cf. section 4.2.2). The purpose of ecosystem accounting in the SEEA is probably to remove controversial issues from the central framework, holding out against the criticism of skirting environmental degradation.

The non-monetary evaluation of ecosystems by experts and stakeholders – outside any accounting system – has flourished therefore, especially at the local level. Subjective evaluations (e.g. Maynard et al. 2015; Raymond et al. 2014; Iniesta-Arandia et al. 2014) bundle the changes in ecosystem quality by weighting ecosystem conditions and services. Alternatively, easier-to-measure surrogates are advanced. Proposed carbon accounts focus on the carbon cycle through the biosphere, atmosphere, geosphere and the oceans to provide a measure of the condition of ecosystems, and, in particular, its biota. It remains to be seen if these surrogate accounts can show at least a partial picture of the quality and health of natural systems.[14]

So far there are no regularly compiled accounts that could provide indicators of overall environmental impact at different regional levels. Much of the ecosystem evaluation remains judgmental. It can be useful, though, at local levels. Stakeholders and experts might agree there on the significance of particular features of an ecosystem for the wellbeing of the local community.

6.3.3 Overuse of energy – a surrogate for depletion?

The energy theory of value claims that the flow of energy into human and non-human uses provides a measure of the value of nature. Different attempts at assessing this value, based on this theory, did not yield practical measures of the value of nature's functions and services. Narrowing down the focus on energy uses for economic production and consumption, i.e., on available "exergy," provides a clearer picture of the efficiency of energy use by economic activity.

Wall (2001, plate 30) presents an exergy system for Sweden. The system shows the loss of energy from extracting primary natural resources through various processes of production and high-quality energy (electricity) generation to their final uses by industries and households. The overall efficiency of the energy sector comes to less than 15 percent as indicated by the diminishing widths of the exergy flows towards final use. Note that compared to energy carriers other material flows (timber, ores and iron scrap) are quite insignificant in their exergy content.

Exergy, the measure of energy efficiency, might stimulate the search for more efficient processes of energy supply and use. It does not get, though, into assessing the depletion of energy sources and the emission of pollutants in the production and use of energy. Distinguishing between renewable and non-renewable energy sources brings embodied energy (emergy) accounts (see section 6.1.1) closer to measuring actual impact. It appears that the use (flows) of non-renewables (mostly sub-soil resources) exceeded the use of renewables (solar, deep earth heat, tidal) since the mid-1960s. In 1995 global flows of non-renewable energies amounted to 68 percent of total energy flows, leaving 32 percent to the flow of renewables (Brown and Ulgiati 1999, Table 2). Given that emergy stores of non-renewables amount to about 20 percent of the total there seems to be a risk that we might run out of non-renewables, needed for particular production processes. We would have to use instead the vast stock of renewables, notably solar energy. Actual energy consumption by the economy confirms these conclusions with about 90 percent of energy consumed consisting of non-renewables (Our Finite World 2012).

Measurement problems increase when tracing energy uses and their emissions down to different production and consumption processes. The reason is the difficulty of obtaining reliable data on the exergy content of energy carriers like oil, gas or wood, and also of minerals, metals and pollutants. Problems of making energy accounts a standard tool of environmental assessment thus include

- converting matter and different energy sources into a common energy unit;
- lack of knowledge about, and differing measurement methods for, a multitude of energy transformation processes; and
- incomparability of the theory of energy value with economic choice and preferences.

6.3.4 Climate change – a surrogate for degradation?

Global warming is often considered the embodiment of environmental decline. The reason is "carbon's central place in ecosystem and other environmental processes and its importance to economic and other human activity" (United Nations et al. 2014b, para. 4.92). Carbon accounts focus on the carbon cycle through natural systems of the biosphere, atmosphere, geosphere and the oceans. Changes in carbon stocks might signal changes in the conditions of ecosystems, especially in the biosphere, whereas economic production and consumption can be the causes of these changes by carbon emissions into the atmosphere. The balance of carbon inputs and outputs in nature might therefore not only be an indicator of ecosystem condition but also a broader measure of environmental quality. But can one topic in the limelight really represent other environmental concerns such as deforestation, loss of genetic resources, water shortage, pollution and nuclear energy risks?

88 Ecological sustainability

Global energy balances (U.S. National Weather Service 2010) show that 23 percent of all incoming solar energy is absorbed by vapor, clouds, dust and ozone before reaching the earth. Then 46 percent is absorbed by the ocean and land. The rest (31 percent) is reflected back into outer space. The trapping of heat reflected from the earth by greenhouse gases, in particular CO_2 and methane, is responsible for the greenhouse effect that keeps the earth at a comfortable average temperature of about 27 °C. Increasing greenhouse gas emissions, notably from fossil fuel use in production, transportation and consumption, is responsible, however, for pushing up the equilibrium temperature. The result has been global warming since the beginning of the industrial revolution − a sign of potential non-sustainability of climate change (see section 7.1.3).

The Intergovernmental Panel on Climate Change (IPCC 2014) puts current global warming at between 0.6 °C and 1.1 °C since the nineteenth century. The same report also gives "very likely" estimates of a decrease of cold days and nights and an increase of hot ones, and "likely" estimates of higher sea levels, incidents of tropical cyclones and heavy precipitation. Contrary to previous reports no clear trends of changes in Antarctic sea ice was observed. These are hardly accurate measures of the state and trend of the environment, let alone sustainability, even if one should not deny the potential severity of climate change.

Rather than modeling the complex connections between greenhouse gas emissions and climate change, the Carbon Footprint component of the Ecological Footprint measures the forest and sea area required to safely absorb CO_2 emissions. The Carbon Footprint avoids aggregation of diverse and differently measured environmental pressures and has therefore been used as a surrogate for environmental deterioration. However, the difficulty of estimating the absorptive capacity of different land and water areas makes converting CO_2 emissions into areal units problematic; it also disregards the severity of other environmental impacts and differences, and changes in human preferences for tolerating them (Bartelmus 2015b).

Still, Table 6.8 gives an indication of the significance of carbon emissions for environmental deterioration and its origins in world regions. The global Carbon Footprint(s) is about half the total Ecological Footprint in 2012. The CO_2 emissions of 27 percent of total material output in Europe's 1996 material flow accounts (Bringezu 2002) seem to tell a different story. In North America, China, and the Middle East and Central Asia the Carbon Footprint makes up over two-thirds of their Ecological Footprints. Developing countries in Africa and Latin America have lower Carbon Footprint shares because of relatively low industrialization and corresponding use of fossil fuels. The second column of Table 6.8 shows that most of the Carbon Footprint is made by Asia, and within Asia by China. Europe and North America come in next. The Carbon Footprint in developing regions are very low because of their pre-industrial state of development.

As indicated in Table 6.3, high CO_2 emitters are responsible for most of the total carbon damage valued at social avoidance cost. This damage counts for 23 percent of the comprehensive wealth estimates by the World Bank. However damage values differ considerably from estimates of mitigation cost. A green accounting

How much nature do we use? **89**

TABLE 6.8 Carbon Footprint, 2012

	Carbon Footprint	
	% of regional Ecological Footprints	% of global Carbon Footprint
EU-27	58.3	18.1[a]
North America	70.7	17.0
USA	72.0	10.1[b]
Other Europe	64.6	–
Asia-Pacific	60.9	46.7
China	67.6	28.0
Middle East/Central Asia	66.7	0.3[c]
Africa	28.6	4.0[d]
Latin America	42.9	5.0[b]
WORLD TOTAL	49.4	91.1[e]

Source: Global Footprint Network (2003–2017).

Notes
a Europe.
b 2009.
c 2010.
d 2013.
e Coverage by "world total" estimate.

study (Bartelmus 2009) found only a 7 percent share of global CO_2 costs over total environmental cost. These estimates do not show who ultimately bears the damage. A recent publication now claims that poor states in the USA and poor countries in the world bear most of the damage caused by the rich ones (Hsiang et al. 2017).

Of course the challenge of these estimates is their assumptions, notably about the valuation of human welfare and its detractions. There are also glaring discrepancies in climate change evaluations by physical indicators and by estimates of the emission costs caused and borne by economic agents.

Notes

1 The analysis of available energy and its efficient use in economic processes has tradition (e.g. Slesser 1975; Martinez-Alier 1987). More recently Ayres et al. (1998) and various contributors to the *Encyclopedia of Life Support Systems* (Brodianski 2001; Frangopoulos 2001; Szargut 2001; Wall 2001) advanced "exergy" for the valuation and sustainability analysis of "useful" energy in energy accounts. Valero (2006) suggests exergy replacement cost to assess energy use before extraction and the occurrence of any externalities of its production or use.
2 The 1992 Convention on Biological Diversity (no date) sets out from the notion of an intrinsic value to justify the conservation of species and ecosystems. In a similar vein, the Earth Charter (Earth Charter Initiative 2012–2016) affirms in its first principle that "every form of life has value regardless of its worth to human beings." Recognizing the intrinsic value of nature is a strong motive of its conservation (Sandler 2012).
3 See section 6.3.1 for the use of "equivalent factors" for measuring the significance of environmental services and their losses.

90 Ecological sustainability

4 The World Bank (2011, p. 88) bases the estimate of the damage function on an optimal growth model, which even its author characterizes as "extremely conjectural" (Nordhaus 2008, pp. xiii, 42). Note that the IPCC (2014) seems now to have abandoned any costing of climate change damage.

5 The social view of metabolism extends the original concept of biological metabolism, i.e., the biochemical processes of energy generation in a living organism, to the economy or society. Fischer-Kowalski (2002, p. 16) even claims that such metabolism "cuts across 'the great divide' ... between natural and social sciences."

6 Unused flows of overburden can create considerable environmental disturbances, amounting to two-thirds of total material input in some countries (Bringezu et al. 2004). The question is how a large amount and weight of overburden would affect the level and significance of actual environmental impacts. Note that the "compilation guide" of Eurostat (2013) does not include any more these "unused extractions" in its questionnaire.

7 More detailed analyses of material extraction and consumption at different regional levels and for different materials can be found in the regularly updated database of SERI et al. (2016/2017).

8 The term Material *Footprint* might be misleading as it should be reserved for impacts on an *area* (as for the Ecological Footprint), rather than for the weight of resource flows and uses.

9 This is probably the reason why the SEEA seems to have doubts about the application of comprehensive material flow accounts: in practice such accounts "tend to focus either on particular materials or on specific types of flows" (United Nations et al. 2014a, para. 3.224). The development and compilation of "economy-wide material flow accounts" is therefore left to Eurostat (2013) and the OECD (2015). On the other hand, a coalition of material flow accountants claims that material flow accounts could monitor progress towards achieving the sustainable development goals (Schandl et al. 2017, in prep.).

10 Structural decomposition, applied to time series of input–output tables, reveals the driving forces of economic activity as factors whose product affects economic output and growth. For environmental quality, de Haan (2001) "explains" CO_2 emission in the Netherlands by mainly economic growth. Dietzenbacher and Los (1998) warn, however, against relying on one of many forms of equivalent decompositions. Note also that explaining the change in a product of factors can generally not explain the actual (additive or otherwise) contributions of the factorial variables to that change.

11 Exports minus imports of 393 million tons (not shown in Table 6.5).

12 See for a critique of and response to the footprint calculations a special feature of the *Journal of Industrial Ecology* 18 (1), 2014.

13 Other assessments of environmental impacts apply similar aids. For example, the European Environment Agency (EEA, no date) uses overlay maps and directional arrows for assessing pressures of resource use on the environment and their effects on human wellbeing.

14 The SEEA's ecosystem accounts consider carbon and biodiversity accounts, based on the carbon cycle through natural and human-made systems and land use, "suitable" for assessing the quality (conditions) of ecosystems (United Nations et al. 2014b, sections 4.4, 4.5). See Bartelmus (2015a) for a detailed review and critique of the proposed ecosystem accounts.

References

Ayres, R.U. (1976). *Environment Statistics: Draft Guidelines for Statistics on Material/Energy Balances*, Report of the Secretary-General, New York: United Nations.

Ayres, R.U., Ayres, L.W. and Martinás, K. (1998). Energy, waste accounting and life-cycle analysis, *Energy* 23 (5): 355–63.

Bartelmus, P. (2009). The cost of natural capital consumption: accounting for a sustainable world economy, *Ecological Economics*, 68: 1850–7.

Bartelmus, P. (2013). *Sustainability Economics: An Introduction*, London and New York: Routledge.

Bartelmus, P. (2015a). Do we need ecosystem accounts? *Ecological Economics* 118: 292–8.

Bartelmus, P. (2015b). How bad is climate change? *Environmental Development* 14: 53–62.

Bateman, I.J. and Nunes, P.A.L.D. (eds.) (2016). Special issue on valuing ecosystems for improved national accounting, *Environmental and Resource Economics* 64 (1): 1–80.

Borucke, M., Moore, D., Cranston, G., Gracey, K., Iha, K., Larson, J., Lazarus, E., Morales, J.C., Wackernagel, M. and Galli, A. (2013). Accounting for demand and supply of the biosphere's regenerative capacity: the national footprint accounts, *Ecological Indicators* 24: 518–33.

Bringezu, S. (2002). Towards sustainable resource management in the European Union, *Wuppertal Papers* No. 121, Wuppertal, Germany: Wuppertal Institute for Climate, Environment and Energy.

Bringezu, S. and Moriguchi, Y. (2002). Material flow analysis, in R.U. Ayres and L.W. Ayres (eds.), *A Handbook of Industrial Ecology*, Cheltenham, UK: Edward Elgar: 79–90.

Bringezu, S., Schütz, H., Steger, S. and Baudisch, J. (2004). International comparison of resource use and its relation to economic growth, *Ecological Economics* 51: 97–124.

Brodianski, V. (2001). Earth available energy and the sustainable development of life support systems, in M.K. Tolba (ed.), *Our Fragile World: Challenges and Opportunities for Sustainable Development*, Oxford: Eolss: 471–504.

Brown, M.T. and Ulgiati, S. (1999). Emergy evaluation of the biosphere and natural capital, *Ambio* 28: 486–93.

Convention on Biological Diversity (no date). Online: www.cbd.int/convention/articles/default.shtml?a=cbd-00 (accessed 5 October 2017).

Costanza, R. (1980). Embodied energy and economic valuation, *Science* 210: 1219–24.

Costanza, R., d'Arge, R., de Groot, R., Farber, S., Grasso, M., Hannon, B., Limburg, K., Naeem, S., O'Neill, R.V., Paruelo, J., Raskin, R.G., Sutton, P. and van den Belt, M. (1997). The value of the world's ecosystem services and natural capital, *Nature* 387: 253–60.

Costanza, R., de Groot, R., Sutton, P., van der Ploeg, S., Anderson, S.J., Kubiszewski, I., Farber, S. and Turner, R.K. (2014). Changes in the global value of ecosystem services, *Global Environmental Change* 26: 152–8.

Daly, H.E. (1996). *Beyond Growth*, Boston, MA: Beacon Press.

De Groot, R., Brander, L., van der Ploeg, S., Costanza, R., Bernard, F., Braat, L., Christie, M., Crossman, N., Ghermandi, A., Hein, L., Hussain, S., Kumar, P., McVittie, A., Portela, R., Rodriguez, L.C., ten Brink, P. and van Beukering, P. (2012). Global estimate of the value of ecosystems and their services in monetary units, *Ecosystem Services* 1: 50–61.

De Haan, M. (2001). A structural decomposition analysis of pollution in the Netherlands, *Economic Systems Research* 13 (2): 181–96.

Dietzenbacher, E. and Los, B. (1998). Structural decomposition techniques: sense and sensitivity, *Economic Systems Research* 10 (4): 307–23.

Earth Charter Initiative (2012–2016). The Earth Charter. Online: www.earthcharterin action.org/content/pages/Read-the-Charter.html (accessed 1 August 2017).

European Environment Agency (EEA) (no date). SOER 2015: The European environment – state and outlook 2015. Online: www.eea.europa.eu/soer (accessed 19 July 2017).

Eurostat (2013). *Economy-wide Material Flow Accounts (EW-MFA): Compilation Guide 2013*. Eurostat, Luxembourg. Online: http://ec.europa.eu/eurostat/documents/1798247/6191

533/2013-EW-MFA-Guide-10Sep2013.pdf/54087dfb-1fb0-40f2-b1e4-64ed22ae3f4c (accessed 29 October 2017).

Ewing, B., Moore, D., Goldfinger, S., Oursler, A., Reed, A. and Wackernagel, M. (2010). *Ecological Footprint Atlas 2010*, Oakland, CA: Global Footprint Network. Online: www.footprintnetwork.org/images/uploads/Ecological_Footprint_Atlas_2010.pdf (accessed 29 October 2017).

Fischer-Kowalski, M. (2002). Exploring the history of industrial metabolism, in R.U. Ayres and L.W. Ayres (eds.), *A Handbook of Industrial Ecology*, Cheltenham, UK: Edward Elgar: 16–26.

Fischer-Kowalski, M., Krausmann, F., Giljum, S., Lutter, S., Mayer, A., Bringezu, S., Moriguchi, Y., Schütz, H., Schandl, H. and Weisz, H. (2011). Methodology and indicators of economy-wide material flow accounting, *Journal of Industrial Ecology* 15 (6): 855–76.

Frangopoulos, C. (2001). Exergy, energy system analysis, and optimization, in M.K. Tolba (ed.), *Our Fragile World: Challenges and Opportunities for Sustainable Development*, Oxford: Eolss Publishers: 427–52.

Georgescu-Roegen, N. (1979). Energy analysis and economic valuation, *Southern Economic Journal* 45: 1023–58.

Global Footprint Network (2003–2017). Data and methodology. Online: www.footprint-network.org/resources/data/ (accessed 27 March 2017).

Guerry, A.D., Polasky, S., Lubchenco, J., Chaplin-Kramer, R., Daily, G.C., Griffin, R., Ruckelshaus, M., Bateman, I.J., Duraiappah, A., Elmqvist, T., Feldman, M.W., Folke, C., Hoeksra, J., Kareiva, P.M., Keeler, B.L., Li, S., McKenzie, E., Ouyang, Z., Reyers, B., Ricketts, T.H., Röckstrom, J., Tallis, H. and Vira, B. (2015). Natural capital and ecosystem services informing decisions: from promise to practice, *Proceedings of the National Academy of Sciences* 112 (24): 7348–55.

Hoekstra, R. and van den Bergh, J.C.J.M. (2006). Constructing physical input–output tables for environmental modeling and accounting: framework and illustrations, *Ecological Economics* 59: 375–93.

Hsiang, S., Kopp, R., Jina, A., Rising, J., Delgado, M., Mohan, S., Rasmussen, D.J., Muir-Wood, R., Wilson, P., Oppenheimer, M., Larsen, K. and Houser, T. (2017). Estimating economic damage from climate change in the USA, *Science* 356 (6345): 1362–9.

Iniesta-Arandia, I., García-Llorente, M., Aguilera, P.A., Montes, C. and Martín-López, B. (2014). Socio-cultural valuation of ecosystem services: uncovering the links between values, drivers of change, and human well-being, *Ecological Economics* 108: 36–48.

Intergovernmental Panel on Climate Change (IPCC) (2014). *Synthesis Report*, Geneva: IPCC. Online: www.ipcc.ch/pdf/assessment-report/ar5/syr/SYR_AR5_FINAL_full_wcover.pdf (accessed 11 March 2017).

Kubiszewski, I., Costanza, R., Anderson, S. and Sutton, P. (2017). The future value of ecosystem services: global scenarios and national implications, *Ecosystem Services* 26: 289–301.

La Notte, A., D'Amato, D., Mäkinen, H., Paracchini, M.L., Liquete, C., Egoh, B., Geneletti, D. and Crossman, N.D. (2017). Ecosystem services classification: a systems ecology perspective of the cascade framework, *Ecological Indicators* 74: 392–402.

Latham, J., Cumani, R., Rosati, I. and Bloise, M. (2014). Global land cover share (GLC-share) database beta-release version 1.0–2014. Online: www.glcn.org/downs/prj/glcshare/GLC_SHARE_beta_v1.0_2014.pdf (accessed 12 January 2017).

Lovelock, J.E. (2009). *The Vanishing Face of Gaia: A Final Warning*, New York: Basic Books.

Martinez-Alier, J. (1987). *Ecological Economics: Energy, Environment and Society*, Oxford and Cambridge: Blackwell.

Maynard, S., James, D. and Davidson, A. (2015). Determining the value of multiple eco-system services in terms of community wellbeing: who should be the valuing agent? *Ecological Economics* 115: 22–8.

Millennium Ecosystem Assessment (MEA) (2005). *Ecosystems and Human Well-being: Synthesis*, Washington, DC: Island Press. Online: http://millenniumassessment.org/documents/document.356.aspx.pdf (accessed 1 December 2017).

Naess, A. (1976). The shallow and the deep, long-range ecology movement: a summary, *Inquiry* 16: 95–100.

Nordhaus, W.D. (2008). *A Question of Balance: Weighing the Options on Global Warming Policies*, New Haven, CT: Yale University Press.

Odum, H.T. (1996). *Environmental Accounting, Emergy and Decision Making*. New York: Wiley.

Organisation for Economic Co-operation and Development (OECD) (2015). *Material Resources, Productivity and the Environment*. Online: www.oecd.org/environment/waste/material-resources-productivity-and-the-environment-9789264190504-en.htm (accessed 7 October 2017).

Our Finite World (2012). World energy consumption since 1820 in charts. Online: https://ourfiniteworld.com/2012/03/12/world-energy-consumption-since-1820-in-charts/ (accessed 10 November 2017).

Patterson, M.G. (2002). Ecological production based pricing of biosphere processes, *Ecological Economics* 41: 457–78.

Raymond, C.M., Kenter, J.O., Plieninger, D., Turner, N.J. and Alexander, K.A. (2014). Comparing instrumental and deliberative paradigms underpinning the assessment of social values for cultural ecosystem services, *Ecological Economics* 107: 145–56.

Sander, J., Dendoncker, N., Martin-López, B., McGrath, F.L., Vierikko, K., Geneletti, D., Sevecke, K.J., Pipart, N., Primmer, E., Mederly, P., Schmidt, S., Aragão, A., Baral, H., Bark, R.H., Briceno, T., Brogna, D., Cabral, P., De Vreese, R., Liquete, C., Mueller, H., Peh, K.S.-H., Phelan, A., Rincón, A.R., Rogers, S.H., Turkelboom, F., Van Reeth, W., van Zanten, B.T., Wam, H.K. and Washbourne, C.-L. (2016). A new valuation school: integrating diverse values of nature in resource and land use decisions, *Ecosystem Services* 22: 213–20.

Sandler, R. (2012). Intrinsic value, ecology, and conservation, *Nature Education Knowledge* 3 (10): 4. Online: www.nature.com/scitable/knowledge/library/intrinsic-value-ecology-and-conservation-25815400 (accessed 9 May 2017).

Schandl, H., Fischer-Kowalski, M.F., West, J., Giljum, S., Dittrich, M., Eisenmenger, N., Geschke, A., Lieber, M., Wieland, H., Schaffartzik, A., Krausmann, F., Gierlinger, S., Hosking, K., Lenzen, M., Tanikawa, H., Miatto, A. and Fishman, T. (2017). Global material flows and resource productivity: forty years of evidence, *Journal of Industrial Ecology* (doi: 10.1111/jiec.12626).

Slesser, M. (1975). Accounting for energy, *Nature* 254: 170–2.

Stahmer, C., Kuhn, M. and Braun, N. (1998). Physical input–output tables for Germany, 1990, Eurostat Working Papers No. 2/1998/B/1, European Commission.

Strassert, G. (2000). Stoffflüsse und Systempreise: produktionstheoretische Zusammenhänge von monetärer und physischer Input-Output-Rechnung, in S. Hartard, C. Stahmer and F. Hinterberger (eds.), *Magische Dreiecke, Band 1: Stoffflussanalysen und Nachhaltigkeitsindikatoren* [Material flows and system prices: production theoretical relations of monetary and physical input–output tables, in *Magical Triangles, Volume 1: Material Flow Analyses and Sustainability Indicators*], Marburg, Germany: Metropolis Verlag: 93–126.

Sustainable Europe Research Institute (SERI), WU, Ifeu, Wuppertal Institute (2016/2017). www.materialflows.net, the online portal for material flow data. Online: www.material

94 Ecological sustainability

flows.net/trends/analyses-1980-2013/shares-of-global-material-extraction-by-world-region-1980-2013/ (accessed 26 December 2017).

Szargut, J. (2001). Exergy analysis of thermal processes and systems with ecological applications, in M.K. Tolba (ed.), *Our Fragile World: Challenges and Opportunities for Sustainable Development*, Oxford: Eolss Publishers: on CD.

United Nations, European Commission, Food and Agriculture Organization of the United Nations, International Monetary Fund, Organisation for Economic Co-operation and Development and World Bank Group (2014a). *System of Environmental-Economic Accounting 2012: Central Framework*. New York: United Nations. Online: http://unstats.un.org/unsd/envaccounting/seeaRev/SEEA_CF_Final_en.pdf (accessed 19 March 2017).

United Nations, European Commission, Food and Agriculture Organization of the United Nations, International Monetary Fund, Organisation for Economic Co-operation and Development and World Bank Group (2014b). *System of Environmental-Economic Accounting 2012: Experimental Ecosystem Accounting*, New York: United Nations. Online: http://unstats.un.org/unsd/envaccounting/eea_white_cover.pdf (accessed 19 March 2017).

United Nations Environment Programme (UNEP) (2016). *Global Material Flows and Resource Productivity*. Online: www.actu-environnement.com/media/pdf/news-27256-pnue-matieres-premieres.pdf (accessed 21 October 2017).

United Nations Environment Programme (UNEP) and UNU-IHDP (2014). *Inclusive Wealth Report 2014: Measuring Progress Toward Sustainability*, Cambridge: Cambridge University Press.

United Nations Statistics Division (UNSD) (2016). *Framework for the Development of Environment Statistics (FDES 2013)*, New York: United Nations. Online: http://unstats.un.org/unsd/environment/FDES/FDES-2015-supporting-tools/FDES.pdf (accessed 29 October 2017).

U.S. National Weather Service, JetStream – online school for weather (2010). The earth–atmosphere energy balance. Online: www.srh.noaa.gov/jetstream//atmos/energy.htm (accessed 15 January 2017).

Valero, A. (2006). Exergy accounting: capabilities and drawbacks, *Energy* 31 (1): 164–80.

van den Bergh, J.C.J.M. and Grazi, F. (2013). Ecological Footprint policy? Land use as an environmental indicator, Yale University, research and analysis. Online: www.cei-bois.org/files/03_van_de_Berg_et_al_2013.pdf (accessed 26 February 2017).

Wall, G. (2001). The use of natural resources in society, in M.K. Tolba (ed.), *Our Fragile World: Challenges and Opportunities for Sustainable Development*, Oxford: Eolss Publishers: 183–208.

Wiedmann, T.O., Schandl, H., Lenzen, M., Moran, D., Suh, S., West, J. and Kanemoto, K. (2015). The material footprint of nations, *Proceedings of the National Academy of Sciences* 112 (20), 6271–6. Online: www.pnas.org/content/112/20/6271.full.pdf?with-ds=yes (accessed 19 October 2017).

World Bank (2011). *The Changing Wealth of Nations: Measuring Sustainable Development in the New Millennium*, Washington, DC: World Bank. Online: http://siteresources.worldbank.org/ENVIRONMENT/Resources/ChangingWealthNations.pdf (accessed 1 September 2017).

7

SUSTAINABILITY

Reaching the limits?

Environmentalists take environmental impact indicators as evidence that we transgressed the limits of ecological sustainability. They claim that the human appropriation of 40 percent of the terrestrial net primary productivity leaves little or no environmental space for human expansion (Vitousek et al. 1986; Weterings and Opschoor 1992). Consequently our planet should be treated as a self-contained spaceship rather than an ever-expanding production system (Boulding 1966). Daly (1996) bases his view of a previously empty world, now filled with people and their disastrous activities, on his "pre-analytic vision" of a dramatically expanding human subsystem of nature. The "core belief" of ecological economists is that our economies have "already reached or exceeded the maximum sustainable scale" (Røpke 2005, p. 267). Such reasoning reveals personal convictions that appear to motivate the normative and sometimes moralistic argumentation of many environmentalists.

Scientific assessments of ecological sustainability should find measures that tell us when, where and by how much we overshot the limits of nature's capacity to maintain its services to people. Confronting capacity with impacts will indicate if the impacts have been or can be safely absorbed. This is the topic of section 7.1. In the absence of unequivocal measures of biocapacity, section 7.2 looks into setting sustainability standards or targets. The standards and targets remain essentially judgmental but allow examining compliance with these judgments. Section 7.3 narrows down the notion of ecological sustainability to maintaining at least nature's source and sink services to the economy; it treats nature as a type of capital used in the production of goods and services. The price of this practical simplification is restricting ecological sustainability to the support of economic activities and their objectives.

96 Ecological sustainability

7.1 Transgression of biocapacity

Biocapacity is about the availability of nature's benefits. The assumption of measuring ecological sustainability is that this capacity can be measured, linked to its uses and monitored over a lengthy period of time in the past. Models could extend past trends into the future.

7.1.1 The Ecological Footprint

The footprint calculations are the only attempt at recurrently confronting biocapacity with increasing demand for environmental services at sub-national, national and global levels. The question is, when does an ecological deficit turn into ecological non-sustainability? The ecological deficit of a region can be misleading as one does not know if and when excessive demand for environmental services will be met by regeneration, importing source and sink services, or reducing and replacing the use of exhaustible natural assets. Figure 7.1 indicates that we might need about half a

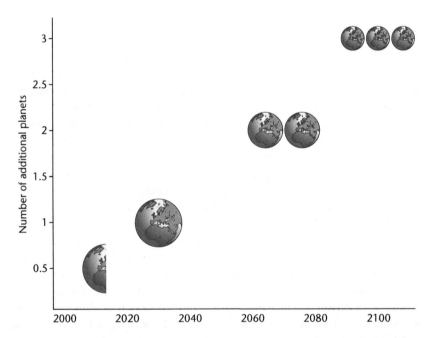

FIGURE 7.1 Ecological Footprint trend. With business as usual and continuing population growth, we might need one more planet in the 2030s and two more in the 2070s to maintain our lifestyles during one year. This looks indeed like non-sustainability of our current needs and wants for the next decades

Source: Bartelmus (2013), with permission from the Taylor & Francis Group.

Notes
Data source until 2050: World Wide Fund for Nature et al. (2010); two- and three-planets trend: own linear extrapolation.

planet's additional biocapacity to compensate for an annual ecological overshoot. In other words it would take one-and-a-half years to meet the current annual demand for nature's services. This may indeed lead to depletion and degradation of the environment.

Future environmental impacts and sustainability need to be modeled. Figure 7.1 presents trend extrapolations of the global footprint. According to the World Wide Fund for Nature et al. (2010), the projection for the 2030s is based on international forecasts of population, land use, land productivity, energy use, diet and climate change. If business as usual continues, we will overshoot the available biocapacity by 100 per cent in the 2030s; in other words, we would then require another planet to meet the needs of our current lifestyles. A further linear extrapolation indicates that the business-as-usual scenarios would require the need for two more planets in the 2070s and possibly even three by the end of the century. But we do not know if such needs will be met by further policy intervention or resource-reducing technologies, i.e., if human demand will be sustainable or will generate permanent or at least long-term depletion and degradation.

The Ecological Footprint ignores wisely the implications for human welfare, except for general statements that ecological overshoot would bring about losses of ecosystem services and future wellbeing of people (ibid., pp. 9, 12). Still, the problems of estimating biocapacities, actual impacts by footprints and their sustainability made some authors question the validity of the calculations. For instance, van Kooten and Bulte (2000, p. 385) consider the Ecological Footprint more a political call for action than a scientific measure of environmental impact and sustainability. It may alert to non-sustainability but does not tell when or where it would actually happen.

7.1.2 Land cover and land use

A summary of estimates and projections of global land use confronts land availability in the year 2000 with demand for land in 2030 (Table 7.1). Total land available for crops, pasture, forests, built-up and unused land in 2000 amounts to about 8800 million ha. Deducting projected additional land demand of 539 million ha from available unused productive land (401 million ha) obtains a non-sustainable

TABLE 7.1 Sustainability of global land use (million ha)

(1) Total land use in 2000	8802 (7701 to 9903)
(2) *thereof: unused productive land*	401 (356 to 445)
(3) Total additional land demand in 2030	539 (285 to 792)
(4) Sustainability: (2)–(3)	−138 (71 to −347)
(5) *with deforestation*	*90 (223 to −44)*

Source: Lambin and Meyfroidt (2011, Table 1).

Note
Figures in parentheses show the range of estimates.

98 Ecological sustainability

overuse of 138 million ha by the year 2030. If we take "unavoidable deforestation," which may create productive land, into account non-sustainability turns into a positive land reserve of 90 million ha. The picture becomes more uncertain when considering the large variations in projected land use. Sustainability without deforestation then ranges from +71 million ha to non-sustainability of −347 million ha and with deforestation still ranges between 223 million ha and −44 million ha. Uncertainty about future trends and different assumptions about attaining food security prevent a clear assessment of the sustainability of agricultural land use and its effects on ecological sustainability.

Linking land use to the final consumption of land-based products would determine sustainability as the safe supply of these products, i.e., as food security. UNEP (2014, p. 68) thus defines the minimum sustainability limit of global cropland use as the availability of 1640 million ha of agricultural land. Out of the total continental surface area of about 15,000 million ha, one-third (4100–5051 million ha) is agricultural land of croplands and pastures. UNEP also believes that for business-as-usual net expansion of cropland,[1] this limit will be overshot in the 2020s.

A report for the Food and Agriculture Organization (FAO) indicates variations in cropland use at regional levels. Different ecological characteristics, production and consumption patterns and abilities for developing and adopting innovative technologies are the reasons. During 1961–2004 cropland increased by 11 percent (Bindraban et al. 2009, Fig. 2.9). The use of cropland in the European Union (EU), North America and Eastern Europe declined during this period whereas it increased in South America, Asia, Africa and Oceania. North America, Oceania and Central America and the Caribbean have leveled off in recent years. One can hardly come to an overall conclusion about the sustainability or non-sustainability of current and future food security from these cropland changes. One reason is uncertainty about food trade in a globalizing world.

7.1.3 Energy use and climate change

Assessing the availability of energy for potential human and non-human use requires measuring the stock of useful energy embodied in natural resources plus solar energy influx. The concept of energy embodied in natural capital and products, i.e., "emergy" (Odum 2002), links the "stores" of energy to their use. The purpose is to determine the sustainability of energy uses. Section 6.3.3 indicated that the high use of non-renewable energies might eventually deplete their stocks.

Brown and Ulgiati (1999) suggest a number of sustainability indices that are essentially ratios of renewable and non-renewable emergies. An "emergy yield ratio" indicates the benefits of using energy as total emergy of output, constrained (divided) by the use of non-renewable energy. The global yield ratio declined from 3.7 in 1950 to 1.6 in 1995. An "environmental loading ratio" shows a corresponding increase; it indicates how much non-renewables are used by the economy in relation to the use of renewables.[2] The use of non-renewables surpassed renewable energy use since the 1960s. But the authors do not indicate when we would run out of non-renewables. This might be due to the difficulty of predicting energy uses as well as the general problem of comprehensive accounting for the energy value of material inputs (see section 6.3.3). Unsurprisingly, energy accounting has not become as popular as material flow accounting.

The use of fossil fuels and their carbon content and emission are the main causes of climate change. Climate change has been taken as a surrogate for environmental decline (see section 6.3.4). The question here is whether such a decline indicates the non-sustainability of environmental quality and its health and welfare effects – in other words, when and at what level CO_2 concentration in the atmosphere should be held constant to attain sustainability (World Wide Fund for Nature 2012, p. 137). To determine the sustainability threshold of climate change a maximum level of global warming of 2°C and its causes since pre-industrial times are usually specified. Section 7.2.2 will further discuss this threshold as a key boundary of an "environmental space."

7.2 Standards and targets of ecological sustainability

If capacity measures for environmental services are questionable or not available at all, one cannot directly assess the sustainability of capacity maintenance. In this case, one could resort to expert advice or politically negotiated standards, telling when excessive uses of nature become "intolerable" abuse. Sustainability standards advanced to this end represent of course the judgments of the standard setters.

7.2.1 Limits for material throughput

Section 6.2.1 described material flows through the economy as an indicator of pressure on environmental source and sink functions. Further analysis of the dependence on natural resources and concomitant carbon emissions found that in the long run developing and emerging countries show a stronger correlation of material consumption and economic growth than industrialized ("mature") nations (Steinberger et al. 2013). Most countries (at any stage of development) could or did not dematerialize and decarbonize over the 1970–2004 period. The authors find this trend "fundamentally unsustainable" (ibid., p. 9). Of course, modeling the future with different policy interventions might paint a different picture.

Environmental pressures are proxies only for actual impacts that might undermine ecological sustainability. The opaque connection between pressure and impact and the lack of a meaningful overall stock measure for materials encouraged statements about how much pressure is tolerable for a growing economy. A number of "factors" for delinking economic growth from material input were suggested to this end. The objective is indeed to dematerialize the economy by increasing resource productivity, i.e., gross domestic product (GDP) per unit of natural resource input, and perhaps also to reduce in this way the emission intensity of residuals per GDP.

A radical suggestion is to attain a "steady-state economy" where material throughput does not increase for an economy deemed to be at the edge of a

100 Ecological sustainability

non-sustainable state (Daly 1996). In such an economy a Factor 0 (zero) through-put increase would ensure sustainability. Other factors suggest attaining sustainability or an otherwise desirable state, setting out from different evaluations of the current situation and future developments. The popular Factor 4 connects long-term planetary equilibrium with economic growth: material input into the economy could be halved with the help of innovative technology while facilitating a doubling of wealth or output within the next few decades (von Weizsäcker et al. 1997). A Factor 10 reduction of material inputs for industrialized countries is supposed to enable developing countries to catch up with industrialized ones (Factor 10 Club 1994). Unfortunately the authors do not specify what such equilibrium would look like, i.e., what kind and amount of environmental impacts can be expected and how much economic growth would actually be possible from reduced material input.

The United Nations Environment Programme (UNEP 2011) uses a simple model of different scenarios based on anticipated population growth and stable material consumption. Table 7.2 presents global resource use and per-capita resource consumption for the baseline situation in 2000 and three scenarios for 2050. The assumption is that the average resource consumption of developing countries will converge to the projected consumption of industrialized countries.

The business-as-usual scenario shows relative dematerialization of industrialized countries by maintaining their average consumption of 13–24 tons[3] with continuing economic growth. At the same time developing countries adopt the consumption pattern of industrialized nations. Their annual global resource use would nearly triple in this scenario, generating "an unsustainable future in terms of both resource use and emissions" (ibid., p. 29). Average resource consumption will double (to 16 tons) in 2050, and continuing relative decoupling will exhaust annual resource availability by 2050. The UNEP report calls therefore for a "tough" reduction of

TABLE 7.2 Projections of resource capacity and consumption, 2000–2050[a]

	Baseline 2000	BAU: relative decoupling 2050	Factor 2 reduction 2050[b]	Factor 3–5 reduction 2050[b]
Global annual resource use (gigatons per year)	49	141[c]	70	49
Average per-capita resource consumption (tons)	8	16	8	5.5
industrialized countries (tons)	13–24	13–24	6.5–12	5–8
developing countries (tons)	5–9	13–24	6.5–12	5–8

Source: UNEP (2011, Table 2.1).

Notes

a Global population is assumed to increase from 6 billion in 2000 to 8.9 billion in 2050.

b For industrialized countries.

c Maximum available resource use by the year 2050.

annual resource use in industrialized countries by a "factor of 3 to 5" to maintain the global annual resource use of 49 gigatons of the year 2000 by 2050. This scenario is supposed to succeed in maintaining present global natural resource use by actually decreasing average resource consumption from 8 tons to 5.5 tons.

The underlying assumption of both the business-as-usual and the sustainable resource use (Factor 3–5) scenarios is a capacity of 141 gigatons of natural resources available annually.[4] The justification of this assumption is odd: it is "most compatible with the existing *if unknown* [own emphasis] limits to the Earth's resource base," even if it is "a glaring unsubstantiated assumption" about long-term resource extraction (ibid., pp. 32, 28). The purpose is to show a "hypothetical barrier" rather than an actual estimate of global resource availability. The anchor to reality seems to be the linkage of the highest reduction scenario to the resource use required to keep the proxy of global warming below 2 °C (ibid., p. 27).

The different assumptions may not stand empirical tests. Admittedly the model is only to provoke such validation, notably of the convergence of standards of living (a kind of social justice that would eradicate poverty) and of the setting of an available global resource capacity at 141 gigatons per year. The latter is to avoid introducing resource constraints but actually replaces them with an overall global limit that does not seem to be grounded in actual measurement. Still more important is the issue of translating pressure of tons of material flows into environmental impact and possibly human wellbeing. Perhaps it is not unreasonable to evoke the picture of "ton ideology" (Gawel 1998) when normative standards of Factor X resource productivity are set for meeting "the needs of nine billion people."

Nonetheless, international organizations picked up the idea of dematerializing economic growth. They seem, however, to abandon the idea of determining sustainability by means of concrete factors or targets. The EU's natural resource strategy recognizes that lack of knowledge and data precludes setting quantitative targets (Commission of the European Communities 2005). Its call for a *relative* decoupling indicates that member states are not willing to decrease the use of materials which might entail a significant slow-down of economic growth. Similarly, the Organisation for Economic Co-operation and Development (OECD 2002, p. 5) admits that its "decoupling concept lacks an automatic link to the environment's capacity to sustain, absorb or resist pressures of various kinds." Even former followers see the Factor 4 delinking more as a "directional guide" than a concrete policy prescription (Hinterberger et al. 2000; Bringezu 2002).

7.2.2 Thresholds of environmental space

Environmental limits or thresholds denote an "environmental space" (Weterings and Opschoor 1992). In principle, human activities can be carried out within this space without impairing the carrying capacity of a territory. Carrying capacity is basically a property of ecosystems. It is related to their limited resilience to heavy shocks, especially by human activity. Section 2.1 described ecosystem resilience as an ingredient of ecological sustainability. The widely differing and complex nature

102 Ecological sustainability

of ecosystems and their vulnerabilities thwart the measurement of resilience at national and global levels. The analysis of carrying capacity has therefore more narrowly focused on the biophysical limits to environmental impacts from economic activity. Even then, differing and mostly judgmental assumptions about standards of living and their distribution, technology, economic preferences and policies, environmental conditions and prediction techniques impair the meaning and validity of carrying capacity estimates (Cohen 1995).

This did not deter environmentalists from setting limits to avoid overtaxing ecosystems. According to Perrings (1995) "safe minimum standards" would "hold back" human activity and could ensure the maintenance of carrying capacities and resilience of natural systems. Ekins (2011) advanced a "sustainability gap," which could provide the evidence. The sustainability gap applies safe minimum standards to environmental themes and compares the standards to actual environmental conditions. For the Netherlands, the sustainability gap decreased by 18 percent from 1980 to 1991 (ibid., Table 4). Equal weighting of different concerns and their gaps obscures, however, the meaning and validity of the indicator.

A global framework of "planetary boundaries" attempts to set limits to environmental use and abuse; their transgression might cause abrupt catastrophic changes of the earth system (Rockström et al. 2009). The planetary framework defines a safe operating space for humanity, within which human activities could be carried out (ecologically) sustainably. The scientists, who determined the boundaries, admit that normative judgments influence the definition and position of the boundaries (ibid., Fig. 3). They also believe that we have already crossed three (out of nine) boundaries for:

- climate change, exceeding atmospheric CO_2 concentration of 350 ppm, which would push global warming to more than 2 °C,
- biodiversity, where the loss rate is higher than ten extinctions per million species per year, and
- nitrogen pollution, when removal of the pollutant from the atmosphere for human use is greater than 35 million tons per year.

Nordhaus et al. (2012) point out that except for climate change no global limits can be set since most environmental impacts are local and regional in nature and most "boundaries" are not based on inherent thresholds. Even staying within the limits of environmental space can condone low welfare effects for particular strata of a population that are largely excluded from the benefits of ecosystem services. Environmental space has therefore been connected with a "fair earthshare" for countries and their people (Sachs et al. 1998; Vale and Vale 2013). But such connection did not lead to any suggestion how an inequitable distribution of environmental impacts and benefits could be specified. This is a matter of general social equity, which will be examined in section 10.1 as part of the broader development paradigm.

Boundaries and representative impact indicators suffer not only from judgmental standard setting and distributional questions but also from the murky weighting of boundaries and indicators, expressed in different units of measurement. Selecting a representative issue and setting a limit for it may be easier to interpret and assess, but it is also a simplification: it reduces the multi-dimensional space of ecological sustainability to one particular concern.

Climate change, the preferred surrogate for environmental decline, has been used in particular to this end. Stabilizing global average temperature below a 2 °C increase since pre-industrial times is usually proclaimed as the level at which one would avoid disaster (IPCC 2014, p. v; UNFCCC 2014). Past trends (during 1880–2012) indicate that global land and water surface temperature increased by 0.85 °C (within a 90 percent likelihood range of 0.65 °C to 1.06 °C). So far, this has kept us below the non-sustainability level.

Projections change the story. "Representative concentration pathways" for greenhouse gas emissions and their atmospheric concentrations predict different degrees of global warming by the end of the century. "Stringent mitigation" generates greenhouse gas concentration of 430–530 ppm CO_2 equivalents that could keep global warming below 2 °C. Higher greenhouse gas emissions and concentrations might drive global warming over the sustainability threshold and up to 5 °C for "very high emissions" with concentrations of more than 1000 ppm. The ellipses of Figure 7.2 show total anthropogenic warming in different projections based on various assumptions about atmospheric concentrations of CO_2 and corresponding emission. To stay below 2 °C would mean that no more than 2900 gigaton CO_2 should be emitted. The actual emission of 1900 gigatons in 2011 is still well below this limit.

But which of the reduction scenarios will come true in the future, and what will be the overall effect of diverse impacts? Economists turned to pricing and modeling the effects of climate change, but the wide range of results reflects different time frames and model assumptions, data gaps and incompatible valuations of mitigation costs and damages. Table 7.3 shows examples of global cost estimates in the past and for the future. Even the wide ranges of results call for taking greater caution by preventing current trends from continuing. But "economics appears to be unable to determine how much caution is needed" to lower greenhouse gas emissions to sustainable levels (Bartelmus 2015, p. 59). Uncertainties about future greenhouse gas emissions and their effects on human health, wellbeing and the sustainability of human activity prevail.[5]

7.3 The cost of maintaining nature's services

Treating nature as a provider of capital inputs for the economy calls economic preferences and corresponding pricing into the arena of ecological economics. When nature thus enters the realm of the economy its maintenance becomes a feature of economic sustainability. Applying a price to diverse natural assets and flows allows aggregation and usually assumes substitutability of environmental services, i.e., weak sustainability.

On the other hand, exhaustible "critical" natural capital that cannot be replaced can play an important role in maintaining the level of economic activity

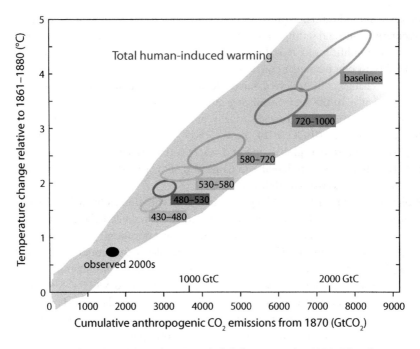

FIGURE 7.2 CO_2 emission and projected global warming by 2100. The plume containing the ellipses of projections (defined by ranges of CO_2 concentrations) indicates the spread of model results. Average global temperature increased since 1870 to the current level by 0.85 °C. By 2100, a "stringent" scenario allows stabilizing temperature below 2 °C (concentration of 430–480 ppm CO_2-eq). Higher emission and concentration scenarios generated higher temperature increases

Source: IPCC (2014, Fig. SPM 5, contribution of Working Groups I, II and III to the Fifth Assessment Report of the IPCC, with permission from the IPCC).

and resulting welfare. Its preservation requires separate identification for measuring strong sustainability (cf. section 2.2). Despite its potentially limiting role in pursuing economic growth, the use of critical capital is generally ignored in monetary terms at national and international levels. The reason might be the relative abundance and substitutability of depletable natural capital such as fossil fuels, or else the difficulty of determining and pricing critical irreplaceable capital.

The original System for integrated Environmental and Economic Accounting (SEEA) (United Nations 1993) treated the loss of sinks for wastes and pollutants as part of natural capital consumption and suggested their valuation as a cost of capital maintenance. The revised SEEA (United Nations et al. 2014) relegated such valuation to inconclusive experimental ecosystem accounts. The argument is that it is difficult to find a monetary value for nature's sinks which are usually not traded in markets. The Economics of Ecosystems and Biodiversity (TEEB 2010, p. 26) team concedes that the complexity of ecosystems and their services could create "radical

Reaching the limits? **105**

TABLE 7.3 Global cost of climate change (% of world GDP)

	Past cost 2006	Expected cost	
		2100	2200
IPCC (2007)	–	1–5[a]	–
IPCC (2014)	–	1.9[b]	–
Stern (2006)	–	2.9[c]	13.8[c]
Nordhaus (2008)	–	2.5[d]	–
Bartelmus (2009)	0.45[e] (0.15)[f]	–	–
World Bank (2010)	0.4[g]	–	–

Source: Bartelmus (2015, Table 3), with permission from Elsevier.

Notes

a Global mean loss (macro-economic cost) for 4°C global warming in the second half of the 21st century.

b Difference of mitigation costs in terms of consumption losses between best and worst scenario (430 ppm CO_2-eq vs. 580–650 ppm), converted to percent of GDP.

c "High-climate" scenario (mean: 4.3°C global warming).

d "Best guess" of economic damage in 2100 with no intervention of emission control.

e Maintenance cost in greened national accounts at $35 per ton of CO_2-eq, 2030 estimate for the 550 ppm stabilization goal (IPCC 2007, p. 61).

f Maintenance cost at $12 per ton of CO_2-eq (average value for 2005, range: $–3 to $95) (IPCC 2007, p. 69).

g Social cost in 2006 in adjusted net savings accounts at marginal damage cost of $5.4 per ton of CO_2.

uncertainty"; in this case, marginal economic valuation might be "less useful" for a precautionary setting of safe minimum standards.

Nonetheless, at least one attempt at implementing the SEEA at the global level estimated the cost of total (source and sink) depreciation of natural capital. Table 7.4 indicates that Asia (including China) and "other" industrialized countries

TABLE 7.4 The cost of natural capital maintenance

	1990		2006	
	billion US$	% of GDP	billion US$	% of GDP
EU-25	43.4	0.60	120.5	0.84
USA	81.7	1.42	310.0	2.35
Other industrialized countries	190.2	3.66	681.1	7.69
China	39.6	9.80	332.3	12.46
Asia and Oceania, developing countries[a]	169.2	9.05	835.0	15.33
Africa	62.5	12.16	306.6	28.10
Latin America and the Caribbean	74.0	6.41	381.4	12.39
WORLD	660.6	2.99	2966.9	6.10

Source: Bartelmus (2009, annex tables).

Note

a Excluding China.

106 Ecological sustainability

(excluding the USA and EU-25 countries) incurred most of the costs of environmental depletion and degradation. The situation does not seem to be sustainable in terms of maintaining the value of natural capital, at least for the 1990–2006 period, globally and in some of the high-environmental-cost regions. For developing countries the picture is particularly gloomy when examining the share of environmental cost over GDP: their economic strength is unlikely to tackle their environmental problems.

Of course, these are only first rough estimates that need improvements in the coverage of environmental functions and in finding appropriate (and deflated) cost values. The objective is less to provide stand-alone values than to combine natural capital consumption with conventional (fixed) capital consumption for measuring a broader concept of economic sustainability (section 4.2.2). On their own, environmental depletion and degradation costs can assess the expenditure necessary to maintain the supply of natural resources and environmental quality; but the economic preferences represented by these expenditures need to be weighed against those of maintaining other forms of capital and assets to obtain a full picture of the sustainability of economic performance and socioeconomic development.

Changes in the per-capita value of natural wealth might be closer to ecological sustainability by indicating a change in the capacity of nature to meet people's demand for environmental services. Stock values of natural wealth are not routinely measured, though, even if the environmentally expanded national accounts discuss natural resource wealth in some detail.

Table 7.5 provides a limited picture of the distribution of marketed natural wealth over world regions.[6] South Asian and sub-Saharan countries lost considerable natural capital per person owing to high population growth and mismanagement of natural resources. The latter includes overexploitation, notably for exports to industrialized countries, which may shift the environmental burden to developing nations (Bringezu et al. 2004). As these countries' economies depend on the

TABLE 7.5 Natural wealth per person in world regions, 1995 and 2005

	1995 (constant US$)	2005 (constant US$)	Change (%)	Increase in population (million)
East Asia and the Pacific	3243	4401	35.7	154
Europe and Central Asia[a]	15,226	15,330	0.7	0
Latin America and the Caribbean	10,523	12,063	14.6	72
Middle East and North Africa	6475	9895	52.8	37
South Asia	3230	2637	−18.4	228
Sub-Saharan Africa	5393	3686	−31.7	147
WORLD[b]	6045	6568	8.7	639

Source: World Bank (2011, Tables 2A.1 and 2A.2).

Notes

a 2000–2005.

b Includes only countries for which wealth data are available.

high share of natural wealth (notably agricultural land) in total wealth these shifts impair their economic growth. In other regions gains in natural capital are through discovery of subsoil resources, notably oil in the Middle East and Northern Africa, and the expansion of agricultural land in East Asia and the Pacific. However, as the available data exclude the loss of sink services they do not say much about the decline or improvement of nature in world regions.

Section 13.2 will discuss briefly the modeling of system-inherent pricing of an ecological system to find nature's own valuation of its functions and services, which could ensure the maintenance of ecosystems by reproduction. While intriguing, such pricing has to cope with the absence of a standard value and the difficulty of assessing large numbers of interdependent ecological processes and quantities. Estimates of the value of "ecological inputs" attempt to approximate intrinsic values. They reach values that may exceed global GDP (see section 6.3.2) but do not realistically measure the sustainability or non-sustainability of the use of nature's wealth. Kubiszewski et al. (2017) attempt to model the sustainability of nature by "necessary" policy reforms as an "encouragement" of research (see section 12.3). Progress in measuring ecological sustainability by maintaining nature's functions is indeed still a matter of further research.

Even if one reduces ecological sustainability to one surrogate impact, notably CO_2 emission and corresponding global warming, the question remains whether monetizing this impact reflects environmental damage. The above-described valuations in terms of social avoidance or mitigation cost refer to expenditure needed to attain a desirable sustainability level. It is a matter of strategy and policy, which will be addressed in section 12.3. The assessment of damage, on the other hand, suffers from the problem of measuring and aggregating human wellbeing at global, regional or country levels.

At least one thing seems to be clear: economic sustainability of maintaining natural capital in monetary terms seems to give much lower importance to using up carbon sinks than physical ecological sustainability: the carbon footprint is about half the total Ecological Footprint (see section 6.3.4), whereas the global SEEA study (section 4.3) estimates the cost of greenhouse gas emission at 7.4 percent only of the total environmental cost (Bartelmus 2009, annex tables). It is an open question whether (economic) preferences will do for now to "save the world," or if they need to be combined or replaced with environmental objectives (see section 12.1).

Notes

1 Net expansion takes changes in land productivity and expansion into other bioproductive areas into account.

2 A further "energy sustainability index" combines the two ratios to obtain a benefit–stress indicator. However the resulting quotient of ratios is difficult to interpret.

3 The range refers to the lower average consumption ("metabolic rate") of industrialized countries with high-population density vs. the higher metabolic rate of low-density industrialized countries. Note that the reduction "factors" refer to resource inputs only and not to resource productivity as for instance by the Factor 4 target.

108 Ecological sustainability

4 The intermediate Factor 2 reduction scenario maintains average resource consumption (at 8 tons) halving annual resource availability to 70 gigatons. This reflects a growing trend that might still go beyond the 141 gigatons barrier after 2050. Only the high Factor 3–5 reduction scenario does not increase current resource use (of 49 gigatons).
5 Note that the IPCC (2014) report seems to have given up on damage valuation, which it presented in the preceding report (IPCC 2007).
6 The World Bank estimates of natural capital are not part of the national accounts. They include agricultural land, protected areas, forests, minerals and energy resources and exclude the capacity of nature to provide environmental sink services.

References

Bartelmus, P. (2009). The cost of natural capital consumption: accounting for a sustainable world economy, *Ecological Economics*, 68: 1850–7.

Bartelmus, P. (2013). *Sustainability Economics: An Introduction*, London and New York: Routledge.

Bartelmus, P. (2015). How bad is climate change? *Environmental Development* 14: 53–62.

Bindraban, P., Bulte, E. Conijn, S., Eikhout, B., Hoogwijk, M. and Londo, M. (2009). *Can Biofuels be Sustainable by 2020? An Assessment for an Obligatory Blending Target of 10% in the Netherlands*. Online: www.pbl.nl/sites/default/files/cms/publicaties/500102024.pdf (accessed 29 October 2017).

Boulding, K.E. (1966). The economics of the coming spaceship earth, in H. Jarret (ed.), *Environmental Quality in a Growing Economy*, Baltimore, MD: Johns Hopkins Press for Resources for the Future.

Bringezu, S. (2002). Towards sustainable resource management in the European Union, *Wuppertal Papers* No. 121, Wuppertal, Germany: Wuppertal Institute for Climate, Environment and Energy.

Bringezu, S., Schütz, H., Steger, S. and Baudisch, J. (2004). International comparison of resource use and its relation to economic growth, *Ecological Economics* 51: 97–124.

Brown, M.T. and Ulgiati, S. (1999), Emergy valuation of the biosphere and natural capital, *Ambio* 28: 486–93.

Cohen, J.E. (1995). *How Many People Can the Earth Support?* New York: Norton.

Commission of the European Communities (2005). *Thematic Strategy on the Sustainable Use of Natural Resources*, COM(2005) 670 final. Online: http://ec.europa.eu/smart-regulation/impact/ia_carried_out/docs/ia_2005/sec_2005_1683_en.pdf (accessed 6 October 2017).

Daly, H.E. (1996). *Beyond Growth*, Boston, MA: Beacon Press.

Ekins, P. (2011). Environmental sustainability: from environmental valuation to the sustainability gap, *Progress in Physical Geography* 35 (5): 629–51. Online: http://journals.sagepub.com/doi/pdf/10.1177/0309133311423186 (accessed 16 January 2017).

Factor 10 Club (1994). *Carnoules Declaration*, Wuppertal, Germany: Wuppertal Institute for Climate, Environment and Energy.

Gawel, E. (1998). Das Elend der Stoffstromökonomie: eine Kritik [The misery of material flow economics: a critique], *Konjunkturpolitik* 44 (2): 173–206.

Hinterberger, F., Luks, F., Stewen, M. and van der Straaten, J. (2000). Environmental policy in a complex world, *International Journal of Sustainable Development* 3: 276–96.

Intergovernmental Panel on Climate Change (IPCC) (2007). *Climate Change 2007: Synthesis Report*. Geneva: IPCC. Online: www.ipcc.ch/pdf/assessment-report/ar4/syr/ar4_syr_full_report.pdf (accessed 22 July 2017).

Intergovernmental Panel on Climate Change (IPCC) (2014). *Climate Change 2014: Synthesis Report, Summary for Policy Makers*. Online: www.ipcc.ch/pdf/assessment-report/ar5/syr/ AR5_SYR_FINAL_SPM.pdf (accessed 10 November 2017).

Kubiszewski, I., Costanza, R., Anderson, S. and Sutton, P. (2017). The future value of ecosystem services: global scenarios and national implications, *Ecosystem Services* 26: 289–301.

Lambin, E.F. and Meyfroidt, P. (2011). Global land use change, economic globalization, and the looming land scarcity, *Proceedings of the National Academy of Sciences of the United States of America* 108 (9): 3465–72. Online: www.pnas.org/content/108/9/3465/T1.expansion. html (accessed 26 February 2017).

Nordhaus, T., Shellenberger, M. and Blomqvist, L. (2012). *The Planetary Boundaries Hypothesis: A Review of the Evidence*, Breakthrough Institute. Online: https://thebreakthrough. org/blog/Planetary%20Boundaries%20web.pdf (accessed 20 January 2018).

Odum, H.T. (2002). Emergy accounting, in P. Bartelmus (ed.), *Unveiling Wealth: On Money, Quality of Life and Sustainability*, Dordrecht: Kluwer: 135–48.

Organisation for Economic Co-operation and Development (OECD) (2002). *Indicators to Measure Decoupling of Environmental Pressure from Economic Growth*, (SG/SD(2002)1/ FINAL), Paris: OECD. Online: www.oecd.org/officialdocuments/displaydocumentpdf/ ?cote=sg/sd(2002)1/final&doclanguage=en (accessed 6 October 2017).

Perrings, C. (1995). Ecology, economics and ecological economics, *Ambio* 24: 60–3.

Rockström, J., Steffen. W., Noone, K., Persson, Å., Chapin III, F.S., Lambin, E., Lenton, T.M., Scheffer, M., Folke, C., Schellnhuber, H., Nykvist, B., de Wit, C.A., Hughes, T., van der Leeuw, S., Rodhe, H., Sörlin, S., Snyder, P.K., Costanza, R., Svedin, U., Falkenmark, M., Karlberg, L., Corell, R.W., Fabry, V.J., Hansen, J., Walker, B., Liverman, D., Richardson, K., Crutzen, P. and Foley, J. (2009). Planetary boundaries: exploring the safe operating space for humanity, *Ecology and Society* 14 (2): ART. 32. Online: www.ecologyandsociety.org/vol.14/iss2/art32/ (accessed 29 October 2017).

Røpke, I. (2005). Trends in the development of ecological economics from the late 1980s to the early 2000s, *Ecological Economics* 55: 262–9.

Sachs, W., Loske, R., Linz, M., with Behrensmeier, R., Bierter, W., Bleischwitz, R., Böge, S., Bringezu, S., Burdick, B., Fischedick, M., Hinterberger, F., Jung, W., Kristof, K. and Schütz. H. (1998). *Greening the North: A Post-industrial Blueprint for Ecology and Equity*, London and New York: Zed Books.

Steinberger, J.K., Krausmann, F., Getzner, M., Schandl, H. and West, J. (2013). Development and dematerialization: an international study. *PLoS ONE* 8 (10): 1–11. Online: https://doi.org/10.1371/journal.pone.0070385 (accessed 21 July 2017).

The Economics of Ecosystems and Biodiversity (TEEB) (2010). *Mainstreaming the Economics of Nature: A Synthesis of the Approach, Conclusions and Recommendations of TEEB*. Online: http://doc.teebweb.org/wp-content/uploads/Study%20and%20Reports/Reports/ Synthesis%20report/TEEB%20Synthesis%20Report%202010.pdf (accessed 29 Oct. 2017).

United Nations (1993). *Integrated Environmental and Economic Accounting*, New York: United Nations.

United Nations, European Commission, Food and Agriculture Organization of the United Nations, International Monetary Fund, Organisation for Economic Co-operation and Development and World Bank Group (2014). *System of Environmental–Economic Accounting 2012: Central Framework*. New York: United Nations. Online: http://unstats. un.org/unsd/envaccounting/seeaRev/SEEA_CF_Final_en.pdf (accessed 19 March 2017).

United Nations Environment Programme (UNEP) (2011). *Decoupling Natural Resource Use and Environmental Impacts from Economic Growth*, A report of the working group on decoupling to the international resource panel. Online www.unep.org/resourcepanel/ decoupling/files/pdf/decoupling_report_english.pdf (accessed 14 February 2017).

110 Ecological sustainability

United Nations Environment Programme (UNEP) (2014). *Global Environmental Outlook 6.* Online: www.unep.org/geo/ (accessed 3 October 2017).

United Nations Framework Convention on Climate Change (UNFCCC) (2014). *The Paris Agreement.* Online: http://unfccc.int/paris_agreement/items/9485.php (accessed 16 January 2017).

Vale, R. and Vale, B. (eds.) (2013). *Living Within a Fair Share Ecological Footprint.* Abingdon, UK and New York: Routledge.

van Kooten, G.C. and Bulte, E.H. (2000). The ecological footprint: useful science or politics? *Ecological Economics* 32 (3): 385–9.

Vitousek, P.M., Ehrlich, P.R., Ehrlich, A.H. and Matson, P.A. (1986). Human appropriation of the products of photosynthesis, *Biometrics* 36 (6): 368–73.

von Weizsäcker, E.U., Lovins, A. and Lovins, H. (1997). *Factor Four: Doubling Wealth, Halving Resource Use,* London: Earthscan.

Weterings, R. and Opschoor, P.H. (1992). *The Ecocapacity as a Challenge to Sustainable Development,* Rijkswijk: Netherlands Advisory Council for Research on Nature and Environment.

World Bank (2011). *The Changing Wealth of Nations: Measuring Sustainable Development in the New Millennium,* Washington, DC: World Bank. Online: http://siteresources.worldbank.org/ENVIRONMENT/Resources/ChangingWealthNations.pdf (accessed 1 September 2017).

World Wide Fund for Nature (2012). *Living Planet Report 2012: Biodiversity, Biocapacity and Better Chances,* Gland, Switzerland: WWF International.

World Wide Fund for Nature, Zoological Society of London and Global Footprint Network (2010). *Living Planet Report 2010: Biodiversity, Biocapacity and Development,* Gland, Switzerland: WWF International.

PART IV

Cornucopia from sustainable development?

Sustainable development is like the Holy Grail: it appeals to everyone, many believe in its powers, no one has found it yet. Governments subscribe to sustainable development in Earth Summits and at home. The United Nations adopted Sustainable Development Goals. The European Union made sustainable development part of its Constitution, as did the hardly environment-minded World Trade Organization. Business sees new investment opportunities. Few publications on environment and/or development can resist summoning the concept in support of their arguments. So what makes sustainable development so endearing and elusive at the same time? The answer lies in the cornucopian promise of "development."

Essentially one can pack anything into the concept of development. It is no surprise that development goals are thought to attain human wellbeing and even happiness. Chapter 8 checks the measurability of the ultimate goals of development, i.e., wellbeing, life satisfaction or happiness. Chapter 9 steps down to a more realistic assessment of living standards and their improvement through development. Chapter 10 examines the role of sustainability in turning development into a paradigm of social progress that maintains its economic, environmental and social dimensions.

8

WHAT DO WE WANT

Happiness, wellbeing, the good life?

From a personal point of view it is less a question of what we need, than what we want. We all look for happiness, or, more durably, satisfaction with our lives. The question of what makes us better off might thus best be answered by asking people directly. Answers given in happiness surveys can be expected to be emotional and subjective; they are difficult to evaluate and aggregate within countries and among countries at different stages of development. The recent Nobel-prize laureate in economics, Thaler, and his co-author show that many economic decisions are dominated by irrationality (Thaler and Sunstein 2008, 2009). Moreover, the recent wave of terrorism can shatter our feelings of security in pursuing the goals of prosperity and wellbeing. However, predicting such events and their effects is hardly possible and is therefore not further pursued here.

8.1 Beyond prosperity – the quality of life

8.1.1 Objectives and methods

Policy makers like to show how they will improve the quality of human life as the basis for happiness and wellbeing. Box 8.1 is the example of the USA where the euphoria of independence created belief in potential happiness for all. The more realistic Constitution appears to dampen these expectations with its reference to tranquility, security and the promotion of welfare. The success of industrialization and a concomitant growing materialism reduced the grand notions of happiness and social welfare even more to the pursuit of prosperity as the dominant paradigm of the twentieth century.

The general argument is, however, that indicators of material prosperity such as wealth, income and output fail to measure what is beyond gross domestic product (GDP), i.e., wellbeing, happiness, life satisfaction, the human quality of life or

114 Cornucopia from sustainable development?

BOX 8.1 THE RIGHTS TO HAPPINESS AND WELLBEING

"We hold these truths to be self-evident, that all men are created equal, that they are endowed by their Creator with certain unalienable Rights, that among these are Life, Liberty and the pursuit of Happiness" (*US Declaration of Independence*, 4 July 1776).

"*We the People* of the United States, in Order to form a more perfect Union, establish Justice, insure domestic Tranquility, provide for the common defense, promise the general Welfare, and secure the Blessings of Liberty to ourselves and our Posterity, do ordain and establish this Constitution for the United States of America" (*US Constitution*, Preamble, 17 September 1787).

---

national welfare. The Stiglitz Commission (Stiglitz et al. 2010, p. 12) argued "that the time is ripe for our measurement system to shift emphasis from measuring economic production to measuring people's well-being." The current widespread criticism of GDP appears to reflect the less materialistic welfare vision of the founders of the USA. The so-called Easterlin (1974; Easterlin et al. 2010) paradox claims that in the long term of ten years or more rich countries experience stagnant life satisfaction, despite growth in income and wealth. Suggestions of totally ignoring GDP in policy making and replacing it by welfare measures are not surprising (van den Bergh 2017). However, problems of welfare measurement (cf. section 4.1.1) make such replacement rather illusory.

Only in the short term happiness might move in tandem with the cyclical movements of output and income. However even this modest claim is disputed by more comprehensive data analysis, pointing to a positive long-term correlation between economic growth and happiness within and among countries (e.g. Stevenson and Wolfers 2008; Inglehart et al. 2008). Much of this argument depends on the significance of the relative income hypothesis (Duesenberry 1949), i.e., whether "keeping up with the Joneses" overwhelms the relationship between absolute levels of income and happiness. But did these visions come up with a meaningful alternative to measures of economic prosperity?

Happiness, subjective wellbeing and life satisfaction are hazy concepts ranging from an acute emotional state to the long-term appreciation of one's life. Sometimes a virtuous touch is added when referring to a "good life" of frugality.[1] All these impressions of how to find happiness or satisfaction have one thing in common: a subjective perception of a person's quality of life. Such a perception relates to a wide range of concerns and indicators of personal feelings, but more objective conditions of health and wealth also affect these feelings. Everyone (including this author) refers to individual wellbeing or aggregate welfare when pointing to the ultimate effects of economic activity. Not everyone, including this author, believes that wellbeing and welfare can serve as an accurate measure of social progress.

Rather than entering into a philosophical discussion of what makes us better off, this section looks directly into the scope and coverage of actual surveys of happiness and wellbeing. Unfortunately happiness and its underlying causes and conditions are often used interchangeably. This blurs the analysis of survey results. The following focuses therefore on relatively "pure" happiness surveys before examining the mixing of subjective and objective indicators of material progress and life quality in section 8.2.

Happiness surveys show similarities and differences in happiness concepts and measurement, depending on the type of questions asked and indicators included (Table 8.1). They may refer to a short period of time such as the day before the survey is taken, but could also cover longer periods of satisfaction or wellbeing. They may also include life expectancy and environmental deterioration that reach into conditional constraints. Table 8.1 included these surveys since their main objective is still to capture the subjective experience of happiness or wellbeing.

The World Happiness Report and the World Data Base of Happiness use "Cantril ladder" scores to calculate average life evaluations ranging from best (score of 10) to worst (score of 0) possible lives imagined. Both surveys also measure inequality in the distribution of these averages. The regression analysis of explanatory variables seeks to determine the main factors influencing happiness during 2014–2016 in the World Happiness Report. The variables include, in particular, GDP per capita, a healthy life expectancy and social support, but leave a large unexplained residual. The World Data Base of Happiness, on the other hand, attempts to consolidate happiness measures over the 2005–2014 period. Besides the basic Cantril scores, it also presents inequality-adjusted average happiness and years of a happy and long life.

The Happy Planet Index introduces an objective environmental constraint into happiness by dividing inequality-adjusted happiness by the Ecological Footprint. The index measures the environmental sustainability of leading a long and happy life. It seeks to create an "efficiency measure" of happy life years restricted by environmental factors that diminish happiness.

Gallup polls compile two different happiness measures: one is an average of personal moods experienced the day before the survey, the other takes a longer lasting picture of different "elements" that affect human wellbeing. The use of random samples for each country allows determining sampling errors, contrary to the other surveys that are not clear about how the samples are determined. Subjective wellbeing supposedly reflects thriving in welfare gains and suffering from welfare losses. It is hardly a measure of the average mood and longer-lasting perception of the wellbeing of a population.

8.1.2 Some results

Table 8.2 presents the country rankings obtained by the surveys for the ten highest and five lowest scoring countries, and selected countries that represent big regions.

TABLE 8.1 Happiness surveys

	World Happiness Report 2014–2016	World Data Base of Happiness 2005–2014	Happy Planet Index 2012	Gallup polls 2014	
				Mood	Subjective wellbeing
Concepts and measures	Average life evaluation	Average life evaluation	Sustainable wellbeing (years of long, happy and environmentally sustainable lives)	Experience of positive emotions	Individual perceptions of five elements of wellbeing
Assessment methods	• National average of contributions to Cantril ladder[a] scores • Average available sample of 1000 respondents per country and year	Averages of life enjoyment by Cantril ladder[a] scores	Happy Planet Index: product of Cantril ladder[a] scores, life expectancy and inequality,[b] divided by the ecological footprint	Positive Experience Index: random sample of people with positive experiences the day before the survey	Global Wellbeing Index: random sample of people thriving, struggling or suffering in elements of wellbeing
Analyses	Regression of explanatory variables[c] with Cantril ladder[a] scores	• Happy life years[d] • Inequality-adjusted average life enjoyment[e]	Inequality adjusted happy life years[b] constrained by environmental impact	Personal experiences: well-rested, respected, smiling/laughing, interesting experience, feelings, enjoyment	Elements of wellbeing: purpose of life; social, financial, community, physical wellbeing
	Helliwell et al. (2017)	Veenhoven (2015)	NEF (2016)	Gallup (2015)	Standish and Witters (2014)

Notes

a Score of 0 (worst possible life) to 10 (best possible life).

b Methods and results based on Veenhoven (2015).

c GDP per capita, healthy life expectancy, social support, absence of corruption, social freedom, generosity.

d Life enjoyment×life expectancy.

e Linear combination of mean life enjoyment and standard deviation.

TABLE 8.2 Happiness ranking of countries

World Happiness Report 2014–2016[a]	Happy Planet Index 2012	Gallup Polls		GNI per capita 2014 (purchasing power parity)
		Mood 2014[b]	Thriving 2014 (Global Wellbeing Index)	
1 NO	1 CR	1 PY	1 PA	1 QA
2 DK	2 MX	2 CO	2 CR	2 KW
3 IS	3 CO	3 EC	3 PR	3 LI
4 CH	4 VA	4 GT	4 CH	4 SG
5 FI	5 VN	5 HN	5 BZ	5 BU
6 NL	6 PA	6 PA	6 CL	6 NO
7 CA	7 NI	7 VE	7 DK	7 AE
8 NZ	8 BD	8 CR	8 GT	8 LU
9 AU	9 TH	9 SV	9 AT	9 CH
10 SE	10 EC	10 NI	10 MX	10 HK
AU: 9	*105*	*43–49*	*40*	*19*
US: 14	*108*	*15–25*	*23*	*11*
BR: 22	*23*	*50–54*	*15*	*74*
RU: 49	*116*	*85–89*	*47*	*49*
CN: 79	*72*	*43–49*	*127*	*83*
151 RW	147 MN	140 RS	141 TN	184 LR
152 SY	148 BJ	141 TR	142 TG	185 BI
153 TZ	149 TG	142 TN	143 CM	186 MW
154 BI	150 LU	143 SD	144 BT	187 CD
155 CF	151 TD	144 SY	145 AF	188 CF

Sources: World Happiness Report: Helliwell et al. (2017); Happy Planet Index: NEF (2016); Gallup poll, mood: Gallup (2015); Gallup poll, thriving: Standish and Witters (2014); GNI per capita: UNDP (2015).

Notes

a Ranking of life evaluations by the average Cantril-ladder score.

b Positive experience score.

Country acronyms (Veenhoven 2015):

A: AE United Arab Emirates, AF Afghanistan, AT Austria, AU Australia; **B**: BD Bangladesh, BI Burundi, BJ Benin, BR Brazil, BT Bhutan, BU Brunei Darussalam, BZ Belize; **C**: CA Canada, CD Congo DR, CF Central African Republic, CH Switzerland, CL Chile, CM Cameroon, CN China, CO Colombia, CR Costa Rica; **D**: DK Denmark **E**: EC Ecuador; **F**: FI Finland; **G**: GT Guatemala; **H**: HK Hong Kong, HN Honduras; **I**: IS Iceland; **K**: KW Kuwait; **L**: LI Liechtenstein, LR Liberia, LU Luxembourg; **M**: MN Mongolia, MW Malawi, MX Mexico; **N**: NL Netherlands, NI Nicaragua, NO Norway, NZ New Zealand; **P**: PA Panama, PR Puerto Rico, PY Paraguay; **Q**: QA Qatar; **R**: RS Serbia, RU Russia, RW Rwanda; **S**: SD Sudan, SE Sweden, SG Singapore, SV El Salvador, SY Syria; **T**: TD Chad, TG Togo, TH Thailand, TN Tunisia, TR Turkey, TZ Tanzania; **U**: US United States of America; **V**: VA Vanuatu, VE Venezuela, VN Vietnam.

118 Cornucopia from sustainable development?

The World Happiness Report and its World Happiness Index show high-income countries, including in particular Scandinavian countries, as the happiest and sub-Saharan and war-torn countries as the least happy ones; a four-point Cantril-scale gap separates the high- and low-level country groups. Increases in happiness are reported especially in Latin America and Eastern Europe, whereas the biggest losers can be found, besides crisis-ridden Greece, in Africa and the Middle East. However, the outliers in these regions do not allow an analysis of regional trends (Helliwell et al. 2017, Fig. 2.3).

The Happy Planet Index presents a radically different picture for the high-income countries: happy nations can be found, notably in Latin America, even if the Ecological Footprint introduces the need for living within environmental constraints. The index thus shows high-income and low-income countries as rather unhappy because of environmental impacts in the former and low life expectancy and wellbeing in the latter. Adjustments for equity do not dramatically change the rankings.

The "mood" of people in the Gallup poll seems also to be particularly good in Latin America. This is not a surprise since the Happy Planet Index actually uses the Gallup poll as the basic happiness measure. In contrast, the Global Wellbeing Index (GWI) of the other Gallup poll finds people "thriving" in rich countries but also in the less prosperous ones of Latin America; very poor and war-torn nations obviously do not have much to be happy about. Regional results of the GWI show the Americas as happiest with about one-third of their population thriving in more than three of the poll's elements. Europe is next with 21 percent, followed by Asia and the former Soviet Union (14 percent), the Middle East and North Africa (13 percent); sub-Saharan countries come in last (9 percent). All surveys show large variations among the big countries of the USA, Australia, China, Russia and Brazil.

In principle, positive changes in national happiness or wellbeing could be taken as the ultimate goal and outcome of national development. However, the comparison of national happiness with economic performance is confounding. The last column of Table 8.2 indicates that rankings for national income per capita are dominated by oil-rich countries of the Middle East and high-income Western nations. There is no clear connection with the results of the happiness surveys, except for the lowest ranking nations in sub-Saharan Africa. This throws doubt on the meaning and use of widely differing correlations of happiness or subjective wellbeing with income and wealth, at least in middle- and high-income countries.

Spurious feelings and impressions of the value of life and correspondingly unreliable subjective responses of people impair the validity of happiness surveys. Further breakdowns into detailed categories of people by gender or age, as in the World Happiness Report, are even more speculative. They are probably derived from everybody's belief of knowing about what makes one happy. It is hardly possible, however, to unambiguously quantify and summarize such "knowledge." Adding more questions, as for instance in the World Values Survey (no date), does not help as it makes any combination into an overall wellbeing index even more questionable.

8.2 Combining subjective and objective indicators

Combining both subject feelings about and objective conditions of human and non-human life, could provide a more comprehensive measure of wellbeing. There is general consensus that both subjective perceptions and objective conditions contribute to a person's wellbeing; they should therefore be accounted for in comprehensive measures of human welfare. The question is whether it makes sense to combine subjective and objective indicators to obtain a common index of national progress, welfare, the quality of life or happiness. Indices proliferated but lack agreement on concepts and methods. In many cases the purpose might be more to disqualify conventional economic indicators than to provide alternative scientific measurement and policy support.

The Organisation for Economic Co-operation and Development's (OECD) (2014) Better Life Index intends to provide "a better understanding of people's well-being [which] is central to developing better policies for better lives."[2] Its indicator framework distinguishes 11 dimensions of the quality of life and material living conditions (Box 8.2). The framework would also like to show sustainability support for its dimensions, including different types of economic, human, social and natural capital. However, suitable indicators of capital stock are still lacking

---

BOX 8.2 BETTER LIFE INDEX: TOPICS AND INDICATORS

Material living conditions:

Housing: dwelling without basic facilities, housing expenditures, rooms per person.
Income: net adjusted disposable income and net financial wealth of households.

Quality of life:

Jobs: labor market insecurity, employment rate, personal savings.
Community: social support network.
Education: educational attainment, student skill, years in education.
Environment: air pollution, water quality.
Civic engagement: stakeholder engagement for developing regulations, voter turnout.
Health: life expectancy, self-reported health.
Life satisfaction: life satisfaction.
Safety: feeling safe walking alone at night, homicide rate.
Work–life balance: employees working very long hours, time devoted to leisure and personal care.

Source: OECD (2011, Fig. 1)

120 Cornucopia from sustainable development?

(OECD 2011, p. 5). One could also question the categorization of dimensions as they overlap and might cause double-counting.

The OECD set of indicators represents the perceptions of wellbeing by experts. The original intention was to differentiate between more quantifiable (objective) indicators and difficult-to-assess qualitative (subjective) measures; it seems to have been abandoned now. Wisely, there are no suggestions of aggregating wellbeing beyond the 11 dimensions. Even then, the summary results for each dimension use equal weighting of the underlying indicators, which obviously cannot do justice to their contribution to human welfare.

Still, the OECD authors attempted to rank countries by the number of indicators falling into the top two deciles minus the number that is in the bottom two deciles. The purpose is to reveal the limits of aggregating wellbeing represented by selected indicators. Table 8.3 shows that Oceania, Canada and Scandinavian countries dominate with high welfare levels in OECD member states; at the lower end there are Eastern European countries and low-performance EU countries together with two less developed nations (Turkey and Mexico). The comparison with GDP per capita shows highly divergent results as indicated by rank differences in the last column (in parentheses). Positive rank differences, notably for Luxembourg, Italy and Austria, appear to make them relatively happy countries (in terms of wellbeing), compared to their economic achievement. On the other hand negative differences would indicate that the people living in countries such as New Zealand, Korea and Chile might not be satisfied with their life, even if economic indicators would say otherwise.[3]

The Legatum Prosperity Index (LPI) (Legatum Institute 2015, p. 38) claims to be the only global measure that combines subjective wellbeing and income as "prosperity."[4] The question is whether such prosperity should be interpreted as a measure of wellbeing or development. The LPI seeks to overcome the problem of combining disparate objective and subjective indicators by weighting its 89 variables by their correlation with wellbeing and income. As most indicators are actually objective in nature, the index is treated as a measure of development in section 9.2.1.

Judging by its name the Gross National Happiness (GNH) Index[5] of Bhutan (Centre for Bhutan Studies and GNH Research 2017) might be closest to the happiness surveys described in the preceding section. It was introduced to a wide audience at a High-Level Meeting on Happiness and Well-Being at the United Nations in 2012. The index has now become a standard bearer for those who disdain GDP as a measure of social progress. Other governments mostly ignore the GNH. The reason might be the weighting of indicators that refer to particular Bhutanese "domains" of happiness – in contrast to "Western" values. According to the survey, over 90 percent of the Bhutanese are more or less happy. Except for its first domain of "psychological" wellbeing (happiness and subjective wellbeing), the index still includes mostly objective political, economic, cultural and environmental indicators.

Happiness surveys try to give some impression of the state of wellbeing of a country's people. But the results are inconclusive. For the prosperous strata there

TABLE 8.3 Welfare ranking for OECD member states[a]

	Ranks of Better Life Index[b]	Indicators in top two deciles (no.)	Indicators in bottom two deciles (no.)	Ranks by GDP per capita[c]
Australia	1	11	2	4 (−3)
New Zealand	2	9	1	20 (−18)
Canada	3–4	9	2	10 (−6.5)
Norway	3–4	8	1	2 (+1.5)
Denmark	5–7	7	1	5 (+1)
Sweden	5–7	8	2	6 (0)
Switzerland	5–7	7	1	3 (+3)
Netherlands	8	7	2	7 (+1)
Finland	9–11	4	0	12 (−2)
Iceland	9–11	5	1	16 (−6)
Japan	9–11	6	2	14 (−4)
Belgium	12–13	4	1	13 (−0.5)
USA	12–13	6	3	8 (+4.5)
Ireland	14–15	4	2	9 (+5.5)
Korea, Republic	14–15	5	3	26 (−11.5)
Austria	16–19	2	1	11 (+6.5)
France	16–19	3	2	17 (+0.5)
Slovenia	16–19	2	1	24 (−6.5)
United Kingdom	16–19	4	3	18 (−0.5)
Germany	20–21	1	1	15 (+5.5)
Luxembourg	20–21	2	2	1 (+19.5)
Czech Republic	22	1	2	27 (−5)
Chile	23	3	5	31 (−8)
Greece	24–25	1	4	23 (+1.5)
Spain	24–25	2	5	22 (+2.5)
Israel	26–27	1	5	21 (+5.5)
Italy	26–27	1	5	19 (+7.5)
Poland	28–29	3	8	32 (−3.5)
Portugal	28–29	1	6	25 (+3.5)
Hungary	30	2	8	30 (0)
Estonia	31	3	10	29 (+2)
Slovak Republic	32–33	1	9	28 (+4.5)
Turkey	32–33	3	11	33 (−0.5)
Mexico	34	2	11	34 (0)

Sources: Better Life Index: OECD (2011, Table 1); GDP per capita: UNSD (2017).

Notes

a For different years during 2000–2010; no data available for some indicators.

b Ranked by the difference between number of indicators in the two top and bottom deciles (second minus third column number).

c In 2010, current prices; in parentheses: rank differences of the Better Life Index minus GDP per capita.

122 Cornucopia from sustainable development?

does not seem to be any compelling evidence of happiness or wellbeing and their changes. There is consensus only about the lack of happiness for the poorest people, who cannot satisfy even their basic needs. This is not surprising and does not convey useful information about how to improve their lot. Realizing that wellbeing is "plural" (Stiglitz et al. 2010, p. 12), requiring diverse indicators, does not help since integrative policies need overall indices. The aggregation problem looms large in building compound measures of national (average) wellbeing or social progress.

Notes

1 Implicitly the good life seems to refer to the bad life of overconsumption and greed, responsible for anxiety and unhappiness. Section 12.1.1 will discuss how to approach a good (or at least less greedy) life as a matter of changing our values.
2 It remains to be seen if the Better Life Index will be more successfully implemented than the previous "social indicator" approach to measuring the quality of life (OECD 1973, 1976).
3 Looking more closely at the information conveyed by the indicators in the top and bottom deciles (cf. the second and third column of Table 8.3 and Table 1 of the OECD 2011 publication) might explain the differences; it is not further pursued here because the questionable aggregative rankings presented here serve more to illustrate the limits of measuring welfare than to convey information about its level.
4 There is at least one other index attempting to measure prosperity. The Social Progress Index (Social Progress Imperative 2017) calculates simple averages of 50 indicators of basic human needs, foundations of wellbeing (education and health services, life expectancy, environmental protection) and opportunity (rights and freedoms). The obvious overlap of these equally weighted dimensions obscures the meaning of the overall index and even its dimensions.
5 The meaning of the "gross" attribute is not clear; it might invite comparing the index to its economic counterpart, the GDP.

References

Centre for Bhutan Studies and GNH Research (2017). *Gross National Happiness Index*. Online: www.grossnationalhappiness.com/SurveyFindings/Summaryof2015GNHIndex.pdf (accessed 20 January 2017).

Duesenberry, J.S. (1949). *Income, Saving and the Theory of Consumer Behavior*, Cambridge, MA: Harvard University Press.

Easterlin, R. (1974). Does economic growth improve the human lot? Some empirical evidence, in P.A. David and M.W. Reder (eds.), *Nations and Households in Economic Growth*, New York: Academic Press: 89–125.

Easterlin, R.A., McVey, L.A., Switek, M., Sawangfa, O. and Smith Zweig, J. (2010). The happiness–income paradox revisited, Proceedings of the National Academy of Sciences of the USA. Online: www.pnas.org/content/107/52/22463 (accessed 15 December 2017).

Gallup (2015). Mood of the world upbeat on international happiness day. Online: www. gallup.com/poll/182009/mood-world-upbeat-international-happiness-day.aspx (accessed 22 January 2017).

Helliwell, J.F., Huang, H. and Wang, S. (2017). Social foundations of world happiness, in J.F. Helliwell, R. Layard and J.D. Sachs (eds.), *World Happiness Report 2017*, New York: Sustainable Development Solutions Network: 8–47. Online: http://worldhappiness. report/wp-content/uploads/sites/2/2017/03/HR17.pdf (accessed 29 October 2017).

Inglehart, R., Foa, R., Peterson, C. and Welzel, C. (2008). Development, freedom, and rising happiness, *Perspectives on Psychological Science* 3 (4): 264–85.

Legatum Institute (2015). *The Legatum Prosperity Index 2015.* Online: https://lif.blob.core.windows.net/lif/docs/default-source/publications/2015-legatum-prosperity-index-pdf.pdf?sfvrsn=2 (accessed 12 November 2017).

New Economics Foundation (NEF) (2016). Happy Planet Index. Online: www.happyplanetindex.org/about/ (accessed 29 October 2017).

Organisation for Economic Co-operation and Development (OECD) (1973). *List of Social Concerns Common to Most OECD Countries,* Paris: OECD.

Organisation for Economic Co-operation and Development (OECD) (1976). *Measuring Social Well-being: A Progress Report on the Development of Social Indicators.* Paris: OECD.

Organisation for Economic Co-operation and Development (OECD) (2011). *OECD Better Life Initiative: Compendium of OECD Well-being Indicators,* Paris: OECD. Online: www.oecd.org/std/47917288.pdf (accessed 24 January 2017).

Organisation for Economic Co-operation and Development (OECD) (2014). *How's Life? 2015 Measuring Well-being, Summary.* Online: www.oecdbetterlifeindex.org/media/bli/documents/how_life-2015-sum-en.pdf (accessed 12 November 2017).

Social Progress Imperative (2017). 2017 Social progress index. Online: www.socialprogressindex.com (accessed 13 October 2017).

Standish, M. and Witters, D. (2014). Country well-being varies greatly worldwide (Gallup-Healthways Global Wellbeing Index). Online: www.gallup.com/poll/175694/country-varies-greatly-worldwide.aspx (accessed 29 October 2017).

Stevenson, B. and Wolfers, J. (2008). Economic growth and subjective well-being: reassessing the Easterlin paradox, NBER Working Paper No. 14282. Online: www.nber.org/papers/w14282.pdf (accessed 28 May 2017).

Stiglitz, J.E., Sen, A. and Fitoussi, J.P. (2010). *Report by the Commission on the Measurement of Economic Performance and Social Progress.* Online: http://library.bsl.org.au/jspui/bitstream/1/1267/1/Measurement_of_economic_performance_and_social_progress.pdf (accessed 4 June 2017).

Thaler, R.H. and Sunstein, C.R. (2008, 2009). *Nudge: Improving Decisions about Health, Wealth, and Happiness,* New York: Penguin Group.

United Nations Development Programme (UNDP) (2015). *United Nations Development Report 2015,* New York: UNDP. Online: http://hdr.undp.org/sites/default/files/2015_human_development_report.pdf (accessed 6 October 2017).

United Nations Statistics Division (UNSD) (2017). UNSD environmental indicators. Online: http://unstats.un.org/unsd/ENVIRONMENT/qindicators.htm (accessed 25 August 2017).

van den Bergh, J.C.J.M. (2017). Green agrowth: removing the GDP-growth constraint on human progress, in P.A. Victor and B. Dolter (eds.), *Handbook on Growth and Sustainability,* Cheltenham, UK and Northampton, MA: Edward Elgar: 182–210.

Veenhoven, R. (2015). Happiness in nations, world database of happiness, Erasmus University Rotterdam. Online: http://worlddatabaseofhappiness.eur.nl/hap_nat/nat_fp.php?mode=1 (accessed 15 September 2017).

World Values Survey (no date). Online: www.worldvaluessurvey.org/wvs.jsp (accessed 12 November 2017).

9

WHAT CAN WE GET?

Greater happiness and wellbeing are opaque concepts of social progress. They prompted the search for quantifiable measures whose scope and coverage is similarly broad. Indicators of socioeconomic development assume that measures of the living conditions of people affect ultimately their wellbeing. There have been attempts therefore to include both subjective indicators of wellbeing and objective measures of living conditions in development indices. This murky mixture of indicators could be the reason why governments still prefer aggregate measures of economic growth. Governmental rhetoric does invoke some concern about the distribution of income and wealth, calling for the more rapid development of poor "developing" nations. This chapter explores the meaning and measurement of development as a goal for *all* nations before defining and measuring its sustainability in Chapter 10.

9.1 Development: improving living standards

The objective of development is usually described as improving the standards of living of a nation's people. The commonly accepted objective of increasing social welfare serves as the – hardly transparent – glue that keeps diverse indicators of living conditions together. To make any progress from the opaque notions of wellbeing or welfare one could break them down into primary social objectives such as freedom, health, education and more instrumental secondary objectives of food, housing, environmental protection, income, security etc. (Bartelmus 2008, p. 44). The United Nations (2017a) agreed on a more limited number of criteria to identify "least developed countries." They include low gross national income per capita, human assets in terms of health, nutrition and education, and high economic vulnerability. By 2013, 49 countries met these criteria.

The popular sustainable development paradigm, which aims to go beyond narrow economic growth, characterizes development as generating social welfare.

Costanza et al. (2014, p. 14) describe the "overarching goal" of the new Sustainable Development Goals (SDG) of the United Nations as "equity and human well-being." Similar sentiments are expressed in the transition of the EU Constitution from sustainable growth (of the 1992 Maastricht Treaty, Declaration 20) to sustainable development (in the 1997 Amsterdam Treaty, Title I).

Environmentalists are also highly critical of economic growth. "Qualitative development" – disdaining quantitative economic growth – should improve the wellbeing of people; it would be a better objective of development than destructive economic activity (Daly 1996, p. 13; Daly and Farley 2004, p. 169). This seems to forego comprehensive measurement, letting pre-analytic visions reign? Some authors take the risk of abandoning quantification as a reason for not discarding economic growth. Rather they consider qualitative development as a different kind of growth with different purposes (Meadows et al. 2004, p. 255).

Development theories and international development strategies (IDS) fail, however, to provide a commonly accepted concept and policy for development. Early surveys reveal uncertainty and conflicting views about development (Birou et al. 1977; Jolly 1977; Todaro 1977). Seers (1981) provides a critique of contemporary "dependency theories" in which core dominant industrialized nations exploit peripheral dependent ones. A rejection of the Western development paradigm comes also from the environmental and anti-globalization corner. More down-to-earth attempts at substantiating development refer to human needs (Max–Neef et al. 1989) and even more narrowly to "basic" human needs (ILO 1977). The basic needs approach was doomed, though, when developing countries considered this approach as interference with their development strategies and policies. This did not deter the United Nations from advancing "international development strategies" to improve the situation in poor countries (Box 9.1). The strategies were repeatedly revised since they could not achieve their objectives.

BOX 9.1 INTERNATIONAL DEVELOPMENT STRATEGIES

IDS (United Nations 2017b) failed to reach agreement on development. They set out from economic growth in the first "development decade" of the 1960s, added social justice in the second decade and called for a "New International Economic Order" in the third decade; the fourth and last decade of the 1990s returned to economic growth with some reference to human resources and environmental protection. The main reason for this circularity is that the IDS were not able to reduce the glaring gap between rich and poor countries.

Forty years of IDS were abandoned when looking for new development goals. Millennium Development Goals (MDG) (United Nations 2015a) were thought to do a better job of fostering development. Fifteen years later, SDG are now to implement a new development agenda (United Nations, no date-c).

126 Cornucopia from sustainable development?

Frustration with these failures and conspicuous environmental decline prompted the United Nations to establish in 1983 a World Commission on Environment and Development. The objective was to investigate the reasons for the failures of environmental and developmental policies, and to suggest solutions. Sustainable development was deemed to be the tool of integrating fragmented development policies (WCED 1987). The idea was to add ignored dimensions or pillars of development to obtain a comprehensive development concept. Sustainable development would supposedly cover not only economic and social (especially distributive) development concerns but also environmental ones (see section 10.1). Global "Earth Summits" agreed on the need for sustainable development, but details, including measurement, remain elusive. As a compromise, the recent Rio+20 conference puts (sustainable) economic growth "in the context" of sustainable development (United Nations, no date-b).

In the end, the international debate resorted to the political process and corresponding normative goal setting. Non-binding development goals would apply to countries at all stages of economic growth and development (Box 9.1). Table 9.1 compares the MDG and their successor, the SDG. The main conceptual difference between the two lists is the extension of sustainability – beyond environmental sustainability – into economic and social domains by the SDG.

This might justify switching from M to S in the acronyms but raises crucial questions about the nature of sustainability: are environmental, economic and social sustainability concerns genuine development goals, i.e., "dimensions" of development, or are they "pillars" (United Nations, no date-a, para. 2) whose limited carrying capacity might restrict the development process? The SDG appear to ignore this question. They mix up development and its sustainability introducing further dimensions and conditions into the conventional notion of development. Here we seek to make a clearer distinction between development goals and factors that might impair development in the long run. Crumbling "pillars" would indeed make development unsustainable.

At the same time, referring to global environmental impacts (SDG 13–15) and inclusive sustainable economic growth (SDG 8 and 10) indicates a shift from treating development as the objective of improving the situation in poor countries to make it a concern of nations at any level of prosperity: both poor and rich countries face global environmental problems, social inequities and the need to replace depreciated produced and non-produced natural capital.

Governmental consensus does not eliminate the normative nature of setting development goals.[1] The adoption of goals and targets by the United Nations is the result of political negotiation. The underlying notion of human wellbeing permits packing anything and everything into the development concept. Moreover, expanding the MDG by the SDG from 8 to 17 goals and their targets from 21 to 169 looks like catering to the divergent priorities and pet projects of the negotiating parties. Like its predecessor, the SDG are non-binding declarations that facilitate consensus but throw doubt on the credibility and actual implementation of the goals.[2]

TABLE 9.1 From MDG to SDG

MDG	SDG
1 Eradicate extreme poverty and hunger	1 End poverty in all its form everywhere 2 End hunger, achieve food security and improve nutrition and promote sustainable agriculture
2 Achieve universal primary education	4 Ensure inclusive and equitable quality education and promote lifelong learning opportunities for all
3 Promote gender equality and empower women	5 Achieve gender equality and empower all women and girls
4 Reduce child mortality 5 Improve maternal health 6 Combat HIV/AIDS, malaria and other diseases	3 Ensure healthy lives and promote wellbeing for all at all ages
7 Ensure environmental sustainability	*Environmental sustainability* 6 Ensure availability and sustainable management of water and sanitation for all 7 Ensure access to affordable, reliable, sustainable and modern energy for all 13 Take urgent action to combat climate change and its impacts 14 Conserve and sustainably use the oceans, seas and marine resources for sustainable development 15 Protect, restore and promote sustainable use of terrestrial ecosystems, sustainably manage forests, combat desertification, and halt and reverse land degradation and halt biodiversity loss *Economic sustainability* 8 Promote sustained, inclusive and sustainable economic growth, full and productive employment and decent work for all 9 Build resilient infrastructure, promote inclusive and sustainable industrialization and foster innovation 11 Make cities and human settlements inclusive, safe, resilient and sustainable 12 Ensure sustainable consumption and production patterns *Social (institutional) sustainability* 10 Reduce inequality within and among countries 16 Promote peaceful and inclusive societies for sustainable development, provide access to justice for all and build effective, accountable and inclusive institutions at all levels

continued

128 Cornucopia from sustainable development?

TABLE 9.1 Continued

MDG	*SDG*
8 Develop a global partnership for development	17 Strengthen the means of implementation and revitalize the global partnership for sustainable development

Sources: MDG: United Nations (2015a); SDG: United Nations (no date-c).

9.2 Measuring development

Assessing overall development faces the challenge of combining the indicators of different development dimensions and pillars into an aggregate index. The main methods of aggregation are summing up physical indicators or calculating indicator averages. Other methods might select a "representative" indicator as a surrogate measure of development, use monetary values for commensurability or reduce development dimensions to "factors" that reflect most of the indicator variance. If these methods are deemed unacceptable, visual aids of icons, colors or cobwebs can provide a first summary impression of the levels and trends of indicators.[3]

9.2.1 Development indices

Overall indices typically calculate an equally or differently weighted average of selected indicators assumed to represent the different dimensions of development. To facilitate aggregation they standardize the indicators, compressing them into a common range, e.g., of 1 to 10 or 1 to 100. Table 9.2 summarizes the purposes and methods of popular development indices. It also gives a first indication of pro-claimed sustainability, which will be further discussed in Chapter 10. Different indicators selected and concepts and methods applied do not permit a direct com-parison of indices, apart from the ranking of countries within the range of ranks (Table 9.3).[4]

The Human Development Index (HDI) is deemed to be a measure of human wellbeing and ability. It reduces the measurement of development to three dimen-sions of average life expectancy at birth, education and gross national income (GNI) per capita, measured by four indicators. To calculate the average the HDI normal-izes the indicators to obtain a common indicator range between minimum and maximum levels. Changes in the "goalposts" of maximum and minimum values affect the range and changes the indicator scores from one period to the next. Moreover, applying a logarithmic value to income reduces its importance deemed to be declining.[5]

Table 9.3 shows that the HDI ranks are highest for most of the industrialized countries, even if their GNI per capita ranking is significantly lower (indicated for all indices in parentheses). This tendency is often reversed in low-ranked countries where non-economic factors gain in relative importance. The biggest (emerging)

TABLE 9.2 Development indices, purpose and methods

	HDI	SDI	LPI	GCI	SDGI
Purpose	Assessing human development, beyond economic growth	Measure of progress towards sustainable development	Measure of prosperity from income and wellbeing	Measure of competitiveness that determines potential productivity and prosperity	• Assessing SDG achievement by country ranking • Dashboard: country highlights of SDG challenges
Definition	Geometric mean of achievements in long and healthy life, education and standards of living	Mean of normalized sustainable development indicators	Mean of indicators linked to objective measures of development and subjective wellbeing	Weighted mean of sub-indices of basic requirements, efficiency and innovation	Weighted mean of SDG indicators
Indicators	4 normalized indicators of life expectancy at birth, mean of years of adult schooling, expected years of schooling for children, and GNI per capita	14 indicators, combining 58 variables in economic, demographic, social and political areas	89 objective and subjective indicators across 8 sub-indices that form the "foundation" of prosperity	114 indicators of objective and perceived competitiveness	99 normalized indicators for 17 SDG (incl. externalities of "spillover" effects)

continued

TABLE 9.2 Continued

	HDI	SDI	LPI	GCI	SDGI
Weighting	• HDI: logarithm of income to reduce its importance • IHDI: inequality weighted HDI	Equal weighting of indicators	Indicators weighted by regression with income and wellbeing (life satisfaction); equally weighted average of the sub-indices	• Sub-indices weighted according to stages of development • Pillars with equally weighted sub-indices	Equal weighting of ranks in each indicator and across the SDG
Sustainability concept	"Contextual" environmental sustainability	Sustainable development: high index value	None	Future growth- and innovation-oriented index; separate sustainability adjusted index	Weak and strong sustainability according to aggregation methods
Sources	*UNDP (2016)*	*Nováček and Mederly (2002)*	*Legatum Institute (2015)*	*WEF (2015)*	*Bertelsmann Stiftung and SDSN (2017)*

TABLE 9.3 Development ranks compared[a]

GNI per capita 2015[b]	HDI 2015	SDI[c]	LPI 2015 (GNI per capita)	GCI 2015/16	SDGI 2017
1 QA	1 NO (6)	1 NO (6)	1 NO (6)	1 CH (9)	1 SE (16)
2 SG	2 AU (21)	2 FI (24)	2 CH (9)	2 SG (2)	2 DK (18)
3 KW	2 CH (9)	3 CA (22)	3 DK (18)	3 US (11)	3 FI (24)
4 LI	4 DE (17)	4 SE (13)	4 NZ (32)	4 NL (15)	4 NO (6)
5 BU	5 DK (18)	5 CH (9)	5 SE (16)	5 DE (17)	5 CZ (39)
6 NO	5 SG (2)	6 AT (20)	6 CA (22)	6 SE (16)	6 DE (17)
7 AE	7 NL (15)	7 NZ (32)	7 AU (21)	7 GB (26)	7 AT (20)
8 LU	8 IE (19)	8 IE (19)	8 NL (15)	8 JP (27)	8 CH (9)
9 CH	9 IS (29)	9 NL (15)	9 FI (24)	9 HK (10)	9 SI (38)
10 HK	10 CA (22)	10 DE (17)	10 IE (19)	10 FI (24)	10 FR (25)
US: 11	10 (11)	19	11	3	42
AU: 21	2 (21)	13	7	22	26
RU: 50	49 (50)	57	58	43	62
BR: 78	79 (78)	43	54	81	56
CN: 83	90 (83)	63	52	115	71
188 NE	184 BI (189)	142 ET (180)	138 BI (189)	134 MW (186)	153 MG (183)
189 BI	185 BF (177)	143 HT (172)	139 TD (167)	135 BI (189)	154 LR (190)
190 LR	186 TD (167)	144 BI (189)	140 HT (172)	136 TD (167)	155 CD (191)
191 CD	187 NE (188)	145 AO (123)	141 AF (170)	137 MA (145)	156 TD (167)
192 CF	188 cf. (192)	146 ER (180)	142 CF (192)	138 YE (164)	157 CF (192)

Sources: GNI per capita: UNDP (2016); other indices see Table 9.2.

Notes
a GNI per capita ranks in parentheses.
b 2011 purchasing power parity.
c Survey years mostly in the 1990s.

Country acronyms (Veenhoven 2015):
A: AE United Arab Emirates, AF Afghanistan, AO Angola, AT Austria, AU Australia; **B:** BF Burkina Faso, BI Burundi, BJ Benin, BR Brazil, BU Brunei Darussalam; **C:** CA Canada, CD Congo DR, CF Central African Republic, CH Switzerland, CN China, CZ Czech Republic; **D:** DE Germany, DK Denmark; **E:** ER Eritrea, ET Ethiopia; **F:** FI Finland, FR France; **G:** GB United Kingdom, GN Guinea; **H:** HK Hong Kong, HT Haiti; **I:** IE Ireland, IS Iceland; **J:** JP Japan; **K:** KW Kuwait; **L:** LI Liechtenstein, LR Liberia, LU Luxembourg; **M:** MA Mauretania, MG Madagascar, MW Malawi, MZ Mozambique; **N:** NE Niger, NL Netherlands, NO Norway, NZ New Zealand; **Q:** QA Qatar; **R:** RU Russia; **S:** SE Sweden, SG Singapore, SI Slovenia; **T:** TD Chad, TG Togo; **U:** US United States of America; **Y:** YE Yemen.

economy, China, is approaching the half-way mark in the HDI ranks of 188 countries. As expected from previous analyses of wealth (Part II) and wellbeing (Chapter 8), the lowest ranked countries are all in the sub-Saharan region of Africa.

Weighting the development dimensions by an inequality measure incorporates distributional inequalities in the HDI. The inequality adjusted ("discounted") index (IHDI) (UNDP 2016, Statistical Annex, Table 3; not shown in Table 9.3) hardly

132 Cornucopia from sustainable development?

changes the HDI ranks, except for Iran losing 34 ranks, USA 23 ranks, Namibia 22 ranks, Botswana 21 ranks and the Republic of Korea 20 ranks. But what levels and changes of inequality are unacceptable? Is it when poverty increases over a maximum (tolerable) level (see section 9.2.2)? Another addition to the index is the extensive discussion of environmental concerns in the "context" of sustainable development. One can see this as an attempt to jump on the bandwagon of the new SDG.

The Sustainable Development Index (SDI) is a one-time effort shown here for illustrative purposes. It is an equally weighted average of development indicators. The authors see sustainability as an inherent quality of a comprehensive coverage of development dimensions. In other words, "a higher [index] value means greater progress toward sustainable development" (Nováček and Mederly 2002, p. 50). The SDI rankings are quite similar to those of the HDI, except for the oil-rich nations of Kuwait and the United Arab Emirates where the introduction of CO_2 emissions and natural resource consumption generated a much lower ranking in the SDI. This points to the critique of the HDI as a measure that ignores problems of sustainability (cf. section 10.2.1).

The Legatum Prosperity Index (LPI) does not mention development. Its coverage of income and wellbeing as "prosperity" and its wide range of indicators weighted according to their correlation with wellbeing (life satisfaction) and income make it, however, a de-facto measure of socioeconomic development. No attempt is made to weight the significance of sub-indices,[6] except for the fact that about two-thirds of the indicators are objective measures whereas the remainder reflects subjective perceptions of wellbeing. The notion of "prosperity" as a combination of income and wellbeing is therefore difficult to interpret. The country ranking is quite similar to the HDI ranks, placing industrialized countries into the top ranks and sub-Saharan countries into the bottom ones.

Like the LPI the Global Competitiveness Index (GCI) avoids calling the index a measure of development. It sees competitiveness as leading to higher productivity and on to prosperity, the key objective of development. The connection with development is more openly shown in its weighting of sub-indices, which are based on correlation with stages of development. The index is future-oriented, and sustainability means overcoming environmental and social restrictions of economic growth. Sustainability is, however, measured separately by adjusted GCIs (see section 10.2.1). Development stages, based on per-capita gross domestic product (GDP), generate a high ranking of industrialized countries and low ranking of sub-Saharan countries (and war-torn Yemen). The different areas ("pillars") of the GCI include, besides economic efficiency and innovation, non-economic concerns of institutions, education and health. The index deviates therefore considerably from the income (GNI per capita) rankings.

An attempt to produce an index for meeting the SDG is currently underway. The Sustainable Development Goals Index (SDGI) provides an average ranking for selected indicators, equally weighted across the SDG. A particular feature is the inclusion of international environmental, economic, governmental and security "spillovers," i.e., external effects between countries (Bertelsmann Stiftung and

SDSN 2017, p. 5). The HDI and SDGI ranks are highly correlated as indicated in Figure 9.1. Some of the oil-rich countries that seem to fare better in the SDGI rankings are the exception. The four indicators of the HDI might thus represent development as well as (if not better than) the 39 indicators of the SDGI.

Taking happiness or wellbeing as the ultimate objective of human striving and socioeconomic development, one would expect some connection between subjective measures of social welfare and more objective ones of development. However, happiness indices do not provide a clear picture of the connection between happiness and economic performance (in terms of GNI per capita, see Table 8.2). The World Happiness Report and its World Happiness Index are exceptions possibly due to the significant role of GDP per capita in the "Cantril ladder" evaluation of the quality of life. Figure 9.2 compares the ranking of selected countries in terms of Gallup's Global Wellbeing Index (GWI) and UNDP's HDI. Except for sub-Saharan countries, Switzerland and Russia, one would be hard pressed to find any correlation in the scatter diagram along the diagonal line. Extreme poverty of the poorest countries in the sub-Saharan region is the main cause of diminished wellbeing and correspondingly low ranks (high rank numbers).

Table 9.4 summarizes and confirms the differences in measuring perceived wellbeing, human development and economic performance for world regions. The HDI shifts Asia from third down to fourth place, giving oil-rich Middle Eastern and

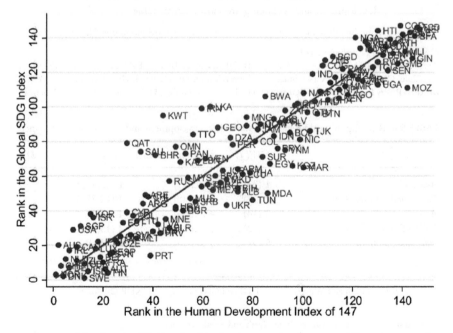

FIGURE 9.1 Meeting the SDG and achieving human development. The country rankings of the SDGI and the HDI are highly correlated with some exceptions of oil-rich countries

Source: Sachs et al. (2016, Fig. 3), with permission from the authors.

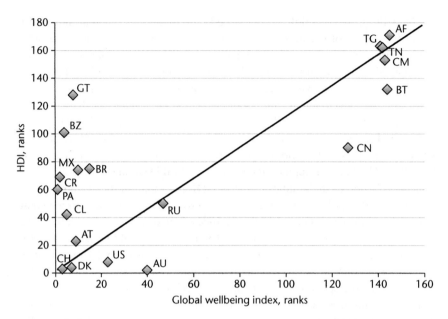

FIGURE 9.2 Subjective wellbeing and human development. The HDI and the Global Wellbeing Index show no significant correlation in their rankings. Human development and wellbeing are hardly comparable

Sources: wellbeing: Standish and Witters (2014, Gallup); human development: UNDP (2015).

Country acronyms (Veenhoven 2015):
A: AF Afghanistan, AT Austria, AU Australia; **B**: BR Brazil, BT Bhutan, BZ Belize; **C**: CH Switzerland, CL Chile, CM Cameroon, CN China, CR Costa Rica; **D**: DK Denmark **G**: GT Guatemala; **M**: MX Mexico; **P**: PA Panama, **R**: RU Russia, **T**: TG Togo, TN Tunisia; **U**: US United States of America.

TABLE 9.4 Ranking of world regions by wellbeing, development and economic performance

	GWI (%)	HDI (index value)	GNI per capita (US$)
Americas[a]	**1** (33)	**1** (0.831)	**1** (30,897)
Europe and Central Asia	**2** (18)[b]	**2** (0.748)	**3** (12,791)
Asia	**3** (14)	**4** (0.659)	**4** (8527)
Middle East and Northern Africa	**4** (13)	**3** (0.686)[c]	**2** (15,722)[c]
Sub-Saharan Africa	**5** (9)	**5** (0.518)	**5** (3363)
WORLD	*17*	*0.711*	*14,301*

Sources: GWI: Standish and Witters (2014); HDI and GNI per capita: UNDP (2015).

Notes
a Standish and Witters (2014) combine North and South America.
b Europe and former Soviet Union.
c Arab states.

North African countries a higher ranking. National income (GNI) gives the oil-rich regions an advantage over Europe, which is ranked second to the Americas by the GWI and HDI. All indicators show worst performance in subjective and objective measures for the poorest, notably sub-Saharan, countries.

9.2.2 Poverty, the measure of underdevelopment

Chapter 3 looked into the distribution of personal income and wealth as the result of a country's economic performance and policy. The conclusion was that economic inequality was generally on the increase, representing a decline in prosperity of parts of a country's population. When an increase in inequality is perceived as inequity in the distribution of income and wealth it could be treated as a normative evaluation of the social dimension of sustainable development.[7]

An extreme aspect of distributional inequality, poverty, could be considered as unsustainable. Poverty is often taken as an overriding problem of development which makes it a surrogate for "under-development." The World Bank, for example, describes its mission, carved in stone at its headquarters, as "Our Dream is a World Free of Poverty." Both, the MDG and SDG, present poverty reduction as their number one goal. Poverty is usually measured as the concentration of income in the lowest quantiles of income distribution and can therefore not fully represent distributional inequality. In fact, poverty reduction can be accompanied with an increase in overall income inequality due to an increased concentration of wealth and income in the hands of the richest. The Oxfam International (2013) alliance of non-governmental organizations finds therefore that the "inequality crisis" could undermine social and economic progress.

The MDG did reach their target of halving the proportion of people living on less than US\$1.25 a day. Table 9.5 shows the percentage of people living below two different poverty lines in world regions. Raising the line from living on less than US\$1.25 a day to US\$1.90 increases the number of poor people, an indication of the judgmental character of setting poverty lines. According to the World Bank (2015), the share of extremely poor people (below the \$1.25 line) in developing countries fell from 22 to 5 percent during 1990–2012. The MDG report calculated a worldwide decrease from 47 to 14 percent for the 1990–2015 period (United Nations 2015b).

Despite methodological differences,[8] both assessments confirm meeting the MDG target of halving extreme poverty, albeit to a different extent. Reductions between 70 and 96 percent for 1990–2012 in the developing regions of East Asia and the Pacific, Latin America and South Asia confirm this success of development. However the sub-Saharan region did not meet the MDG goal of halving poverty (at least by 2012) with reducing the number of people living on less than \$1.25 a day from 35 to 24 percent, and those on \$1.90 a day from 54 to 43 percent according to World Bank data.

There is disagreement about how to handle the distribution of income and wealth. This book treats distributional questions in principle as an objective of personal economic wellbeing (section 3.2.1). At the national level the reduction of

136 Cornucopia from sustainable development?

TABLE 9.5 Poverty in world regions (%)

Region	1990		2012	
	People below poverty line (%)[a]		People at and below poverty line (%)[a]	
	$1.25	$1.90	$1.25	$1.90
East Asia and Pacific	32.87	61.38	1.31	7.24
Europe and Central Asia	0.34	1.74	0.79	2.44
Latin America and Caribbean	8.73	15.96	2.74	5.06
Middle East and North Africa	0.92	6.18	0.46	2.55
South Asia	15.08	44.64	2.57	17.51
Sub-Saharan Africa	34.89	54.37	23.64	42.64
Developing world	22.06[b]	42.45	15.23[b]	14.66
TOTAL WORLD	17.43	35.28	4.45	12.55

Source: World Bank (2017).

Notes

a Poverty (in 2011 purchasing power parity): percent of population living in households with consumption or income per person a day below the poverty lines of $1.25 and $1.90.

b In 2005 purchasing power parities (World Bank 2015).

inequality is seen as an objective of the social dimension of development. The prevailing focus on poverty looks like a return to treating development as a concern of poor countries. However, poverty and its "lines" will not capture inequality in the distribution of income and wealth. Section 3.3.2 indicated that inequality could be rising explosively by the end of the century as returns to capital might exceed economic growth rates. Such inequality could indeed undermine social and economic progress and, hence, the sustainability of development.

9.2.3 Other assessments of development

As explained in section 9.2.1, the LPI attempts to combine income with wellbeing in an index of "prosperity," whose indicator weights are based on the correlation of income and wellbeing. A better approach would be to use the covariance of *all* indicators to do the weighting, letting the strength of covariances decide how to reduce the number of indicators to one or two "factors." Such factor analysis has not been able, however, to substitute for the average or surrogate indices described above. The reason is that usually more than one factor is needed to reflect most of the total variance of indicators. Moreover, the substantive meaning of the factors for representing the overall index remains obscure.

Other evaluations of large sets of indicators resort to visual aids. This would leave the decision about the direction and strength of development to the judgment of individuals or experts designing and analyzing the images. The SDG dashboard thus presents "traffic lights" of the ability of countries to reach SDG thresholds of the indicators. The lowest indicator score is usually taken to represent the total score, which is considered to be a "tough grading" of all indicator values (Bertelsmann Stiftung and SDSN 2017, p. vii). Overall color codes obviously hide relatively good performances in the other SDG. The GCI uses cobwebs to show country performance for its 12 pillars and compares the overall performance to the regional results. As an example, Figure 9.3 shows China exceeding the scores of "emerging and developing Asia" in all dimensions.

Monetary valuations of economic welfare look into extended capital categories as measures of sustainability. However, the application of monetary values refers to people's willingness or ability to pay for goods and services. Consequently these measures remain relatively narrow indicators of economic performance rather than development unless economic valuation is applied, however obscurely, to non-economic concerns (cf. section 6.1.1).

The next chapter discusses the sustainability notions applied to the above-discussed development measures. This will help answer our key concern of whether we can expect to be at least as well off in the future as we are now.

FIGURE 9.3 GCI profile of China. China exceeds the development of Asian developing countries, notably in terms of its market size, infrastructure and the macro-economic environment

Source: WEF (2015, p. 140), with permission from the *Global Competitiveness Report 2015–2016*.

138 Cornucopia from sustainable development?

Notes

1 Nor do attempts at extending consensus to non-governmental organizations and "philanthropists" as, for instance, by the Copenhagen Consensus Centre (www.copenhagen consensus.com).
2 Just consider gender equality in both the MDG and SDG: can one really assume compliance by some Middle Eastern states that agreed formally to this goal?
3 International organizations usually avoid the thorny issue of indicator aggregation and advance large and small sets of indicators (United Nations 2007; UN ECE 2014); they leave the combination or summarization of indicators to other organizations or experts.
4 The last row of Table 9.3 indicates the lowest-ranked country and thus the range of countries covered.
5 See, for the methods applied by the HDI, UNDP (2013, technical note 1).
6 The areas covered by "sub-indices" are economy, entrepreneurship and opportunity, governance, education, health, safety and security, personal freedom and social capital. An equally weighted average of these indices obtains the overall LPI.
7 Distributional concerns of the quality of life and access to environmental services also affect socioeconomic development and human wellbeing. As there is a lack of valid measurement and evaluation tools for non-economic distributional concerns at national and international levels, these concerns are not further pursued here.
8 For example, the MDG report uses 2005 purchasing power parities whereas the World Bank uses those of 2011.

References

Bartelmus, P. (2008). *Quantitative Eco-nomics: How Sustainable are Our Economies?* Dordrecht: Springer.

Bertelsmann Stiftung and Sustainable Development Solutions Network (SDSN) (2017). *SDG Index and Dashboards Report 2017, Global Responsibilities*. Online: www.sdgindex. org/assets/files/2017/2017-SDG-Index-and-Dashboards-Report-full.pdf (accessed 3 December 2017).

Birou, A., Henry, P.M. and Schlegel, J.P. (eds.) (1977). *Towards a Re-definition of Development*, Oxford: Pergamon.

Costanza, R., McGlade, J., Lovins, H. and Kubiszewski, I. (2014). An overarching goal for the UN sustainable development goals, *Solutions* 5 (4): 13–16.

Daly, H.E. (1996). *Beyond Growth*, Boston, MA: Beacon Press.

Daly, H.E. and Farley, J. (2004). *Ecological Economics*, Washington, DC: Island Press.

International Labour Organization (ILO) (1977). *Employment, Growth and Basic Needs: A One-world Problem*, New York: Praeger.

Jolly, R. (1977). Changing views on development, in J.J. Nossin (ed.), *Surveys of Development: A Multidisciplinary Approach*, Amsterdam: Elsevier: 19–48.

Legatum Institute (2015). *The Legatum Prosperity Index 2015*, London: Legatum Institute. Online: http://media.prosperity.com/2015/pdf/publications/PI2015Brochure_WEB. pdf (accessed 6 October 2017).

Max-Neef, M., Elizalde, A. and Hopenhayn, M. (1989). Human scale development: an option for the future, *Development Dialogue* 1: 5–80.

Meadows, D., Randers, J. and Meadows, D. (2004). *Limits to Growth: The 30-years Update*, White River Junction, VT: Chelsea Green Publishing.

Nováček, P. and Mederly, P. (2002). *Global Partnership for Development: Sustainable Development Index*, Olomouc, Czech Republic: Palacky University (for: American Council for the United Nations University). Online: www.researchgate.net/publication/39894478_Global_Partnership_for_Development (accessed 17 September 2017).

Oxfam International (2013). Global leaders shirk responsibility to tackle global inequality crisis. Online: www.oxfam.org/en/pressroom/pressreleases/2013-05-30/global-leaders-shirk-responsibility-tackle-global-inequality (accessed 30 May 2017).

Sachs, J.D., Schmidt-Traub, G. and Durand-Delacre, D. (2016). *Preliminary Sustainable Development Goal (SDG) Index and Dashboard*. Online: http://unsdsn.org/wp-content/uploads/2016/02/160215-Preliminary-SDG-Index-and-SDG-Dashboard-working-paper-for-consultation.pdf (accessed 17 September 2017).

Seers, D. (ed.) (1981). *Dependency Theory: A Critical Reassessment*, London: Oxford University Press.

Standish, M. and Witters, D. (2014). Country well-being varies greatly worldwide (Gallup-Healthways Global Wellbeing Index). Online: www.gallup.com/poll/175694/country-varies-greatly-worldwide.aspx (accessed 18 October 2017).

Todaro, M.P. (1977). *Economic Development in the Third World: An Introduction to Problems and Policies in a Global Perspective*, London: Longman.

United Nations (2007). *Indicators of Sustainable Development: Guidelines and Methodologies*. New York: United Nations. Online: www.un.org/esa/sustdev/natlinfo/indicators/guidelines.pdf (accessed 10 July 2017).

United Nations (2015a). *The Millennium Development Goals Report 2015*, New York: United Nations. Online: www.un.org/millenniumgoals/2015_MDG_Report/pdf/MDG%202015%20rev%20(July%201).pdf (accessed 6 October 2017).

United Nations (2015b). We can end poverty, Millennium Development Goals and beyond 2015. Online: www.un.org/millenniumgoals/ (accessed 9 February 2016).

United Nations (2017a). Criteria for identification and graduation of LDCs. Online: http://unohrlls.org/about-ldcs/criteria-for-ldcs/ (accessed 14 November 2017).

United Nations (2017b). Encyclopedia of the Nations. Online: www.nationsencyclopedia.com/United-Nations/Economic-and-Social-Development-FOURTH-UN-DEVELOPMENT-DECADE.html (accessed 14 September 2017).

United Nations (no date-a). *Plan of Implementation of the World Summit on Sustainable Development*. Online: www.un.org/esa/sustdev/documents/WSSD_POI_PD/English/WSSD_PlanImpl.pdf (accessed 6 October 2017).

United Nations (no date-b). Sustainable development: future we want – outcome document. Online: https://sustainabledevelopment.un.org/rio20/futurewewant (accessed 6 October 2017).

United Nations (no date-c). Sustainable development goals. Online: www.un.org/sustainabledevelopment/sustainable-development-goals/ (accessed 27 August 2017).

United Nations Development Programme (UNDP) (2013). *United Nations Development Report 2013*, New York: UNDP. Online: http://hdr.undp.org/sites/default/files/hdr_2013_en_technotes.pdf (accessed 14 November 2017).

United Nations Development Programme (UNDP) (2015). *United Nations Development Report 2015*, New York: UNDP. Online: http://hdr.undp.org/sites/default/files/2015_human_development_report.pdf (accessed 6 October 2017).

United Nations Development Programme (UNDP) (2016). *United Nations Development Report 2016*, New York: UNDP. Online: http://hdr.undp.org/sites/default/files/2016_human_development_report.pdf (accessed 15 September 2017).

United Nations Economic Commission for Europe (UN ECE) (2014). *Conference of European Statisticians Recommendations on Measuring Sustainable Development*, New York and Geneva: UN ECE. Online: www.unece.org/fileadmin/DAM/stats/publications/2013/CES_SD_web.pdf (accessed 7 April 2017).

Veenhoven, R. (2015). Happiness in nations, world database of happiness. Erasmus University Rotterdam. Online: http://worlddatabaseofhappiness.eur.nl/hap_nat/nat_fp.php?mode=1 (accessed 15 September 2017).

World Bank (2015). PovcalNet, Regional aggregation using 2005 PPP and $1.25/day poverty line. Online: http://iresearch.worldbank.org/PovcalNet/index.htm?1 (accessed 31 July 2017).

World Bank (2017). PovcalNet. Online: http://iresearch.worldbank.org/PovcalNet/pov DuplicateWB.aspx (accessed 14 November 2017).

World Commission on Environment and Development (WCED) (1987). *Our Common Future*, Oxford: Oxford University Press.

World Economic Forum (WEF) (2015). *The Global Competitiveness Report 2015–2016*, Geneva: World Economic Forum. Online: http://reports.weforum.org/global-competitiveness-report-2015-2016/ (accessed 19 October 2017).

10

SUSTAINABLE DEVELOPMENT

Blueprint or fig leaf?

Measures of sustainable development refer to different dimensions or supportive pillars of development. The former expand the conventional concept of socio-economic development; the latter determine its long-term sustainability. Development components identified in this manner can be economic, environmental and social, but may also include other cultural, political or ethical objectives. These components refer often to hardly measurable human welfare, which makes them difficult, if not impossible, to combine in an overall index. Taking alternatively judgmental development goals as the ultimate objectives creates a normative concept of sustainable development. In the absence of a practical objective measure, sustainable development might alert to the need of looking beyond gross domestic product (GDP), but might also distort our vision of socio-economic progress.

10.1 A murky concept

How did sustainability get into development? One reason could be the realization that conventional indicators of economic growth fail to capture changes in social welfare, the ultimate objective of development. Economic indicators ignore significant dimensions of development and distort therefore the assessment of overall development. Expanding economic development under the label of sustainability turns the concept into an alluring aspiration. Everyone can subscribe to it, taking credit for contributing to a cornucopian paradigm without being held accountable for its failure. To industry, sustainable development offers opportunities for investing in environmental protection; governments adopt it for pacifying environmentalist objections to an unfair distribution of economic output; and civil society uses it to argue against globalization. With sustainable development "all [is] in harmony" (WCED 1987, p. 46).

142 Cornucopia from sustainable development?

Adding ignored dimensions of development could indeed enhance the coverage of human welfare. The problem is measurability. One step of finding indicators could break down the opaque concept of sustainable development into more specific components such as human needs or more normative development goals. Another step would try to find measurable components of human wellbeing as the ultimate objective of development; these components could include human needs and wants such as health, education, distributional equity etc. The final step would have to combine the indicators thus determined into a composite index of development.

The popular concept of sustainable development, advanced by the World Commission on Environment and Development (WECD), seeks to integrate fragmented economic, environmental and social policies. It defines sustainable development as "development that meets the needs of the present without compromising the ability of future generations to meet their own needs" (ibid., p. 43). The objective is to meet "essential" human needs of employment, food, energy supply, housing, water supply and sanitation, food, clothing, shelter and jobs (ibid., pp. 54–5).

The WCED definition treats sustainability as a matter of inter-generational equity to ensure that future generations enjoy at least the same standards of living as the current one. It sees intra-generational equity largely as a matter of reducing poverty, which undermines meeting human needs. The "inter-national" distribution of prosperity could also be made part of social sustainability. However, it is the result of historic and political events, on whose inequity governments and experts cannot be expected to agree. Still, country rankings by development levels (Table 9.3) might give a first indication of what political events have brought about. In theory, one could further add a political dimension to sustainable development. But, lacking any agreement on the inequity of past and future power struggles, political sustainability is not pursued here.

Parts II and III discussed the sustainability of the economy and the natural environment as separate concerns of maintaining produced and natural capital for economic growth, and preserving nature for its own purpose or for delivering services to people. Integrating economic and environmental sustainability with social sustainability would lead us closer to the overall sustainability of development. However, attempts at defining sustainable development in terms of social wellbeing, using wealth or human needs to measure such wellbeing, fail in providing a valid integrated measure of development. It is not clear how economic growth, social equity and environmental quality combine to meet human needs and wellbeing now and in the future. The trade-offs and conflicts among different needs and goals, and stakeholders and decision makers are not known, and there are no clear time frames and thresholds for sustainability.[1]

Depending on how and by whom human needs are identified, they might reflect physiological and psychological perceptions of individuals or might be set as national or international goals for development. Millennium Development Goals (MDG) (United Nations 2015) and Sustainable Development Goals (SDG) (United Nations, no date-b) attempt the latter; however, they treat sustainability differently. The MDG present environmental sustainability explicitly as a development goal, whereas the

SDG use "sustainable" or "for sustainable development" as supportive attributes in most of its goals. Table 9.1 groups the SDG into environmental, economic and social sustainability. Economic and social sustainability can thus be clearly identified in addition to environmental sustainability, the only sustainability goal of the MDG.

Development goals are, however, often confounded with development restrictions. Placing a green economy in the "context" of sustainable development by the latest Earth Summit does not help: it treats the greening of the economy as "one of the important tools" of sustainable development, an option that "should not be a rigid set of rules" (United Nations, no date-a, para. 56). The image of "pillars" of development (United Nations 2003) appears to refer to *sustaining* development rather than introducing further dimensions or goals. The pillar metaphor is often used interchangeably, though, with notions of dimensions or goals of sustainable development (ibid.; Adams 2006).

Contrary to the maintenance of capital for economic growth and environmental quality, the social dimension of development is difficult to specify and measure. This book treats poverty and its distributive implications as a social goal of development rather than a supportive pillar. Poverty mitigation might enhance economic growth, but is still more in the nature of a social goal of equity than a supportive factor for economic growth. Poverty is often treated, therefore, as a surrogate for the complex and hardly quantifiable notion of development (cf. section 9.2.2).

Another question is if sustainability at low levels of development is a meaningful objective: should one not set out from meeting at least "basic" or otherwise defined adequate needs of a country's population before talking about sustainability? The setting of minimum limits for desirable development goals and maximum limits that restrain their achievement could provide a more realistic definition of sustainable development. The model of "outer limits," suggested in section 5.2.1 for economic sustainability, could be expanded to this end: it would specify minimum economic and non-economic needs and maximum environmental and other limits to create a development space within which the development process could proceed sustainably. This would also open the environmental space discussed in section 7.2.2 to further development processes and restrictions.

One might also specify a minimum speed for development that would enable convergence by poor countries towards rich countries' levels within a "reasonable" time frame. Getting closer to these levels might indicate that we are on the right path. But even "developed" countries look for more ambitious goals that can only be modeled for some time in the uncertain future. Shifts in the goals and targets are a further indication of the judgmental character of both the goals and their sustainability. For poverty, the MDG specify goal attainment and hence sustainability as halving the proportion of people living in extreme poverty by 2015. The SDG now raise the goal to "end poverty in all its forms everywhere" by 2030. Different poverty "lines" support different distributional objectives (World Bank 2017). In the case of environmental deterioration international declarations stick to a 2°C global warming target, while unofficially admitting that a 3°C limit is the realistic option. Judgmental norms can change with the perceptions of the goal setters and their constituencies.

144 Cornucopia from sustainable development?

Setting out from welfare as the ultimate objective of development (e.g., UN ECE 2014; Sala et al. 2015) cannot provide a valid and commonly agreed picture of sustainable development. Widely differing concepts and measures of economic and non-economic welfare reflect different views about what generates human well-being. This makes development and its sustainability an elusive concept when it comes to assessing success or failure. Setting development goals and limits for reaching or evaluating them are judgmental about their importance. Suggested indicators and indices of sustainable development might warn us about possible "tipping points" of sustainable development (Adams 2006, p. 8). But their results can hardly be trusted as valid measures of the level and trend of sustainable development.

10.2 Measuring sustainable development

Doubts about the concepts and validity of development indices (Böhringer and Jochem 2007; Stiglitz et al. 2010;[2] Fleurbaey and Blanchet 2013; Sala et al. 2015) do not augur well for exploring time series or modeling trends for assessing sustainable development. Table 9.2 included a first indication of the kinds of sustainability adopted by selected development indices. This section explores in greater detail how sustainability could be inferred from development measures.

10.2.1 Trends of indices

The need to normalize indicators for aggregation into indices distorts their contribution to overall development and obscures the meaning of the indices. Development indices are therefore mostly used for a comparative ranking of countries. But do changes in country ranks reflect sustainability better than changes in index levels? Table 10.1 shows changes in ranks, whereas Figure 10.1 compares growth in happiness, human development and GDP.

A rather confusing picture emerges from Table 10.1. The common feature of economic growth in both the Human Development Index (HDI) and the Legatum Prosperity Index (LPI) creates distinct blocks of high ranked industrialized and low-ranked poor countries in each index. It does not create, however, a clear pattern of rank *changes*. Longer time series would of course be preferable for assessing trends and sustainability but are not available for all indices. Changes in ranks vary for the "big" nations, except for China and to a lesser degree Germany, which show considerable progress across all indices. A forecast for GDP per capita (to 2020) (Knoema 2011–2016) presents high gains in rank for China and Russia, but is less optimistic about oil-rich countries (Brunei Darussalam, United Arab Emirates). All in all, it does not make much sense to further explore country rankings for assessing trends in development and corresponding sustainability.

Looking at the growth of index levels might be a better approach to measuring sustainable development. Figure 10.1 presents changes in life satisfaction by the World Happiness Index (WHI), human development by the HDI, and economic standards of living by GDP per capita.

TABLE 10.1 Changes in country ranks

Country codes	HDI (188 countries)		LPI (142 countries)		GDP per capita[a] (202 countries)	
	Rank 2014	Δ Rank 2009–2014	Rank 2015	Δ Rank 2009–2015	Rank 2015	Δ Rank 2009–2015
NO	1	0	1	0	8	−1
AU	2	0	7	−2	19	−1
CH	3	0	2	+6	9	0
DK	4	+1	3	−1	20	−4
NL	5	0	8	+3	14	−2
DE	6	+3	14	+2	17	+8
IE	6	−2	10	−1	12	+2
US	8	−3	11	−1	11	−1
CA	9	+1	6	0	21	+2
NZ	9	−1	4	−1	29	+4
RU	50	+8	58	+4	50	−4
BR	75	+3	54	−9	77	−3
CN	90	+13	52	+6	81	+19
BI	184	0	138	−1[b]	185	−1
TD	185	+1	139	0[b]	161	0
ER	186	−5	–	174	−2	–
CF	187	0	142	−33	186	−4
NE	188	–	114	0[b]	182	+1

Sources: HDI: UNDP (2015); LPI: Legatum Institute (2015); GDP per capita: Knoema (2011–2016).

Notes
a Constant prices, purchasing power parities.
b 2012–2015.

Country acronyms (Veenhoven 2015):
A: AU Australia; **B**: BI Burundi, BR Brazil; **C**: CA Canada, CF Central African Republic, CH Switzerland, CN China; **D**: DK Denmark, DE Germany; **E**: ER Eritrea; **I**: IE Ireland; **N**: NE Niger, NL Netherlands, NO Norway, NZ New Zealand; **R**: RU Russia; **T**: TD Chad; **U**: US United States of America.

The WHI assesses national happiness as the average life satisfaction of a country's inhabitants. It claims to provide a measure of sustainable development in "a holistic approach to well-being" (Helliwell et al. 2016, p. 4). The 2005–2014 period covers the global economic recession. This could give an impression of how people coped with the economic downturn in their personal feelings. Rich countries showed mixed reactions. Latin American nations withstood the global economic downturn especially well, with an actual increase of happiness according to the World Happiness Report (Helliwell et al. 2015). Some transition countries and even some sub-Saharan countries also gained happiness; the reason is probably the less pronounced effects of the recession in their regions. Happiness "losers" are Middle Eastern and North African, hard-hit Western European (Greece, Spain, Italy) and sub-Saharan countries.

146 Cornucopia from sustainable development?

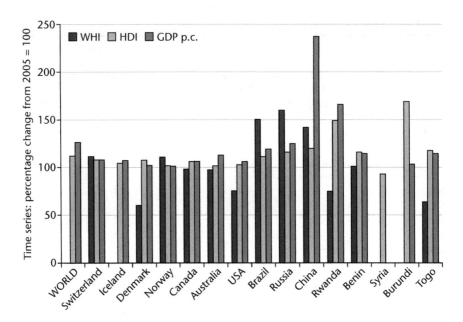

FIGURE 10.1 Growth in average happiness, human development and GDP per capita, 2005–2015 (2005 = 100). Growth of the indices is similar in economically developed countries, except for the WHI in Denmark and the USA. Other countries differ considerably in these measures. High economic growth and human development in developing countries, makes for some convergence with industrialized ones. China's accelerated economic growth does not seem to translate into happiness and human development. It is an open question whether economic growth contributes to the sustainability of development and wellbeing

Sources: WHI: Helliwell et al. (2017, Fig. 2.3) (2005/2007–2014/2016); HDI: UNDP (2010, 2016); GDP per capita: World Bank (2017) (purchasing power parities 2011).

The selected data of Figure 10.1 confirm (or at least do not contradict) this assessment. Figure 10.1 also shows that countries seem to be in most cases less happy than what would be indicated by an increase of GDP per capita. Conspicuously, happiness did not follow China's accelerated economic growth. This looks like the workings of the Easterlin (1974) paradox, according to which national happiness remains stationary after reaching a certain level of income and economic growth. However, as discussed in section 8.1.1, statistical evidence appears to refute the paradox. On the other hand, poor countries suffering from an unsatisfactory life need to catch up with rich countries' – desirable or maximally possible – level of life satisfaction.

The question of sustainability is indeed one of level and continuation. Should we take the tenth-ranked Uzbekistan in the WHI rankings of change in happiness by 74 percent from 2005–2007 to 2012–2014 as a sustainability threshold, or is Norway's situation of a 12 percent increase in happiness (ranked 57) a better indicator? On the other hand, the situation of 56 nations, whose happiness decreased, does not look sustainable. Happiness indices do not give a clear answer to the sustainability question, as subjective perceptions of the growth of happiness or well-being are difficult to measure, interpret and compare.

The HDI has the advantage of using a smaller number of objective indicators. It is an average of four indicators that allows a more immediate interpretation of development as progress in life expectancy, education and income. Measuring the growth of HDI levels thus provides a clearer picture of trends. Globally, the HDI increased by 12 percent between 1990 and 2015, compared to a 26 percent increase in GDP per capita. Developing countries converged on rich countries through a 30 percent increase. Figure 10.2 shows sub-Saharan and South Asian countries remaining at low HDI levels, whereas Latin American and European/Central Asian countries are closing in on rich nations. East Asian countries have now overtaken Arab countries in HDI values. Large differences in national developments impair, however, the significance of regional averages.

The question remains what reflects sustainability in HDI trends.[3] Notably for poorer regions and countries the steady development of Figure 10.2 should not (yet) be taken as sustainable development. One could choose, for instance, a rather arbitrary HDI level of 0.7 as the sustainability threshold. This would suggest that East Asia has joined Latin America and Europe/Central Asia in the club of sustainable development nations. One could also claim that no region has reached the "very high" 0.8 level, even if the first 51 countries are ranked individually above this level (UNDP 2016).

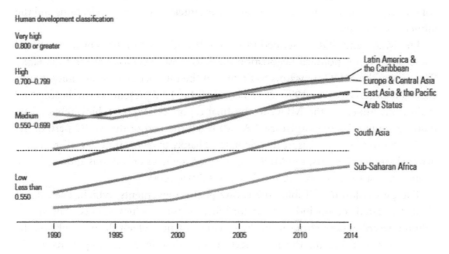

FIGURE 10.2 Regional changes in HDI levels. All regions have progressed in terms of human development since the 1990s. The South Asian and sub-Saharan regions remain still at relative low levels of development, whereas all other regions appear to converge at high HDI levels

Source: UNDP (2015, Fig. 2.1).

148 Cornucopia from sustainable development?

Rather than deriving the sustainability of "human development" from high rankings or index growth, Togtokh and Gaffney (2010) introduce environmental sustainability explicitly by including per-capita carbon emission in the HDI. This "cost" of global environmental impact reduces the original HDI scores and corresponding ranking of countries responsible for high CO_2 emissions. A typical conflation of non-sustainability with climate change is the result, but such deterioration ignores other types of pollution and natural resource depletion (cf. section 6.3.4).

One could accept such simplification, given that the HDI itself is a simplified measure of development. But there is another more conceptual problem with introducing an (environmental) impact indicator in an outcome measure of human wellbeing. The two are certainly not additive (deductible from each other) since they lack common ground such as the production function of economic output and its *cost* of produced and natural capital consumption. Ultimately the mixing of hardly measurable wellbeing with physical impacts (whose connection to either notion is opaque) generates difficult-to-interpret measures of their sustainability.[4]

10.2.2 Meeting development goals

The preceding section questioned the validity and usefulness of averaging selected indicators into an overall index of sustainable development. Another way of measuring sustainable development is to directly reflect the priorities of decision makers by setting goals and targets for development. Such judgmental goal setting might reflect hidden agendas, and so would attempts at aggregation. At the national level, more or less democratically elected governments are supposed to represent popular consensus, but government policies and their targets change with elections and the influences of lobbies.

The MDG and SDG described in section 9.1 appear to represent international consensus, even if political negotiation seeks to satisfy everyone around the table. We can use the MDG indicators to find out if the international community met its goals and targets over the 1990–2015 period. Table 10.2 presents key indicators and evaluations linked to the MDG in the final report on MDG achievements. The report is quite self-congratulatory: "As we reach the end of the MDG period, the world community has reason to celebrate. Thanks to concerted global, regional, national and local efforts, the MDGs have saved the lives of millions and improved conditions for many more" (United Nations 2015, p. 4).

The plus column of Table 10.2 shows goal achievements, which, even if not explicitly stated, could indicate sustainability in these achievements. The minus column describes detractions from these achievements, which throw doubt on the sustainability of achieving the goals. Section 9.2.2 described halving poverty and its attainment as the main MDG success. Percentages of goal achievements and the qualitative description of gaps in achievement do not provide an overall picture of progress or failure in meeting development goals and their sustainability.

Table 10.3 uses visual icons to make sense of the net effects of positive and negative indicator values. Up- and down-arrows serve to evaluate more comprehensively

TABLE 10.2 Selected indicators of MDG achievements, 1990–2015

MDG	+ (achievements)	– (detractions)
1 Eradicate extreme poverty and hunger	• People living in extreme poverty:[a] **−56.6%** • Proportion of undernourished people: **from 23.3% to 12.9%**	Millions of people still live in extreme poverty and hunger; rising inequality in income and wealth is ignored
2 Achieve universal primary education	Out-of-school children of primary school age: **−43%**[b]	Large differences between poorest and richest households
3 Promote gender equality and empower women	• Gender disparity in education has been eliminated in developing regions • Women gained ground in parliamentary representation in **90%** of countries	Overall, gender inequality persists
4 Reduce child mortality	Under-5 mortality reduced by **52.8%**	Large differences between poorest and richest households
5 Improve maternal health	Maternal mortality rate declined by **44.7%**	Large differences between poorest and richest households
6 Combat HIV/AIDS, malaria and other diseases	HIV infections fell by **40%**, malaria incidence by **37%**, tuberculosis prevalence rate by **41%**[c]	Only 36% of HIV infected people receive antiretroviral therapy

continued

TABLE 10.2 Continued

MDG	+ (achievements)	– (detractions)
7 *Ensure environmental sustainability*	• Ozone depleting substances eliminated • Substantial increase in protected areas • Improved drinking water use of world population: **from 76% to 91%** • **2.1 billion** people have gained access to improved sanitation • Urban slum dwellers decreased **from 39.4% to 29.7%**[d]	• CO_2 emissions up 50% since 1990 • Poor people most affected by natural resource depletion
8 *Develop a global partnership for development*	• Official development assistance increased by **66.7%**[e] • Internet penetration up **from 6% to 43%**[f]	International conflicts remain a big threat to human development

Source: United Nations (2015).

Notes

a People living on less than **$1.25 a day.**
b 2000–2015.
c Different time periods.
d By 2014.
e 2000–2014.
f 2000–2015.

Blueprint or fig leaf? **151**

TABLE 10.3 MDG evaluation, 1990–2015

Goal 1: Eradicate extreme poverty and hunger ↗

Target 1.A: Halve, between 1990 and 2015, the proportion of people whose income is less than $1 a day ↑

Target 1.B: Achieve full and productive employment and decent work for all, including women and young people ↓

Target 1.C: Halve, between 1990 and 2015, the proportion of people who suffer from hunger ↗

Goal 2: Achieve universal primary education ↓

Target 2.A: Ensure that, by 2015, children everywhere, boys and girls alike, will be able to complete a full course of primary schooling ↓

Goal 3: Promote gender equality and empower women ↓

Target 3.A: Eliminate gender disparity in primary and secondary education, preferably by 2005, and in all levels of education no later than 2015 ↓

Goal 4: Reduce child mortality ↓

Target 4.A: Reduce by two-thirds, between 1990 and 2015, the under-5 mortality rate ↓

Goal 5: Improve maternal health ↓

Target 5.A: Reduce by three-quarters, between 1990 and 2015, the maternal mortality ratio ↓

Target 5.B: Achieve, by 2015, universal access to reproductive health ↓

Goal 6: Combat HIV/AIDS, malaria and other diseases ↗

Target 6.A: Have halted by 2015 and begun to reverse the spread of HIV/AIDS ↑

Target 6.B: Achieve, by 2010, universal access to treatment for HIV/AIDS for all those who need it ↓

Target 6.C: Have halted by 2015 and begun to reverse the incidence of malaria and other major diseases ↑

Goal 7: Ensure environmental sustainability ↓

Target 7.A: Integrate the principles of sustainable development into country policies and programs and reverse the loss of environmental resources ↓

Target 7.B: Reduce biodiversity loss, achieving, by 2010, a significant reduction in the rate of loss ↓

Target 7.C: Halve, by 2015, the proportion of people without sustainable access to safe drinking water and basic sanitation ↗

Target 7.D: By 2020, to have achieved a significant improvement in the lives of at least 100 million slum dwellers ↗

Goal 8: Develop a global partnership for development ↓

Target 8.A: Develop further an open, rule-based, predictable, non-discriminatory trading and financial system ↓

Target 8.B: Address the special needs of the least developed countries ↓

Target 8.C: Address the special needs of landlocked developing countries and small island developing states ↓

Target 8.D: Deal comprehensively with the debt problems of developing countries through national and international measures in order to make debt sustainable in the long term ↗

continued

152 Cornucopia from sustainable development?

TABLE 10.3 Continued

Target 8.E: In cooperation with pharmaceutical companies, provide access to affordable essential drugs in developing countries	↓
Target 8.F: In cooperation with the private sector, make available the benefits of new technologies, especially information and communications	↗

Notes
Vertical upward arrows ↑, full achievement of targets; rising upward arrows ↗, close to achievement; downward arrows ↓, non-achievement.

MDG successes and failures in terms of complying (or not) with its goals and targets. Once we look inside the goals into targets the optimistic picture of the MDG report turns pessimistic. Only three targets of extreme poverty reduction (1.A), decreases in HIV (6.A) and malaria (6.C) are met. Of these, "eradication of poverty" could be taken as meeting the global goal of social sustainability. This ignores, however, more differentiated distributional equity and other sustainability targets unless one takes poverty mitigation as a surrogate for development (cf. section 9.2.2). The reduction of hunger, access to drinking water and sanitation, and improvement of slums come close to meeting their targets. Total development remains non-sustainable, though, failing to attain all other targets, and in fact all goals.

The question is what does this really mean for the evaluation of past and future development. Table 10.3 reveals the difficulty of coming to an overall conclusion about progress made or to be made, even with a relatively narrow range of key indicators. Imagine the information overload and the difficulty of assessing progress for the next 15 years by the 169 SDG targets.

Section 9.2.1 discussed the treatment of sustainability as dimensions of development. If sustainability were an inherent property of development the indices of Chapter 9 could indeed assess sustainable development. As discussed, it is not. The rather cavalier treatment of sustainability goals by both the MDG and SDG suggests nonetheless relying more on actual index trends than ad-hoc measurements of goal achievements. It remains to be seen if the newly advanced 230 indicators (United Nations 2016) can be turned into a meaningful overall development index (Sachs et al. 2017). For now, the ability of such an index to assess sustainable (or unsustainable) development remains questionable.

10.3 Has it run its course?

"It" is of course sustainable development. The arbitrariness of setting sustainability thresholds in terms of ranks, index levels or political goals discourages an objective assessment of development and its sustainability. Those still not discouraged explain sustainable development in terms of selected indicators. They summon further development issues and dimensions – such as natural and political disasters, climate change, inequalities and social networks – and refer to particular deprivations as non-sustainabilities of a murky concept of development. The problems increase when the analysis looks into the future of the long-term prospects for sustainable development.

The close connection between wealth and economic growth and the costs of using up wealth as capital consumption are the reasons why in the past governments tended to equate development with economic growth. Widespread bashing of growth and its epitome GDP seems to make governments give in now, at least rhetorically, to calls for replacing unsustainable economic growth by broader sustainable development. Impacts of diminished environmental services and inequities in the distribution of the fruits of economic growth are held responsible for environmental and social non-sustainability of economic activity.

Treating environmental decline as natural capital consumption leaves us in the realm of green growth, whereas adding inequities leads into socioeconomic development. Green growth treats sustainability as a matter of maintaining natural capital in addition to produced ("fixed") capital. The social dimension of development might judge inequality as an inequity in the distribution of income and wealth, but does not generally provide a clear definition and measure of non-sustainable inequity. Nor can this dimension specify when high environmental damage, caused or borne by economic agents (see Table 6.3), generates inequity within and among countries. Governments appear to wish for both green growth and comprehensive development. They placed therefore the greening of the economy into the "context of sustainable development" (United Nations, no date-a, section III).

Further cultural, political, ethical or visionary dimensions feed into a broad development notion that caters ultimately to human wellbeing and national welfare. A clear distinction in the welfare effects of economic growth and development could identify the boundaries of narrow economic performance vs. all-encompassing development of nations. Economic growth would generate *economic* wellbeing and welfare from the use and consumption of goods and services, whereas development would seek to improve *human* (and possibly also non-human) wellbeing more comprehensively as a result of consumption and other activities, processes and events. Economic and developmental sustainability could then be defined as non-decline in the respective notions of wellbeing. Unfortunately such a distinction is difficult to make, given the problems of welfare measurement. Confusion about the significance of more or less adjusted economic growth vs. more or less sustainable development thus remains.

The problem of overcoming this confusion shows up in an attempt by the United Nations and OECD to link environmental, social and economic "themes" with conceptual dimensions of a framework for measuring sustainable development; the sustainability dimensions include current wellbeing, capital (future wellbeing) and transboundary impacts (UN ECE 2014, Table 1). However the framework cannot clearly connect wellbeing to the different dimensions and "dashboard" indicators. Moreover, the addition of "political voice and governance" would further obscure the combination of indicators in an overall sustainability index.

Conveniently the hardly measurable notion of wellbeing serves as the fig leaf, behind which a continuing focus on economic growth can be concealed.

154 Cornucopia from sustainable development?

"Formalizing" sustainability as "a discounted sum of well-being over all future periods" by means of a "social utility function" (Stiglitz et al. 2010, p. 73) serves less to clarify the concept than to provide a hiding place of non-quantifiable jargon. On the other hand, governments readily subscribe to non-material development goals like equity or culture but fail to define and quantify them for a comprehensive operational development concept. They tend, therefore, to ignore these goals in policy making. Are we then going to see a repeat of the fate of the international development strategies (IDS) of the 1960–1990 development decades? As described in Section 9.1, the IDS set out from economic growth, attempted to introduce social justice and ended up calling again for economic growth with eradication of poverty and hunger and adding environmental protection. This looks indeed quite similar to the 2012 Earth Summit's call for a green economy "in the context" of sustainable development.

In the end, the paradigm of sustainable development might draw attention to ignored dimensions, goals or pillars. This omission would indeed make economic growth quite irrelevant for assessing total welfare, whereas ignoring the pillars would undermine economic growth, development and human wellbeing. Better indicators would help assess to what extent particular needs and wants are met or violated. The "data revolution" demanded by an expert group established by the Secretary-General of the United Nations (Data Revolution Group, no date) would improve assessing particular goals and targets. It will not be able to measure overall sustainable development. Bartelmus (2013, p. 123) concludes that "non-countables [of broad wellbeing] count, but we do not know how much."

At best, sustainable development will stimulate the goodwill of nations in caring about the environment and poor countries; at worst, it will serve as a fig leaf of good intentions, never intended to be acted upon (cf. section 11.3).

Notes

1 The WCED (1987, p. 63) seems to hope that democratic participation in decision making, notably at the local levels, will solve problems in agreeing on development strategies and policies.
2 The Stiglitz report avoids the term "development" but focuses instead on trends of wellbeing in its economic, environmental and social dimensions; these trends could therefore represent a broad development paradigm and its sustainability.
3 Since 2011 UNDP adjusts the HDI for inequality and presents separately indicators of environmental sustainability. Not to be left behind by the Millennium Summit of the United Nations, UNDP (2015, Ch. 5) now tries to link the HDI to the MDG and SDG. As shown below, Togtokh and Gaffney (2010) correct the HDI for the decline in environmental sustainability.
4 Nonetheless the HDI is used as a measure of wellbeing in the limits-to-growth model, where it is confronted, but not integrated, with the environmental impact measures of the Ecological Footprint.

References

Adams, W.M. (2006). *The Future of Sustainability: Re-thinking Environment and Development in the Twenty-first Century*, IUCN Report. Online: http://cmsdata.iucn.org/downloads/iucn_future_of_sustanability.pdf (accessed 4 June 2017).

Bartelmus, P. (2013). *Sustainability Economics: An Introduction*, London and New York: Routledge.

Böhringer, C. and Jochem, P.E.P. (2007). Measuring the immeasurable: a survey of sustainability indices, *Ecological Economics* 63: 1–8.

Data Revolution Group (no date). Data revolution report. Online: www.undatarevolution.org/report/ (accessed 7 October 2017).

Easterlin, R. (1974). Does economic growth improve the human lot? Some empirical evidence, in P.A. David and M.W. Reder (eds.), *Nations and Households in Economic Growth*, New York: Academic Press: 89–125.

Fleurbaey, M. and Blanchet, D. (2013). *Beyond GDP: Measuring Welfare and Assessing Sustainability*, Oxford: Oxford University Press.

Helliwell, J., Layard, R. and Sachs, J. (2015). *World Happiness Report 2015*. Online: http://worldhappiness.report/wp-content/uploads/sites/2/2015/04/WHR15.pdf (accessed 16 November 2017).

Helliwell, J., Layard, R. and Sachs, J. (2016). *World Happiness Report 2016*. Online: http://worldhappiness.report/wp-content/uploads/sites/2/2016/03/HR-V1_web.pdf (accessed 16 November 2017).

Helliwell, J., Layard, R. and Sachs, J. (2017). *World Happiness Report 2017*. Online: http://worldhappiness.report/wp-content/uploads/sites/2/2017/03/HR17-Ch2.pdf (accessed 16 November 2017).

Knoema (2011–2016). GDP per capita ranking 2016, data and charts. Online: https://knoema.com/sijweyg/gdp-per-capita-ranking-2016-data-and-charts (accessed 7 October 2017).

Legatum Institute (2015). *The Legatum Prosperity Index 2015*, London: Legatum Institute. Online: http://media.prosperity.com/2015/pdf/publications/PI2015Brochure_WEB.pdf (accessed 6 October 2017).

Sachs, J.D., Schmidt-Traub, G., Kroll, C., Durand-Delacre, D. and Teksoz, K. (2017). *SDG Index and Dashboards Report 2017*, New York: Bertelsmann Stiftung and Sustainable Development Solutions Network (SDSN). Online: http://sdgindex.org/assets/files/2017/2017-SDG-Index-and-Dashboards-Report-full.pdf (accessed 1 October 2017).

Sala, S., Ciuffo, B. and Nijkamp, B. (2015). A systemic framework for sustainability assessment, *Ecological Economics* 119: 314–25.

Stiglitz, J.E., Sen, A. and Fitoussi, J.P. (2010). *Report by the Commission on the Measurement of Economic Performance and Social Progress*. Online: http://library.bsl.org.au/jspui/bitstream/1/1267/1/Measurement_of_economic_performance_and_social_progress.pdf (accessed 4 June 2017).

Togtokh, C. and Gaffney, O. (2010). Human sustainable development index (United Nations University, Our World). Online: http://ourworld.unu.edu/en/the-2010-human-sustainable-development-index (accessed 29 October 2017).

United Nations (2003). *Johannesburg Declaration on Sustainable Development and Plan of Implementation of the World Summit on Sustainable Development*, New York: United Nations.

United Nations (2015). *The Millennium Development Goals Report 2015*, New York: United Nations. Online: www.un.org/millenniumgoals/2015_MDG_Report/pdf/MDG%202015%20rev%20(July%201).pdf (accessed 6 October 2017).

156 Cornucopia from sustainable development?

United Nations (2016). *Report of the Inter-Agency and Expert Group on Sustainable Development Goal Indicators*, Economic and Social Council document E/CN.3/2016/2. Online: https://unstats.un.org/unsd/statcom/47th-session/documents/2016-2-IAEG-SDGs-E.pdf (accessed 7 October 2017).

United Nations (no date-a). Sustainable development: future we want – outcome document. Online: https://sustainabledevelopment.un.org/futurewewant.html (accessed 16 November 2017).

United Nations (no date-b). Sustainable development goals. Online: www.un.org/sustainabledevelopment/sustainable-development-goals/ (accessed 27 August 2017).

United Nations Development Programme (UNDP) (2010). *Human Development Report 2010*, New York: UNDP. Online: http://hdr.undp.org/en/content/human-development-report-2010 (accessed 16 November 2017).

United Nations Development Programme (UNDP) (2015). *United Nations Development Report 2015*, New York: UNDP. Online: http://hdr.undp.org/sites/default/files/2015_human_development_report.pdf (accessed 6 October 2017).

United Nations Development Programme (UNDP) (2016). *United Nations Development Report 2016*, New York: UNDP. Online: http://hdr.undp.org/sites/default/files/2016_human_development_report.pdf (accessed 15 September 2017).

United Nations Economic Commission for Europe (UN ECE) (2014). *Conference of European Statisticians Recommendations on Measuring Sustainable Development*, New York and Geneva: UN ECE. Online: www.unece.org/fileadmin/DAM/stats/publications/2013/CES_SD_web.pdf (accessed 7 April 2017).

Veenhoven, R. (2015). Happiness in nations, world database of happiness. Erasmus University Rotterdam. Online: http://worlddatabaseofhappiness.eur.nl/hap_nat/nat_fp.php?mode=1 (accessed 15 September 2017).

World Bank (2017). Data. GDP per capita, PPP (constant 2011 international $). Online: https://data.worldbank.org/indicator/NY.GDP.PCAP.PP.KD?end=2015&start=2005&view=chart&year_high_desc=false (accessed 15 November 2017).

World Commission on Environment and Development (WCED) (1987). *Our Common Future*, Oxford: Oxford University Press.

PART V

What should we do about it?

Strategies or policies that would deliver sustainable prosperity and wellbeing depend on what we know about the factors affecting our wellbeing. The purpose of the preceding parts was to obtain this knowledge by means of measures of income, wealth, the environment, needs and happiness. Such knowledge makes it possible to determine more clearly what can be quantified when assessing the sustainability of an economy.

Part V examines the ability of available data to assist rational policies of sustaining the economy and the environment and their effects on wellbeing. It focuses on strategies and policies that are the immediate consequence of the assessments in the preceding chapters. Chapter 11 reviews the meaning and validity of key measures of prosperity, environmental quality and wellbeing. It seeks to clarify their messages for informed policy making. Chapter 12 evaluates different strategic options and policies. It leads from vision to integrative policy at national and international levels. Chapter 13 looks for ways of opening a dialogue between environmentalists and economists that might help overcome their polarization.

Chapter 14 presents conclusions about the validity of data and their role in policy making. All in all, it seems that combined economic and environmental accounting might be the best way to provide systematic, albeit limited, support to integrative policy. Other social and political concerns have to be left to politics.

11

WHAT DO THE INDICATORS TELL US?

Do the indicators tell us that we are better off, better than before and better than other people or other countries? Will it last? This chapter summarizes and explores the knowledge accumulated in the preceding chapters by monetary accounts of income and wealth, non-monetary indices and models that generate advice about ensuring future sustainability. The gloomy outlook for the environment and sustainable development contradicts the optimistic picture provided by conventional economic indicators.

11.1 Accounting for prosperity

Prosperity is the economic aspect of being better off. Measuring income and wealth as indicators of prosperity has the advantage of using a monetary accounting *system* of interacting economic stocks and flows. Money serves as the common unit of measurement, and the underlying prices tend to reflect the preferences of economic agents for goods and services. The "net" aggregates of the accounts combine positive (output, income, assets) and negative (costs, liabilities) outcomes of economic activities. Countries compile regularly most of these aggregates for use in national and international economic policies. Part II examined the sustainability of personal income and wealth and the sustainability of our economies in terms of modified ("greened") economic aggregates. This section summarizes and evaluates the use and usefulness of these measures for assessing economic prosperity and its sustainability.

11.1.1 Sustaining personal wealth and income

Chapter 3 presented data on personal income and wealth. It found the value of global personal wealth to be about three times the value of what it generates,

160 What should we do about it?

i.e., income and output. Since wealth and income seem to move in tandem they could both be used as indicators of changes in economic prosperity. Wealth per adult increased from the year 2000 to 2016 to reach a global average of US$52,800 per adult. Of course, this average varies widely among people and regions.

Wealth grew in all global regions since the year 2000, fell during the financial crisis of 2008/2009 and slowed down in the following years (cf. Figures 3.1 and 3.2). Growth of wealth has been most pronounced in China. Inequality has also been rising, especially in North America and Europe, which hold most wealth in the highest deciles. In contrast, Africa and India have most people in the four lowest wealth deciles. A more equal spread of wealth can be observed in Asia (without China) and Latin America.

Within countries, the USA stands out with increasing concentration of income and wealth in the hands of the rich since the 1970s – much more than in European nations (Table 3.1). China shows a concentration of wealth in high deciles, but not the highest one, quite in contrast to India's concentration in the lower deciles. Economic growth in developing and emerging countries with concomitant increasing inequality points to a risk of additional wealth and income ending up with the rich strata of the population.

What does all this mean for the sustainability of prospering economically in the future? Unexpected windfalls of discoveries, afflictions of disasters, natural resource depletion and degradation, and policy changes make it difficult to predict the sustainability of personal income. Piketty (2014) confirms that there are no plausible models of anticipating the future distribution of personal income and wealth. Distribution depends crucially on socioeconomic policy and politics, and the spread of knowledge and skills. It is therefore quite impossible to predict whether nations will move closer to equality in income and wealth, especially in the long term. This applies also to the great polarization of the distribution of income and wealth between labor and capital. Marxian class struggle would make conventional economic activity unsustainable, but such struggle did not spread and persist. The distribution of income and wealth is therefore better explained and managed by the productivity of production factors and distributional policies.

Past developments indicate that the concentration of wealth in the high-income strata created increasing inequality in industrialized countries. Developing countries seem to follow the example of the USA. The Credit Suisse Research Institute predicts sustained growth in wealth, an analysis which Picketty obviously discourages. Apart from the difficulty of predicting future trends, there is no clear objective way to determine at what level inequality turns into – non-sustainable – inequity. Section 11.2.2 will discuss the normative implications of setting equity goals of reducing poverty as a criterion of sustainable development.

11.1.2 The sustainability of our economies

Assessing sustainability at the national level can set out from some of the well-established indicators of aggregate economic performance. Final consumption could bring about national (economic) welfare; capital inputs would support production and economic growth. Welfare is based on notions of utility or disutility obtained from the use of final goods and services. The consumption of produced and natural capital represents a cost of production that needs to be netted out to obtain the benefits of economic activity.

Direct welfare measures add and subtract positive and negative welfare effects from national indicators such as gross domestic product (GDP) or final consumption. The Genuine Progress Indicator (GPI) and its original version of an Index of Sustainable Economic Welfare (ISEW) were first advanced in the USA. Other countries picked up and sometimes modified these measures. The indicators generally show a scissor movement of declining or stagnating welfare and growing GDP since the 1970s. One could see this as a manifestation of the Easterlin (1974) paradox, according to which national happiness, an even broader notion of welfare, remains stationary after the economy has reached a certain level of national income.

Major flaws of judgmentally selecting positive and negative welfare effects and applying rather inconsistent valuations are the reason why the GPI was not taken up by national statistical services. Compiling the GPI remains in most cases a one-time effort of non-governmental experts and organizations. Doubts about the validity of the Easterlin paradox and other hypotheses about the correlation of income and wellbeing persist. All in all, the welfare indices look more like a call for going "beyond GDP" than a valid assessment of the sustainability of social progress.

Two wealth indices, the World Bank's Comprehensive Wealth Measure (CWM) and UNEP/UNU's Inclusive Wealth Index (IWI) seek the help of welfare economics to establish the validity of these indices in terms of current and discounted future wellbeing. To make these measures measurable wellbeing is replaced by the consumption of goods and services. The indices remain thus within the realm of production and final consumption. They differ, however, in their treatment of economic growth. The CWM is based on optimal (efficient) economic growth made possible by the use of produced and natural capital and residual "intangible" wealth. The objective is to facilitate constant – sustainable – consumption generated by the use of different capital assets. The IWI uses shadow prices for directly measuring the welfare (consumption) effects of marginal capital use to assess the availability and use of produced and non-produced (human and natural) capital stocks.

Both indices see environmental decline mostly as a matter of climate change, which threatens the sustainability of economic growth. They treat this threat differently, though. The IWI calculates an adjusted measure by deducting the damage of CO_2 emissions as a kind of depreciation of natural capital. The CWM estimates the social accumulated and discounted avoidance cost of national CO_2 emission. It calculates these costs separately as a percentage of the stock value of CO_2 remaining in the atmosphere. The indices also differ in the treatment of financial capital; the CWM includes it as a type of productive capital whereas the IWI simply ignores it. Results differ therefore considerably. Globally, the level of inclusive wealth is lower

162 What should we do about it?

than that of comprehensive wealth by about 20 percent in 2005; also, the growth rate of the IWI is 15 percent during 1995–2005 whereas it is 25 percent for the CWM. For different income groups the shares of wealth also differ. High- and upper-middle-income countries show relatively low concentration of wealth for the CWM; in contrast, the IWI indicates much higher concentrations of wealth in these countries.

The theoretical reliance on all-encompassing but hardly measurable welfare thwarts measuring the sustainability of wealth and welfare. The purpose is mostly to draw attention to the omission of significant components of – natural, human and social – capital in the conventional national accounts. The relatively new green accounting methods of the System of Environmental-Economic Accounting (SEEA) still leave out non-measurable intangible capital categories. The SEEA includes natural capital, though, for which consistent accounting methods were developed and data availability is deemed sufficient for implementation. The SEEA thus permits staying within the definitions and checks and balances of the national accounts. The original SEEA introduces natural capital as a provider of environmental source and sink services to the economy. Consequently it treats the depletion and degradation of natural capital as a further form of capital consumption.[1]

Deducting the value of natural capital consumption, together with produced capital consumption, from gross indicators obtains measures of Environmentally adjusted *net* Domestic Product (EDP) and Environmentally adjusted *net* Capital Formation (ECF). Positive ECF indicates that countries were able to fend off produced and natural capital losses by new capital formation – a measure of weak sustainability of economic growth. The results of a first rough global application of the original SEEA (cf. section 4.2.2) indicate that economic growth has been globally sustainable in terms of produced and natural capital maintenance during 1990–2006. However, at regional and country levels non-sustainability shows up in African and Latin American countries. These countries appear to sacrifice long-term capital maintenance to short-term final consumption. Global environmental cost almost quadrupled. This presents a challenge for environmental protection in all countries and, in particular, for China whose environmental cost amounted to 12.5 percent of GDP in 2006. Nor should one forget that much of the growth of industrialized countries stems from the import of natural resources from and the export of environmentally hazardous production to developing countries.

Weak sustainability maintains thus only the value of produced and natural capital. It assumes that investments in other forms of capital could compensate for the consumption of exhaustible resources. Weak sustainability thus ignores the existence of irreplaceable "critical" natural capital. The existence of non-substitutable capital would require measuring strong sustainability separately, maintaining its physical amount in hybrid accounts. Ignoring difficult-to-define and -measure human and social capital and their "consumption" further confines the analysis of sustainability of economic activity and growth.

Hybrid accounts link material flows to economic activity. They could lead to the roots of non-sustainability resulting from physical environmental depletion and degradation. However, they would not be able to determine the level of non-sustainability, which would require a common measuring rod for physical impacts and monetary evaluation. Still, linking these flows in a common framework could help overcome the persisting polarization of environmentalists and economists (see section 13.2).

The picture becomes less certain when predicting the future, which is the real concern of sustainability analysis and policy making. Personal economic wealth might increase globally and for most countries in the short run. However, environmental and other social constraints observed in the past pose major challenges to maintaining productive wealth and sustainable economic growth in the long run. Econometric models described in Chapter 5 come to contradictory conclusions. The environmental Kuznets curve (EKC) hypothesis claims that there is an automatic environmental improvement with continuing economic growth after an initial deterioration. The limits-to-growth (LTG) model, on the other hand, predicts economic and social disaster by the end of the twenty-first century with correspondingly improved environmental conditions. Its business-as-usual scenario claims that we could end up with standards of living of the 1900s. Pollution, natural resource depletion and a corresponding decrease in food production are the main reasons.

Both models drew heavy critique about their assumptions, coverage of welfare effects and data availability. The EKC hypothesis seems to apply only to a few local pollutants. Some environmental impacts might actually correlate with economic growth at higher levels of income and output. Max-Neef (1995) claims that the ISEW confirms his "threshold hypothesis" of declining welfare in rich and growing economies. Considering that environmental quality contributes significantly to human welfare the threshold hypothesis tends to invert the EKC hypothesis of environmental improvement through economic growth. For the LTG model, mainstream economists criticized the neglect of adaptive behavior of economic agents and the assumptive bridging of data gaps.

Optimal growth models couch opaque welfare in notions of wealth, defined as the sum of (discounted) welfare effects generated over the lifetime of wealth components. The models include the use of natural capital as the result of utility and welfare maximizing behavior. Most models stress the role of technology as the culprit of generating environmental impacts or as a savior from environmental decline. They generate contradictory results depending on assumptions about the type and effects of old and new technologies and of anticipated policy making. Meyer and Ahlert (2016) find that a prevailing dichotomy in models, which assumes perfect market conditions vs. market imperfections, comes to almost opposite conclusions. Future research needs to examine these assumptions and contradictions, particular with regard to the role of non-substitutable vs. renewable resources in assessing the sustainability of economic activity.

11.1.3 USA: an illustrative evaluation

The above-described measures provide a mixed picture of the sustainability of past and future economic performance. The example of the USA can serve as an illustration of the different results and validity of key prosperity indicators. Twenty years ago, Cobb et al. (1995) found that "America is down," despite GDP being up. The GPI provided the evidence. The general argument is that GDP fails to measure individual wellbeing and national welfare. Figure 11.1 compares the growth of GDP and GPI in the USA together with other measures of production, wealth and welfare.[2] The GPI stays well below growing GDP in what seems to be a scissor movement of a GPI decrease from 52 to 42 percent of GDP during 1990 to 2004. As mentioned, this could be interpreted as a manifestation of the Easterlin paradox.

However, the GPI makes an arbitrary selection of desirables and regrettables, leaning heavily on the latter. In contrast, an earlier Measure of Economic Welfare of the USA (Nordhaus and Tobin 1973) focused on the positive aspects of leisure and non-marketed goods and services and created a rosier picture of the economy.

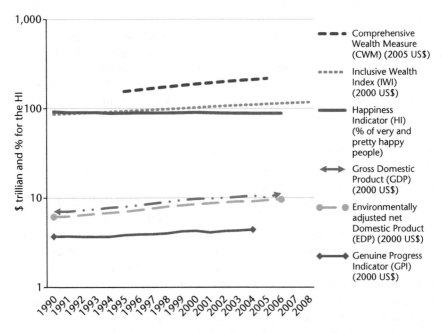

FIGURE 11.1 Comparing indicators for the USA (trillion US$, % for the HI). Except for the happiness indicator all measures seem to show a USA that is "up," rather than down. However, the indicators move at different levels and speed and are not comparable. We do not really know how much prosperity (in a broad sense) has progressed in the country

Sources: CWM: World Bank (2011); IWI: UNEP and UNU-IHDP (2012); HI: GSS (2017); EDP: Bartelmus (2009); GPI: Talberth et al. (2007).

Another reason for the pessimistic outlook of the GPI is its treatment of "defensive expenditures" as a cost. But such expenses could and should realistically be seen as welfare generating since they improve less-than-perfect real-life conditions. And where should one draw the limits? Should one further deduct expenditures on "unhealthy" food and drink, "tasteless" entertainment and "useless" defense? Who is to judge?

A more modest measure of the "greened" national accounts, the EDP, deducts the costs of fixed capital depreciation, environmental degradation and natural resource depletion from GDP. The EDP estimates for the USA reduce the annual GDP by 12–14 percent during 1990–2004. These reductions are much lower than the decreases of about 50 percent brought about by the GPI. The reason is that – like GDP – the EDP does not attempt to measure welfare but remains firmly in the realm of economic production, consumption and invest-ment.[3] The EDP can be seen as a measure of a more sustainable performance of the economy as it takes the "wear and tear" of produced *and* natural capital into account.

Both GDP and EDP indicate that America is up according to their trend in the past. Figure 11.1 shows that the growth of EDP follows closely GDP growth. The reason is that environmental cost did not change dramatically during the rel-atively short period covered (before the financial crisis). According to World Bank (2015) data, GDP grew at an annual rate of about 3.6 percent during 1990–2000, and slowed down to 1.7 percent during 2000–2013 because of the 2008 economic downturn. The distribution of these indicators is of course another matter; it cannot be lumped into an overall economic "up" or "down." Rather, inequality and equity issues are assessed in section 11.2.2 as part of the social dimension of sustainable development, in particular as the level of extreme poverty.

The IWI and the CWM measure the current value of wealth as the discounted value of welfare generated by a country's economic, human, social and natural capital over the lifetimes of the different types of assets. The indices are therefore much larger (about 25 times for the IWI) than the flow of past annual welfare represented by the GPI. Figure 11.1 also indicates that the growth rates of wealth and production tend to be higher than those of the welfare measures of the GPI and a non-monetary happiness indicator (HI). The HI shows a slightly negative trend but HIs are not really comparable to economic welfare measures (see section 11.2.3). All in all, this is hardly a picture of America being "down," except perhaps in the sense of "it could have been better."

The wide range of results presented in Figure 11.1 stems from applying different concepts and methods, and the judgmental selection of indicators. One could argue that it is too early to predict the final fate of these measures. More importantly, budgetary constraints and well-known inertia of national administrations do not augur well for any radical changes in the official statistics and their uses. Obviously it is easier to suggest new sets of indicators and indices than to ensure their regular compilation, aggregation and policy use.

166 What should we do about it?

The real flaws of the wealth and welfare measures lie deeper. They relate to the age-old failure of economics to confirm the fundamental assumption of welfare (utility) maximization by economic agents with realistic data of economic and social outcomes at the national level. Somewhat disguised as genuine progress, human development, inclusive wealth or happiness, different indices claim to successfully measure national welfare. The CWM and IWI rely on modeling future welfare generated by produced, human, natural and less tangible social capital. They discount future welfare more or less heavily and use surveys of people's subjective willingness to pay or market simulation to value different welfare effects.

We do not really know, therefore, if or by how much the socioeconomic and environmental situation has improved altogether in the USA. The responses of people to questions about their state of happiness are subjective and elude valid quantification; they are discussed in more detail in the following section.

11.2 Beyond prosperity: are we really better off?

Section 11.1.2 discussed modified economic indicators of income and wealth. The latter includes, besides produced capital goods, factor inputs of natural, human and social capital. Using money as the common unit of measurement keeps the analysis within the realm of economic preferences for production, investment and consumption. The purpose is to assess *economic* prosperity and wellbeing and their sustainability. This section, based on Parts III and IV, looks beyond the economy at changes in the quality of the natural environment, sustainable development, wellbeing and happiness. Development and wellbeing are, however, often used interchangeably blurring their meaning and measurement.

A categorization of indicators that look beyond GDP distinguishes different views about what affects the current and future situation of people and countries:

- ecological indicators cover life support by environmental services;
- indices of sustainable development combine environmental, social and economic dimensions of development;
- assessments of happiness and life satisfaction reflect personal impressions of being better (or worse) off.

11.2.1 Environmental quality

Table 11.1 puts together a large variety of diverse indicators and indices that aim at measuring the condition of the natural environment. The focus is here on the natural environment as a stand-alone issue of supporting human and non-human life. The extensive footnoting reveals problems of aggregating and comparing indicators that use different concepts, methods and units of measurement. Assessments of the sustainability of trends in environmental impacts are therefore inconclusive

What do the indicators tell us? **167**

and may even show contradictory outcomes. The main results, compiled in Part III and summarized in Table 11.1, include:

- land use statistics ranging from an average increase of 90 million ha in 2000 to an average overshoot of demand of 138 million ha by 2030;
- global ecological deficits of the Ecological Footprint that could double from eight billion ha in 2012 to 16 billion ha in the 2030s, requiring the biocapacity of one more earth;
- a decrease of renewable energy yield from 3.7 to 1.6 percent (1950–1995);
- CO_2 emission, a major factor in climate change, which would have to stay below 2900 gigatons at a cost of at least US$300 billion to prevent a global warming beyond 2°C;
- material flows, measured in tons, which need to be reduced by at least a factor of three to maintain year-2000 levels of consumption by 2050;
- the current transgression of three out of nine planetary boundaries;
- the value of natural capital, which increased by 11 percent during 1995–2005 according to the CWM and decreased by 0.2 percent during 1992–2010 according to the IWI;
- SEEA estimates that indicate global annual natural capital consumption of 3 percent of GDP in 1990 and over 6 percent in 2006.

Comparing the availability of natural assets with changes brought about by human use is the explicit objective of the Ecological Footprint. In 2012, a footprint of 20 billion ha on available biocapacity of 12 billion ha created a global ecological "deficit" of −8 billion ha. A business-as-usual scenario predicts that the area of impact will exceed the area of biocapacity in the 2030s by one planet, if there is no change in production and consumption patterns. In other words, the Ecological Footprint suggests that we are already acting unsustainably and will need another planet's capacity to meet our long-term needs and wants in about 15 years. Of course, it all depends on the validity of the footprint calculations and our ability to tackle the threat of losing nature's services through adaptive and innovative behavior (cf. section 12.2).

Other physical indicators of sustainability are even more questionable. Prospective land use estimates vary widely and cannot produce a clear indication of an unsustainable overuse or sustainable underuse of land. According to the UNEP (2014), food security could be impaired in the 2020s when demand for land-based products could no more be met by available cropland.

The one-time comparison of available energy with its use relies on controversial estimates of energy embodied (emergy) in produced and natural products. Depending on whether one looks at energy stores, flows or consumption, the shares of non-renewables over total energy stores and energy consumption vary considerably: from 20 percent to 68 percent and 93 percent, respectively. There is also no indication when we would run out of non-renewable energy resources.

TABLE 11.1 Global environmental impact and sustainability

	Use/impact	Ecological sustainability
Land		
• Land cover use (credit/deficit) by 2030 (billion ha)		+90 to −138[a]
• Ecological footprint (billion ha)	20.4[b]	−8 (2012); −16 (2030)[c]
• Ecological footprint, earths required (number)		1.6 (2012); 2 (2030s)[d]
Energy (solar joules)		
• Emergy renewables (%)	31.6[e]	
• Emergy non-renewables (%)	68.4[e]	3.7 (1950); 1.6 (1995)[f]
Carbon		
• Anthropogenic mass of CO_2 (gigatons)	1900[g]	1900 (2011) < 2900[j]
• Anthropogenic value of CO_2 (giga\$; % of consumption)	142.6[h]	336.6;[k] 1.4%[l]
• Carbon footprint (billion ha)	12.0[i]	
Material flows		
• material extraction (billion tons)	85[m]	Factors −3 to −5[n]
Ecosystems		
• Ecosystem services degraded (%)	60[o]	
• Biodiversity (%)	52[p]	
• Planetary boundaries transgressed (number)		3 (out of 9)[q]
Natural capital		
• Comprehensive wealth (%)		+11.3 (1995–2005)[r]
• Inclusive wealth (%)		−0.2 (1990–2010)[s]
• Natural capital consumption (%)	3.0[r]	−3.0 (1990); −6.1 (2006)[t]

Sources: indicated in the notes.

Notes

a With and without deforestation (Table 7.1).

b Ecological Footprint in 2012 = per capita footprint of 2.8 ha times population of 7.3 billion = 20.4 billion ha.

c Global ecological deficit in 2012 and the 2030s.

d Figure 7.1.

e Share of total emergy flows in 1995 (Table 6.8).

f Emergy yield ratio (total emergy output divided by use of non-renewables) (Brown and Ulgiati 1999, p. 490).

g CO_2 emission in 2011 (IPCC 2014b, Fig. SPM.5).

h Damage (social cost) in 2005 (World Bank 2011 and World Bank population data).

i In 2012 (2016 data package of the Global Footprint Network 2003–2017), about 59% of the ecological footprint.

j Limit of CO_2 emission to stay below 2 °C global warming (IPCC 2014, SPM.5).

k Maintenance cost in greened national accounts at $35/t of CO_2-eq, 2030 estimate for the 550 ppm IPCC stabilization goal by 2100 (Bartelmus 2009).

l Cost increase (% of consumption loss) from best scenario of 430–80 ppm CO_2eq (to keep global warming below 2 °C) and 530–80 ppm CO_2eq scenario (of about 4 °C global warming) (IPCC 2014a, Fig. 6.21).

m In 2013 (SERI et al. 2016).

n Business-as-usual scenario for annual resource reduction by industrialized countries to achieve sustainable resource use by 2050 (Table 7.2).

o Percent of ecosystem services degraded or used unsustainably (MEA 2005).

p Decline of vertebrate species measuring life sustainability (WWF et al. 2014).

q Planetary boundaries of climate change, biodiversity, nitrogen pollution (Rockström et al. 2009)

r Natural capital increase (World Bank 2011, Table 1.1) from 1995 to 2005 in 2005 prices.

s Negative contribution to inclusive wealth growth by natural capital in 2005 prices (UNEP and UNU-IHDP 2014, Appendix 1).

t Percent of GDP, at maintenance cost in 1990 and 2006 (Bartelmus 2009).

170 What should we do about it?

Climate change caused in particular by CO_2 emission is often taken as a surrogate for environmental decline. The reason is that carbon cycling through nature is deemed essential for the performance and maintenance of natural systems. Measures of carbon stocks and emission are therefore pulled out of broader accounts of

- ecosystems as part of their carbon cycle,
- energy and material flows as carbon inputs and CO_2 emissions, and
- the Ecological Footprint as a carbon footprint.

IPCC data of CO_2 emission in 2011 of 1900 gigatons indicate that we are still below the sustainability limit of 2900 gigatons for staying below a global warming of 2 °C. A doubling of ambient concentrations in a worst-case scenario from 550 ppm to about 1000 ppm in 2100 might bring about an increase to 5 °C. The IPCC also estimated that damage created by a 4 °C warming in the second half of the twenty-first century could amount to 1–5 percent of global GDP. Such a perspective does not look sustainable for the environment and possibly also for the economy if the economic effects of climate change can be realistically assessed. But where do we draw the policy line, considering also the large variations of scenarios and their data? The carbon footprint measures the land and sea area needed for absorbing CO_2 emissions. Apart from measurement problems it cannot reflect the severity and sustainability of environmental impacts in different regions.

If stock data are not available or are difficult to define, normative limits have to be set to determine tolerable environmental impacts and the sustainable use of environmental services. Policy makers could use "factors" of easier-to-aggregate material flows, limiting natural resource inputs into production and consumption. In this way they would seek to reduce pressure on the natural environment to a tolerable level. So far, most natural resource extraction took place in Asia, pointing to a burden shifting through natural resource imports by other regions from Asia. Natural resource consumption per capita tells therefore another story: the inhabitants of Oceania and USA are the highest (wasteful?) users of natural resources. It is, of course, not clear to what extent the pressure of material flows translates into total impact and non-sustainability, even if ecological economists claim that we have reached the limits of sustainable material throughput (Daly 1996).

Assessments of the instrumental value of nature in terms of its physical ecosystem services fail to find a common unit of measurement. Statements that 60 percent of ecosystems are degraded or used unsustainably or that some planetary boundaries are violated (section 7.2.2) do not carry much information about the global and national resilience of ecosystems to disturbances, i.e., ecological sustainability. Summary descriptions of the state and change of ecosystem services have to resort to qualitative evaluations like the up- and down-arrows of the Millennium Ecosystem Assessment (MEA 2005). For now at least, ecosystem assessments seem to be more useful at local levels, where the significance of particular conditions and impacts can be more clearly perceived and acted upon by concerned inhabitants.

Monetary valuation of natural assets could facilitate the aggregation of nature's services. Heroic attempts at finding a common monetary value suffer – admittedly (de Groot et al. 2012, pp. 56–9) – from hardly compatible valuation methods and data gaps. They may create awareness of ecosystem benefits and benefit losses but are not useful in integrating environmental-economic policies. Assuming substitutability of natural *capital* by other production factors, i.e., weak sustainability, makes a focus on the value of natural capital less relevant for assessing ecological sustainability.[4] Still, green accounting estimates (in current prices) for 1990–2006 present a considerable increase in global natural capital depreciation from 3 to 6 percent of global GDP. However, unlike the conventional national accounts, such green accounting is far from being accepted and implemented at the national level.

All indicators do point to a decline in environmental quality. The underlying assumptions and data gaps make the results difficult to compare. They generate questionable advice about what should be done and what it would cost. We see, perhaps surprisingly, some similarities in the regional distribution of the footprint and material consumption (Table 11.2). This could be an indication that the simpler measure of the weight of material flows could be used instead of assumption-laden global hectares of the Ecological Footprint. But there is hardly any correlation of physical impact in regions with their cost of natural capital consumption. It appears that economic evaluation of impacts seems to be inconsistent with physical measures of environmental quality.

11.2.2 Sustainable development

Development indices combine economic, environmental and social dimensions of human activity. They aim at defining a common notion of social progress. Limits

TABLE 11.2 Regional distribution of environmental impacts (%)

	Ecological Footprint (2012)	Material consumption (2010)	Natural capital consumption (2006)
Africa	7.4	7.0	10.3
Asia and the Pacific	51.2	58.5	39.3
thereof: China	29.3	33.3	11.2
Latin America	8.6	11.2	12.9
Europe	12.3[a]	11.2	4.1[a]
Other industrialized countries[b]	20.5	12.1	33.4
thereof: USA	13.2	8.9	10.4
WORLD	100	100	100

Sources: Ecological Footprint: Global Footprint Network (2003–2017); material flows: www.material-flows.net (2016); natural capital consumption: Bartelmus (2009, Table 7.4).

Notes
a EU-27.
b Including transition economies.

172 What should we do about it?

in providing the benefits of the different dimensions are obstacles in attaining development goals. In theory, minimum limits of attaining needs and wants could be confronted with the maximum availability of resources in a feasibility space for human activities. Such a space could assess the possibilities of implementing constrained development (cf. section 7.2.2).

Difficulties of assessing all dimensions and limits prompted the search for surrogate development measures to avoid arbitrary weighting and aggregation. Income and its easier to measure gross version of domestic product (GDP) are often tacitly interpreted as indicators of development. In contrast, environmentalists assume that the natural environment is providing essential life support; they also see environmental quality as a key ingredient of the quality of human life and a prerequisite of sustainable development. Inequity in the distribution of income and wealth is the motivation for focusing on the social dimension of development. All these measures ignore the other dimensions as well as further political, cultural and ethical concerns.

Nonetheless, the popular Brundtland definition of sustainable development seeks to combine fragmented development policies, referring to meeting human needs and their satisfaction now and in the future. The focus is on intra- and intergenerational equity in meeting the needs. Despite looking for a "global agenda for change" (WCED 1987, p. ix) the report does not suggest compiling an overall measure for development.

Arbitrariness in indicator selection and methodological simplifications enter actual attempts of aggregating indicators into indices. In the end, the indices usually just rank countries by index scores, sometimes presenting correlations among their ranks. However, no clear correlation could be found in these ranks (Table 10.1). Nor do changes in Millennium Development Goals (MDG) achievements provide an overall picture of development (Tables 10.2 and 10.3). Changes in the number of people living below "poverty lines" are sometimes taken as a surrogate for unacceptable levels of development.

The validity of changes in income (often replaced by easier-to-measure GDP per capita) and poverty as surrogates can be examined by comparing their trends with more comprehensive indices such as the Human Development Index (HDI). Table 11.3 shows that, except for Africa's sub-Saharan region, economic growth (GDP per capita) is considerably higher than (human) development during 1990–2015. Health and education effects of extreme poverty in the sub-Saharan region may have offset gains in output and income. South Asia experienced the most dramatic surpassing of human development by economic growth. There is no denying that poverty decreased in all regions. The fall of poverty is particularly dramatic in East Asia and the Pacific. In contrast sub-Saharan Africa has made relatively little progress in alleviating poverty.

What do these development trends mean for the sustainability of development? A choice of a sustainability level of 0.7 in the HDI would include East Asia, Latin America and Europe/Central Asia; raising the level to 0.8 would exclude all regions but would include countries classified as enjoying "very high human development" (cf. section 10.2.1). A rapid rise in index scores indicates that countries like China

TABLE 11.3 Global and regional development (1990 = 100)

	HDI (index score)[a]	GDP per capita (2010 US $)[a]	Poverty decrease[b]
South Asia	142	292	295
East Asia and Pacific	140	220	1720
Sub-Saharan Africa	131	132	132
Arab states[c]	124	154	214[d]
Latin America & Caribbean	120	150	293
Europe and Central Asia	116	141	174[e]
WORLD	120	143	327

Sources: HDI: UNDP (2016, statistical annex, Table 2); GDP per capita: World Bank (2017); poverty: World Bank (2016, Table 2A.2).

Notes
a 1900–2015.
b Decrease in the number of people below poverty line of $1.9/day (1990–2013).
c Middle East and North Africa.
d 1990–2008.
e Eastern Europe and Central Asia.

and Russia might be on their way to attaining sustainability, provided their rise does not falter in the future. Measuring changes in "shortfalls," i.e., the distance from the maximum possible HDI level of 1 (UNDP 2015, p. 60), is an alternative for assessing sustainability: Europe/Central Asia and the sub-Saharan region show the lowest shortfall decrease of 28 percent and 20 percent, respectively, while East Asia seems to converge with developed regions showing the highest decrease of shortfalls by 40 percent. The shortfalls apply, however, to highly different levels of development, which obscures the meaning of shortfall levels when it comes to assessing the welfare of people.

If we take reaching key development goals as a measure of sustainability the reduction of world poverty might point to sustainability. The MDG report indicates that by 2015 the number of people living below US$1.25 per day was halved. Furthermore, the incidence of major diseases was reversed, and the number of hungry people and those lacking drinking water and sanitation are approaching the MDG (Table 10.3). The question is whether we can take MDG achievements as a true measure of diminishing inter-generational equity and lasting sustainability of multi-dimensional development. For instance, an explosive rise of inequality might be on the horizon if returns to capital continue to increase (section 3.3). In fact, looking into further development goals and targets makes for a rather pessimistic picture of attaining the goals and sustainability. Mitigating extreme poverty is an important development goal, but it is not development that would apply to countries at any stage of prosperity.

It seems that the absence of an agreed concept and valid data for overall sustainable development confirms the question of section 10.3: the sustainability of

174 What should we do about it?

development, now and in the future, has indeed run its course. Rather than promoting a broader concept of development, the indicators and indices of sustainable development reveal their shortcomings. It comes as no surprise that decision makers continue to use income or output as the main determinants of socioeconomic performance and development.

11.2.3 Wellbeing and happiness

Looking beyond economic prosperity led to exploring the benefits of the natural environment. Sustainable development goes further. It seeks to meet most of our present and future needs and wants, including those that economic growth cannot deliver. Sustainable development might therefore reveal whether we are and will indeed be "better off." In practice, any number of indicators has been used to assess such development in the hope that together they might reflect the social welfare and perhaps even the happiness of people.

Stocks and flows of wealth and welfare measure wellbeing at a point in time and over a period of time, respectively. The state and flow of wellbeing is, however, not always clearly distinguished when combining the indicators and policy responses. For assessing the sustainability of wellbeing, the assumption is that consecutive happiness surveys provide a picture of lasting average life satisfaction and social welfare. Boulding (1966) is one of the few scholars who distinguishes clearly between stock and flow measures. He prefers assessing the mostly ignored *state* aspect of human welfare. Apart from the fact that eating might also give us pleasure and perhaps even more than having a full stomach, a feeling of wellbeing is obviously more difficult to quantify than the actions and material conditions that create it (see section 4.1).

Happiness surveys ask people about the satisfaction with their lives over a past period or about their happiness just before the surveys are taken. The purpose is to capture all the material and non-material benefits that contribute to satisfaction and happiness. Unfortunately objective and judgmental factors of wellbeing and welfare are often mixed up in overlapping sets of objective and subjective indicators. The results of happiness surveys are therefore volatile and confusing.

Some surveys show Latin America as a particularly happy region. Most agree – unsurprisingly – that very poor countries, notably in sub-Saharan Africa have little to be happy about. Attempts at linking happiness to different levels and stages of development do not seem to succeed, though. For example, no significant correlation could be found between Gallup's Global Wellbeing Index and UNDP's HDI. Nor does the ranking of regions provide a significant connection between wellbeing and the development of world regions. At best the ranks indicate the obvious: fairly rich world regions tend to have relatively content populations, whereas the poorest sub-Saharan region includes rather unhappy ones.

Available data do not confirm the Easterlin paradox, i.e., a connection between stagnating happiness and increasing down-to-earth measures of the consumption and use of economic and non-economic goods and services. Long-lasting happiness cannot be quantified unless one assumes that development goals lend themselves to correctly measuring the conditions for individual and national happiness. Mixing subjective and objective indicators in aggregate indices is not a valid method of capturing both development and welfare. The setting of sustainability standards for happiness such as an increase by 1.5 percent during a lengthy period of time, or attaining top happiness ranks make the assessment of wellbeing and happiness even more arbitrary. All this seems to confirm a suspicion expressed in a previous publication (Bartelmus 2013, p. 124) that "we believe more than we believe."

11.3 Summary and evaluation

The question remains if and how the limited knowledge about the effects of economic and non-economic behavior and policies can be combined to assess progress and formulate and evaluate policy responses. The variety of indices, differing in contents, unit of measurement and validity, makes a comprehensive quantifiable assessment near-impossible. Nonetheless, Table 11.4 risks a qualitative assessment by a very subjective interpretation of the levels and trends of the indicators and indices. The reader could easily come to different conclusions.

Economic prosperity in terms of personal income and wealth increased globally and regionally. However, its distribution tends to be concentrated in the hands of the rich. The well-defined and quantifiable measure of green growth, ECF, indicates a non-sustainable performance in the developing countries of Africa, Asia and Latin America. Future economic sustainability is rather uncertain, given the difficulty of predicting technological progress and policies. The cost of maintaining natural capital for sustaining the generation of income and wealth remains comparatively low (compared to GDP) in Europe and North America but is relatively high and increasing in the other regions. This might be the result of environmental burden shifting by industrialized nations on to developing ones.

Looking beyond economic performance and its sustainability leads into the life-supporting natural environment. Unfortunately, one does not have here the advantage of money as a common denominator for a systematic and comprehensive accounting of changes in environmental quality. The physical indicators of the Ecological Footprint, the carbon footprint and natural resource consumption show increasing environmental impact, globally and in world regions. Oceania (part of Asia/Pacific) and the USA (part of North America) are the most wasteful users of natural resources, possibly because the resources are abundant in their regions. The picture looks better in terms of cropland changes, which increased in developing regions. Again, the data allow no final conclusions about future sustainability of environmental services.

The human development version of development points to some progress in most regions, except sub-Saharan Africa. Setting sustainability limits or goals for human development is rather arbitrary, though. A surrogate index of the number of people living below poverty lines shows progress in this regard. The ultimate

176 What should we do about it?

TABLE 11.4 Indicators and indices – summary results

	Global results	Regional results				
		Africa	Asia-Pacific	Europe	Latin America	North America
Prosperity						
Income and wealth	↑	↗	↗	↑	↗	↑
Distribution of income and wealth	↘	↓	↘	↘	↘	↓[a]
Economic sustainability[b]	↘	↓	↘[c]	→[d]	↘	↗[a]
Environmental quality						
Ecological deficit	↘	→	↘	↘[e]	↑	↓
Carbon Footprint	↓	↘	↓	↓	↘	↓[a]
Cropland change	↗	↗	↑[c]	↓[d]	↑[f]	↘
Material consumption	↘	→	↓	↘	↘	↘
Ecological sustainability	↓	→	↓	↓	↗	↓
Development						
HDI[g]	↑	↘[i]	↑	↑[j]	↑	→
Poverty reduction[h]	↗	↗[i]	↗	→[j]	↗	→
Global wellbeing index	n.a.	↓[i]	↘	↗[j]	↑	
Summary evaluation	↘	↓	↘	→	↗	↘

Notes
a USA.
b ECF.
c Developing countries only.
d Positive ECF in EU-25; negative ECF in transition economies.
e EU-27.
f Excluding Central America and the Caribbean.
g Achievement level for 1990–2014.
h Percent of people below poverty lines 1990–2012.
i Sub-Saharan Africa.
j Europe and Central Asia.
↑ strong improvement, ↗ weak improvement, → no significant change, ↘ weak deterioration, ↓ strong deterioration.

goal of development is of course wellbeing, if not happiness, of a country's people. The fact that such a state of feeling good is hardly quantifiable shows up in widely differing regional results. There are no useful indicators for an overall assessment of development and its sustainability in the past and for the future, nationally and globally. Sustainable development has indeed run its course, at least as far as its measurement is concerned.

All in all, Table 11.4 conveys a rather gloomy answer to the question of whether we are better off. Despite being a developing region, the situation seems to improve in Latin America. Europe looks rather stable. All other regions experienced deteriorating conditions, in particular in sub-Saharan Africa, but also in the USA (as part of North America) if non-economic measures are included. However, the overall evaluation of the conditions of world regions and the globe is obviously based on a personal evaluation of the up- and down-arrows in the table.

Figure 11.2 looks into the future with more or less established indicators. The figure seems to confirm the gloomy outlook when looking beyond GDP. The projections of output and welfare and its environmental detraction (in terms of the original Ecological Footprint) are highly uncertain, though. Data gaps are pasted over (interpolated) and business-as-usual scenarios are just one kind of different projections that could be based on different assumptions, notably about responsive policies. It appears that only economic growth, measured by GDP in constant purchasing power parities, will continue till the end of the century. Is it possible that the cherished economic indicator of progress is misleading?

The decline of the Ecological Footprint when based on the business-as-usual scenario of the LTG model is not really an improvement because it is based on the collapse of the economy in this scenario. The loss of human welfare, represented by a somewhat modified HDI in the LTG model, reflects this collapse. On its own, the Ecological Footprint is in fact forecast to increase with a similar speed as that of GDP. The next chapter will explore what this gloominess means for policies of the sustainability of society and its economic activity.

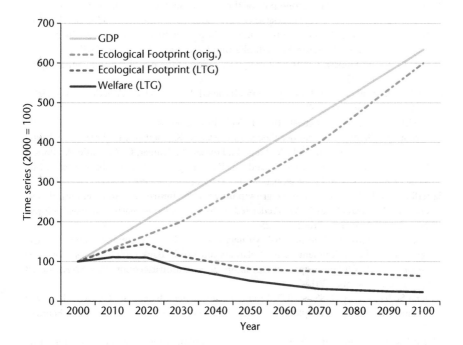

FIGURE 11.2 Will we be better off? A scissor movement between the trends of GDP and human welfare points to a disconnect between economic growth and human welfare. The latter is affected in particular by environmental decline measured by the Ecological Footprint

178 What should we do about it?

Notes

1 As discussed in Section 4.2.2 and contrary to the original version (United Nations 1993), the revised version of the SEEA (United Nations et al. 2014) largely ignores environmental externalities, notably from pollution; it includes as a cost of production only the depletion of (economic) natural resources.
2 The semi-log scale compresses the far-apart values of wealth, welfare and domestic product in a compact presentation and makes growth rates at different indicator levels comparable.
3 The national accounts stress that GDP does not measure welfare (European Commission et al. 2009, para. 1.75); nor is it the objective of the greened accounts and their indicators.
4 Data on the change in value of natural assets, compiled by the World Bank (2011) and UNEP and UNU-IHDP (2014) are not comparable (cf. section 6.1.2); they are also contradictory, with the former pointing to an increase and the latter to a decrease in the value of natural capital (in constant prices).

References

Bartelmus, P. (2009). The cost of natural capital consumption: accounting for a sustainable world economy, *Ecological Economics*, 68: 1850–7.

Bartelmus, P. (2013). *Sustainability Economics: An Introduction*, London and New York: Routledge.

Boulding, K.E. (1966). The economics of the coming spaceship earth, in H. Jarret (ed.), *Environmental Quality in a Growing Economy*, Baltimore, MD: Johns Hopkins Press for Resources for the Future: 3–14. Online: http://arachnid.biosci.utexas.edu/courses/THOC/Readings/Boulding_SpaceshipEarth.pdf (accessed 29 October 2017).

Brown, M.T. and Ulgiati, S. (1999). Emergy valuation of the biosphere and natural capital, *Ambio* 28: 486–93.

Cobb, C., Halstead, T. and Rowe, J. (1995). If the GDP is up, why is America down? *Atlantic Monthly*, October: 59–78.

Daly, H.E. (1996). *Beyond Growth*, Boston, MA: Beacon Press.

De Groot, R., Brander, L., van der Ploeg, S., Costanza, R., Bernard, F., Braat, L., Christie, M., Crossman, N., Ghermandi, A., Hein, L., Hussain, S., Kumar, P., McVittie, A., Portela, R., Rodriguez, L.C., ten Brink, P. and van Beukering, P. (2012). Global estimate of the value of ecosystems and their services in monetary units, *Ecosystem Services* 1: 50–61.

Easterlin, R. (1974). Does economic growth improve the human lot? Some empirical evidence, in P.A. David and M.W. Reder (eds.), *Nations and Households in Economic Growth*, New York: Academic Press: 89–125.

European Commission, International Monetary Fund, Organisation for Economic Co-operation and Development, United Nations and World Bank (2009). *System of National Accounts 2008*. Online: http://unstats.un.org/unsd/nationalaccount/docs/SNA2008.pdf (accessed 29 October 2017).

General Social Survey (GSS) (2017). Data explorer, general happiness, Chicago, IL: Norc. Online: https://gssdataexplorer.norc.org/variables/434/vshow (accessed 9 February 2017).

Global Footprint Network (2003–2017). Data and methodology. Online: www.footprint-network.org/resources/data/ (accessed 27 March 2017).

Intergovernmental Panel on Climate Change (IPCC) (2014a). Climate change 2014: mitigation of climate change. Online: www.ipcc.ch/report/ar5/wg3 (accessed 6 October 2017).

Intergovernmental Panel on Climate Change (IPCC) (2014b). *Synthesis Report*, Geneva: IPCC. Online: www.ipcc.ch/pdf/assessment-report/ar5/syr/SYR_AR5_FINAL_full_wcover.pdf (accessed 11 March 2017).

Max-Neef, M. (1995). Economic growth and quality of life: a threshold hypothesis, *Ecological Economics* 15: 115–18.

Meyer, B. and Ahlert, G. (2016). Imperfect markets and the properties of macro-economic-environmental models as tools for policy evaluation, GWS Discussion Paper no. 2016/09, in cooperation with GWS – Institute of Economic Structures Research, Osnabrück. Online: www.econstor.eu/bitstream/10419/156303/1/875724574.pdf (accessed 3 February 2018).

Millennium Ecosystem Assessment (MEA) (2005). *Ecosystems and Human Well-being: Synthesis*, Washington, DC: Island Press. Online: www.unep.org/maweb/documents/document.356.aspx.pdf (accessed 19 October 2017).

Nordhaus, W.D. and Tobin, J. (1973). Is growth obsolete? *Studies in Income and Wealth* 38: 509–64. Online: www.nber.org/chapters/c3621.pdf (accessed 21 March 2017).

Piketty, T. (2014). *Capital in the Twenty-first Century*, Cambridge, MA and London: Belknap Press of Harvard University Press.

Rockström, J., Steffen. W., Noone, K., Persson, Å., Chapin III, F.S., Lambin, E., Lenton, T.M., Scheffer, M., Folke, C., Schellnhuber, H.J., Nykvist, B., de Wit, C.A., Hughes, T., van der Leeuw, S., Rodhe, H., Sörlin, S., Snyder, P.K., Costanza, R., Svedin, U., Falkenmark, M., Karlberg, L., Corell, R.W., Fabry, V.J., Hansen, J., Walker, B., Liverman, D., Richardson, K., Crutzen, P. and Foley, J. (2009). Planetary boundaries: exploring the safe operating space for humanity, *Ecology and Society* 14 (2): ART. 32. Online: www.ecologyandsociety.org/vol. 14/iss2/art32/ (accessed 29 October 2017).

Sustainable Europe Research Institute (SERI), WU, Ifeu, Wuppertal Institute (2016). www.materialflows.net, The online portal for material flow data. Online: www.materialflows.net/trends/analyses-1980-2013/shares-of-global-material-extraction-by-world-region-1980-2013/ (accessed 6 August 2017).

Talberth, J., Cobb, C. and Slattery, N. (2007). *The Genuine Progress Indicator 2006: A Tool for Sustainable Development*, Oakland, CA: Redefining Progress. Online: www.scribd.com/doc/3061355/Genuine-Progress-Indicator-2006 (accessed 6 October 2017).

United Nations, European Commission, Food and Agriculture Organization of the United Nations, International Monetary Fund, Organisation for Economic Co-operation and Development and World Bank Group (2014). *System of Environmental-Economic Accounting 2012: Central Framework*. New York: United Nations. Online: http://unstats.un.org/unsd/envaccounting/seeaRev/SEEA_CF_Final_en.pdf (accessed 19 March 2017).

United Nations Development Programme (UNDP) (2015). *United Nations Development Report 2015*, New York: UNDP. Online: http://hdr.undp.org/sites/default/files/2015_human_development_report.pdf (accessed 6 October 2017).

United Nations Development Programme (UNDP) (2016). *United Nations Development Report 2016*, New York: UNDP. Online: http://hdr.undp.org/sites/default/files/2016_human_development_report.pdf (accessed 15 September 2017).

United Nations Environment Programme (UNEP) (2014). *Global Environmental Outlook 6*. Online: www.unep.org/geo/ (accessed 3 October 2017).

United Nations Environment Programme (UNEP) and UNU-IHDP (2012). *Inclusive Wealth Report 2012: Measuring Progress Toward Sustainability*, Cambridge: Cambridge University Press.

180 What should we do about it?

United Nations Environment Programme (UNEP) and UNU-IHDP (2014). *Inclusive Wealth Report 2014: Measuring Progress Toward Sustainability*, Cambridge: Cambridge University Press.

World Bank (2011). *The Changing Wealth of Nations: Measuring Sustainable Development in the New Millennium*, Washington, DC: World Bank. Online: http://siteresources.worldbank.org/ENVIRONMENT/Resources/ChangingWealthNations.pdf (accessed 1 September 2017).

World Bank (2015). Data, GDP growth (annual %). Online: http://data.worldbank.org/indicator/NY.GDP.MKTP.KD.ZG (accessed 22 June 2015).

World Bank (2016). *Poverty and Prosperity 2016: Taking on Inequality*, Washington, DC. Online: https://openknowledge.worldbank.org/bitstream/handle/10986/25078/9781464809583.pdf (accessed 28 September 2017).

World Bank (2017). Data. Online: https://data.worldbank.org/indicator/NY.GDP.PCAP.KD?locations=ZJ (accessed 18 November 2017).

World Commission on Environment and Development (WCED) (1987). *Our Common Future*, Oxford: Oxford University Press.

World Wide Fund for Nature (WWF), Zoological Society of London and Global Footprint Network, Water Footprint Network (2014) *Living Planet Report 2014*, Gland: WWF. Online: http://assets.worldwildlife.org/publications/723/files/original/WWF-LPR2014-low_res.pdf?1413912230&_ga=2.226225306.1267642552.1502114198-1951564079.1444570768 (accessed 7 August 2017).

www.materialflows.net (2016). The online portal to material flow data. Online: www.materialflows.net/data/data-download/ (accessed 6 October 2017).

12

STRATEGIES, POLICIES, POLITICS

A topic as broad as this could easily fill a separate volume. This chapter presents just broad strokes of options following from the evaluation of facts and figures in the preceding chapters. Details of how actual policies could be formulated and combined under different circumstances in countries are left – reluctantly – to further reading and research. However, the chapter might motivate decision makers to base the evaluation and strategies of sustainability on facts and figures rather than proclamations of judgmental policy goals.

The picture painted in Chapter 11 might be gloomy; but is it accurate enough to help formulate rational responses? The summary evaluation of a bewildering variety of up- and down-arrows in Table 11.4 indicates that any assessment of a deteriorating world is bound to be, at least partially, subjective. It could be the basis for ethical visions of the future, as discussed in section 12.1. Rather than supporting a unified approach the reality is that different visions contribute to a further diversification of approaches. Section 12.2 examines therefore this reality by "muddling-through" the worst symptoms of economic, environmental and developmental non-sustainability. Section 12.3 looks for possibilities of policy integration and settles for a more systematic, albeit narrow, integration with the help of an expanded national accounts system. Section 12.4 discusses globalization and global governance, an issue that has not been explicitly addressed.

12.1 From vision to mission

The threat of natural and human-made disasters could change our values and priorities. This seems to have happened in the wake of relatively new assessments of the depletion of natural resources, pollution and global warming. The first chapter examined these threats, asking what might be wrong with our planet.

182 What should we do about it?

The environmental movement draws on loosely documented convictions such as a "pre-analytic vision" (Daly 1996, pp. 6, 218; Røpke 2005, pp. 216, 217). It found an exponentially increasing world population which transgressed the carrying capacity of the planet. Only a radical change of our hearts and minds (Adams 2006, p. 14), dominated by economic objectives, would assure sustainability and survival. Suggestions to this end range from finding a symbiotic balance between the biotic and abiotic environment to pursuing the "good life" with changed lifestyles for healing the environment (cf. section 8.1.1). Much of these values are packed into the all-encompassing paradigm of sustainable development.

The ecocentric *gaia* hypothesis believes that the earth's self-regulating ability will offset any human disturbances of nature in the long run. Aware of the threat of global human-made environmental impact, notably of global warming, the *gaia* author (Lovelock 2009) still considers such warming as just a warning to adapt to a hotter face and other deteriorations of the earth. The fittest of the human population would find a way to survive. This ecocentric view appears to believe "that the welfare of *gaia* is more important than the welfare of humankind" (ibid., p. 22).

The ecological balance (homeostasis) could be broken, though, by extreme impacts, threatening human and non-human survival (e.g. Kirchner 2002). An anthropocentric view of attaining lasting wellbeing or at least some satisfaction with one's life takes an active stand therefore. Different visions of changes in lifestyle and corresponding consumption, on one hand, and "responsible" production, on the other hand, can be found to this end.

Sufficiency is the answer to greed and "conspicuous consumption" (Veblen 1967/1899; Frank 1999). The rewards of a simpler and frugal good life would be physical wellbeing and spiritual gratification from solidarity with the world's poor and future generations (Segal 1999; Sachs 1995). Sufficiency seeks to meet human needs, but would restrict consumption deemed to be excessive. More specifically, Sachs (2015) calls for decelerating the speed in our lifestyles, regionalizing production and consumption as opposed to globalizing them, and reorienting households and enterprises towards the common good rather than individual prosperity.

But where are the borderlines of rightful consumption and dutiful frugality? Frugality and moderation have been preached since ancient times without much success. On the other hand, unfettered greed has indeed been the cause for the 2008 economic crisis. Self-interest has also been the engine of unprecedented economic growth, at least in industrialized countries. Who in fact should monitor and control overinvestment and overconsumption? Do we really want – often contradicting – governments, churches and activists to determine what is good for us? Can a democratic grassroots movement weight individual preferences and find a convincing answer (O'Donnell and Oswald 2015)?

The focus of enterprises is profit maximization. It may therefore be surprising that a growing number of corporations seems to subscribe to "corporate social responsibility," possibly in response to calls by international organizations (Crook 2005).[1] Corporate environmental accountants (Gray and Bebbington 2007) are skeptical: despite their sustainability rhetoric, corporations are bound to be accountable to shareholders rather than stakeholders. In reality, caring about stakeholders might work only in times of high profits or for purposes of corporate image building. Still, environmentalists call for going beyond corporate social responsibility with a "new business model" of creating social and environmental value in addition to economic profit (Dietz and O'Neill 2013, p. 148).

The World Business Council for Sustainable Development (no date), a coalition of over 200 international companies, nonetheless coined "eco-efficiency" as an effective environmental strategy of enterprises. Essentially, eco-efficiency is a matter of environmentally sound technology that allows continuing or even increasing economic output with less environmental impact. A more ambitious version of eco-efficiency is "metabolic consistency" (Huber 2004), sometimes propagated under the label of "biomimicry" (Biomimicry Institute 2017). Metabolic consistency ensures that production and consumption are in harmony with nature's metabolism. Such harmony would result in zero emission since nature supposedly does not generate any waste.[2] The Zero Emissions Research and Initiative (ZERI 2013) believes that fully reusing or recycling any waste and pollutants in production can change the mindsets that dominate markets; poverty alleviation and sustainability would be the result. Cradle-to-cradle design of production caters to similar objectives but is probably overoptimistic in vying for the "transformation" of cradle-to-grave economics (Braungart et al. 2007).

At the macro-economic level, sufficiency in production and consumption was invoked by calling for a "steady-state economy" (Daly 1996, p. 31). Such an economy would keep the use of natural resources within ecological capacity limits. Decoupling resource consumption from economic gross domestic product (GDP) growth would attain a desirable qualitative development rather than conventional quantitative growth of the economy. A long list of prescriptions including limiting material throughput and reforming demographic and economic policies might change the destructive ways of humans (Dietz and O'Neill 2013).

A relatively new environmental ethics underlies these approaches. Environmental ethics recognizes an intrinsic value of nature and its biota; it does not necessarily depend on human values such as frugality (Elliot 2001). Nature's values might call for returning to original pristine conditions as invoked by the *gaia* philosophy. More human-oriented approaches stress human rights of access to and equity in the distribution of nature's resources and benefits (Tolba 2001, Chs. 2.10–2.25).

The question is how these visions can be implemented or at least promoted. "Sustainability science" seeks to address the interaction of nature and society by discussing local limits and planetary boundaries, networking and fund raising (Kates et al. 2001). "Ontological, methodological and epistemological" sustainability assessment would bring together the vast fields of sustainability science (Sala et al. 2015). Sustainability science would therefore be based on values and principles that may include a holistic approach, intergenerational equity and good governance. However, such generics and its "subjective and normative dimensions" (ibid., p. 316) do not look very promising for implementation. Bénabou and Tirole (2016, pp. 141, 142) point out that "motivated beliefs and reasoning" can offset accuracy

184 What should we do about it?

in people's arguments when it comes to exploring international behavior. Relatively soft instruments of moral suasion, education and information could facilitate, though, the acceptance of stronger policies. But soft instruments are probably not very effective for radically changing our values, lifestyles and institutions.

Thaler and Sunstein (2008, 2009) seem to think that such radicalization is neither desirable nor possible, at least in democratic societies like the USA. They get this impression from their (Nobel-prize-winning) introduction of human irrationality into economic decision making. They argue that a "libertarian paternalism" could change people's decision without affecting their freedom of choice; a "nudge" from civil society or government would be enough to make people realize what is good for them. The questions are, though, whether small changes can really bring about long-term sustainability of economic growth or development; and who can guarantee that "mild paternalism" does not derail into autocratic rule?

12.2 Muddling through: piecemeal solutions

Internationally agreed development goals provide pieces of a mosaic that we have not (yet) learned to piece together. Diverse policies are listed together in this mosaic but are mostly applied on their own. The evaluation of Millennium Development Goals (MDG) achievements (Table 10.3) shows successes only in the reduction of poverty and hunger, control of HIV/AIDS and malaria, and improvement of slums. More recent strategies of the Sustainable Development Goals (SDG) suggest "early steps for collaboration among stakeholders at local, national and international levels" (Sustainable Development Solutions Network 2015). "Public-private partnership," touted by the 2002 World Summit on Sustainable Development (United Nations 2003), was watered down into a "registry of voluntary initiatives" (United Nations Sustainable Development Knowledge Platform, no date-b). Obviously, these approaches cannot deliver an overall vision and integrated action plan.

Section 10.3 found that the sustainable development concept has become quite irrelevant. The paradigm might have taken on too much. It appears that its main objective, the integration of economic and environmental concerns in decision making (WCED 1987, p. 62) failed not only in its vision but also in its policy mission. Chapter 11 examined what the available indicators tell us about sustaining social progress. The large variety of data for assessing prosperity, environmental quality, development and wellbeing made it necessary to resort to arrows (Table 11.4) when assessing global and regional results. Overall, the situation looks gloomy (section 11.3), except perhaps for Latin American and European countries.

This section explores to what extent tackling different symptoms of economic, environmental and social decline can help address our national and global priority concerns. Section 12.3 will address the possibilities of policy integration. Table 12.1 looks into the different policy responses to the indicators underlying Table 11.4.[3]

The broadest comprehensive but correspondingly vague notion of wellbeing calls for replacing traditional religious values, which promise happiness in the afterlife, by promoting a new secular ethics. The purpose is to increase wellbeing or

TABLE 12.1 Policy responses to selected indicators

	Global result[a]	Policy responses
Wellbeing		
World Happiness Report	n.a.	• New secular ethics, promoted by non-governmental organizations
Development		
Human development index	↑	• Awareness of development concerns beyond economic growth; policies left to countries • Focus on human capital (health and education)
Development goals	↗	• Development goals and conventions, focusing on poverty alleviation (e.g., MDG and SDG); policies left to countries • Official development assistance (0.7% of GNI) – agreed, but implemented only in five countries
Environmental quality		
Ecological deficit (Ecological Footprint)	↘	• No concrete policy recommendation beyond calls for reducing the Ecological Footprint and warnings about non-sustainability
Cropland change	↗	• Agricultural intensification, land use zoning, harnessing globalization
Carbon Footprint	↓	• Global cooperation (conventions), e.g., IPPC adhortations to reduce greenhouse gas emissions • Adaptation and mitigation: technology (low-carbon energy, carbon storage), sustainable production and consumption (market instruments, rules and regulations)
Material consumption	↘	• Dematerialization of the economy: increasing resource productivity
Prosperity		
Income and wealth	↑	• No global policy, but global personal wealth has doubled since 2000 • Regional and national development aid to improve the low income-and-wealth situation in Africa and India
Environmentally adjusted economic indicators	↘	• No global policy based on green accounting indicators • So far, no explicit environmental-accounts-based cost internalization by economic agents
Distribution of income and wealth	↘	• Redistribution of income and wealth (e.g., by taxation), implemented to a different degree in all regions and countries

Note

a Arrows represent the global results of indicators in Table 11.4.

186 What should we do about it?

happiness now or very soon as it is believed to be "the proper measure of social progress and the goal of public policy" (Helliwell et al. 2017, p. 3). As discussed in section 12.1 consensus on such ethics is elusive, even for limited environmental concerns and behavior. Asking people about their individual wellbeing (as in the Gallup polls) might deliver a global wellbeing index as an answer that is derived from ad-hoc expressions of personal feelings. But seeking more objective measures as in the cases of the Better Life Index, the Genuine Progress Indicator or Gross National Happiness quickly leads to long lists of difficult-to-combine indicators (cf. Chapter 8).

How then can social progress be promoted if one does not want to rely on ethical admonition? The hearts and minds of people might be open to moral advice but its diversity makes recommendations rather inconclusive. This book avoids discussing philosophical arguments and leaves the promotion of ethical norms to politics and advocacy by non-governmental organizations.

A multitude of indicators shows up when reducing the search for a better life to sustainable development or just environmental quality. Short or long lists of concerns, goals and indicators focus policy on particular issues. For example, the Human Development Index (HDI) deals with education, health and income, and the 17 goals and 169 targets of the SDG spread themselves over disparate concerns shared to a different degree by most countries. In both cases different suggestions for policies and managerial actions emerge.

Development indices like the HDI turn the attention to human capital, but the index was also used as a welfare measure in the limits-to-growth model (see section 5.1.2). The HDI is probably the most popular practical measure of development. However, its combination, and in particular overlap, of health, education and income indicators is questionable. The different indicators might therefore be more useful on their own for formulating particular policies. Poverty alleviation among countries is often taken as the main objective of the development of poor nations. It is reflected in international agreement on allocating 0.7 percent of the gross national income (GNI) of industrialized countries to financial development assistance (OECD 2016), indicating some responsibility for supporting poor countries. Only a few (Scandinavian nations and the United Kingdom) have so far met the 0.7 percent of the GNI "reference" target of official development assistance. Other development indices seem to be content with assessing the development situation, shying away from giving index-based policy advice.

A multitude of strategies and more managerial actions characterize environmental policies. There is no overall index that could deliver a commonly accepted picture of environmental objectives and policy responses. The Ecological Footprint calls for reducing natural resource consumption and emission of CO_2. It raises awareness of and advocacy for reducing environmental decline by its ecological deficit. Its policy relevance can be questioned because of its methodological flaws and a lack of concrete policy recommendations. In particular, the index does not address the differing significance of spatial policies of land use, infrastructure, trade and transport (van den Bergh and Grazi 2013).

Surrogates for environmental decline are more narrowly designed to account for a particular problem deemed to be "representative" of environmental change. To tackle climate change the Intergovernmental Panel on Climate Change (IPCC) sends out regular exhortations to limit greenhouse gas emissions in all countries for keeping global warming since the nineteenth century below 2°C. A particular "representative concentration pathway" (RCP 6.0) projects what it takes to keep global warming under the 2°C threshold. Its recommendations include an array of policies and institutional changes related to development, innovation and investment, and behavioral choices to adapt to or mitigate climate change (IPCC 2014). Countries agreed to keep global warming below 2°C in the 2015 Paris Climate Agreement. However, the prospects of succeeding look dim now after the rejection of this agreement by the USA. Alternatively, land use policies of intensifying agricultural production in limited land areas and introducing environmentally friendly land zones are suggested to deal with land degradation as a key environmental concern (Lambin and Meyfroidt 2011).

A strategy of decoupling the flows of material inputs and expected environmental impacts from economic growth could set out from simple measures of the total mass (weight) of natural resource use and emissions. Even if such dematerialization measures are quite removed from the effects of environmental depletion and degradation, an international resource panel, established by UNEP (2011), justifies the strategy as being essential for sustainable development and human wellbeing. The objective is to reverse the trends of growing resource extraction and environmental decline by policies of resource substitution and reduction. "Significant changes in government policies, corporate behaviour and consumption patterns" (ibid., p. xiv) would be needed, sometimes expressed by rather subjective "factors" or targets (cf. section 7.2). Presenting material flows and its pressures as physical growth (see section 6.2.1), correlated with economic (GDP) growth, might justify delinking the two types of growth. The problem is measuring the strength of this correlation in order to come up with concrete policy advice.

UNEP (2011) tested the Factor 4 goal of reaching sustainability and a "planetary equilibrium" by halving resource input and doubling economic output (von Weizsäcker et al. 1997). The test indicates that industrialized countries would have to reduce resource consumption by Factors 3–5 to maintain global material consumption at year 2000 levels. This would about double the claim of halving resource inputs to stabilize material flows and their pressure. Business as usual might actually almost triple this flow of resources. The OECD (2015) presents global trends of material flows for its member states. Its report recommends a "relative" decoupling (cf. section 7.2.1) only, enhancing thus "greened" economic growth by reducing, reusing and recycling materials. Identifying the key drivers of material use might help get a hold on decoupling. Wiedmann et al. (2015) find that among wealth, domestic extraction and population density, wealth (GDP per capita) has the greatest influence on material flows per capita. They conclude that "absolute" decoupling is needed "if a growing world population is to make ends meet on a finite planet" (ibid., p. 6275).

188 What should we do about it?

Policies of achieving long-lasting economic prosperity seek to increase and maintain income and wealth. Governments might support this objective internationally by alleviating poverty in developing countries with the help of financial and non-financial aid. A United Nations (2013, p. 112) report admits that there is "no single policy approach," but different policies of employment, social protection and redistribution would have to be applied. Corporate social responsibility could contribute to this objective, but can hardly be expected to substitute for governmental policy.

Environmental deterioration could undermine the achievement of prosperity and could generate greater inequality if it slows down economic growth, whose fruits tend to stay with the rich and powerful. Policies of generating greater equality, e.g., by progressive taxation, could offset the effects of low growth by spending the additional tax revenues into programs of green employment, and environmental infrastructure and research (Pressman and Scott 2017, p. 370). Governments, households and corporations could thus add environmental protection to their sustainability goals. It remains to be seen if their policy will be greened when extended national accounts are widely implemented. To date, the implementation of the System of Environmental-Economic Accounting is at best partial, dealing mostly with the depletion of particular natural resources. Excessive national debt might weaken any resolve to reach economic–environmental sustainability as it would give priority to obtaining a more balanced international investment position.

Awareness of ignored dimensions of human needs and wellbeing motivates most of the suggestions for tackling particular concerns of social progress beyond conventional economic growth. Short or long lists of piecemeal solutions invite, however, advocacy for limited agendas of national and international organizations. International conferences and conventions claim consensus, but are usually not binding and often lack follow-up. For instance, repeating the usual call for official development assistance of 0.7 percent of gross national income has not increased implementation beyond the five countries mentioned above. And the IPCC's call to restrict greenhouse gas emission to less than 2900 gigatons seems hardly achievable, notably with the priorities of the current US administration.

Muddling-through approaches thus dominate governmental policy. They are reactions of policy makers to threats of particular non-sustainabilities, including major disasters, harmful symptoms of environmental degradation and poverty. Non-governmental efforts of academia and activists seem to rely on ad-hoc compilations of indicators and models, which do not reflect the reality of overall social progress or decline. A recent attempt to confront indicators of greening the economy with an evaluation of actual performance reveals large discrepancies between measurement and expert assessment (Table 12.2). The scores (country ranks) do not show any pattern among countries. This might be due to the rather eclectic choice of indicators for leadership and climate change, economic policies and environmental impacts. In the absence of reliable facts and figures, especially for non-economic environmental and social concerns, partial assessments will continue and might end up in politics rather than rational policies.

TABLE 12.2 Measurement and evaluation – score of discrepancy[a]

Rank	Country	Score	Rank	Country	Score
1	Zambia	−71	71	Morocco	0
2	China	52	72	Thailand	0
3	India	49	73	Spain	−1
4	Hungary	−47	74	Costa Rica	−2
5	Cambodia	−44	75	France	2
6	Indonesia	41	76	Chile	2
7	Ethiopia	−39	77	Sweden	−3
8	Australia	39	78	Norway	−3
9	South Africa	39	79	Slovak Republic	3
10	Uruguay	−33	80	Vietnam	3

Rank	"Big" countries	Score
2	China	52
8	Australia	39
17	USA	28
23	Russian Federation	23
57	Brazil	−8

Source: Tamanini and Valenciano (2016, pp. 11–12).

Note

a Scores of discrepancy: rank of performance (measurement) minus rank of evaluation.

12.3 Integrative policy

Broad notions of environmental quality, human wellbeing or development bring about a variety of indicators and indices. Table 12.1 presented a correspondingly large variety of policy options. A common policy framework could connect and evaluate all these options for integrative policy making. Within its reach, economics and its accounting system are well equipped for policy integration. They can base policies on comparable indicators that use money as a common unit of measurement and evaluation. Integrated environmental–economic accounts extend measurement to include environmental externalities. Adjusted market prices and costs could weigh and aggregate economic and environmental outcomes. Influences beyond economic scarcity may, however, still affect markets, environmental quality and human wellbeing.

Environmental decline contributes to market and policy failures in reaching optimal economic conditions.[4] Ecological economists hold that, besides monopolies and other market imperfections, irreversible and disastrous environmental effects render the marginal analysis of economic optimality irrelevant (Funtowicz and Ravetz 1991; Daly 1996). In defense of conventional economic analysis, economists argue that a theoretical "vacuum analysis" can provide insight into complex problems, and a sequence of policy reforms in less-than-perfect situations

190 What should we do about it?

will still help to increase overall economic welfare (cf. section 2.2). Governments may, however, have aggravated problems, for instance by subsidizing environmentally damaging activities. Other cases of policy failure include shortsightedness (notably when ignoring sustainability constraints) and discriminatory yielding to lobbying and corruption.

Letting loose the invisible hand of the market and tackling environmental symptoms by the above-described muddling-through approaches does not provide an optimal solution. Actual policy recommendations differ widely, ranging from highly interventionist regulations to less intrusive market adjustments and combinations thereof. Different schools of environmental and economic thought cannot determine when the levels of environmental impacts become intolerable and what amount of environmental (dis)incentives and regulations could prevent reaching these levels.

Ecological economists favor radical changes in our values. They opt for direct policy interventions by setting constraints and regulations for curbing economic activity.[5] Physical impact indicators reveal and address the limits of environmental source and sink capacities. There is no agreement, though, about how these limits reflect obstacles towards reaching a sustainable economic performance. Environmental economists, on the other hand, seek to adjust markets, notably by price and cost (dis)incentives, which could be obtained from integrated environmental–economic accounts. Markets, rather than judgmental governmental "command-and-control," would make economic agents determine an efficient and sustainable level and pattern of production and consumption by internalizing environment costs.[6]

Table 12.3 summarizes policies tools that go beyond conventional economics, focusing on the economy–environment interface. The table lists and organizes some of the policies that should be combined for integrating environmental and economic objectives. It confronts economic activities with tools that include soft suasion and voluntary action, more intrusive market incentives, and hard instrument of rules and regulations.

Soft instruments elicit and reward voluntary actions. Their benefits are difficult to assess, though. Soft instruments are usually insufficient to control negative externalities. They could pave the way, though, to implementing policies that apply semi-hard and hard tools. Lacking the power of national governments, non-governmental organizations and international conventions have to resort to soft instruments calling for voluntary action.

Governments and their executive arms set and enforce hard instruments. These instruments can serve environmental protection because of their relative simplicity in prohibiting harmful activity. Hard instruments of command and control are rapidly and incisively effective but inefficient in finding the best environmentally sound production and consumption patterns and techniques. They avoid assessing difficult-to-measure and -evaluate environmental damage required for efficient market intervention. They are also judgmental when setting standards, targets and restrictions for economic activities.

Strategies, policies, politics **191**

TABLE 12.3 Environmental–economic policy tools

	Soft instruments	Market instruments	Hard instruments
Production	Voluntary action: • corporate social responsibility • environmental–economic management (eco-efficiency, recycling)	• Fiscal (dis)incentives for environmental cost and benefit internalization • Capping the trade of hazardous products • Creating markets for environmental protection	• Constraints and prohibition of harmful outputs • Regulating production processes • Decoupling environmental impact and economic growth
Final consumption	• Advocacy for environmental education and information • Voluntary implementation: sufficiency, the good life	• Fiscal (dis)incentives for harmful and beneficial goods and services • Capping the trade of hazardous products	• Prohibition of harmful consumption • Rules and regulation for education
Capital formation	Voluntary investment in environmental protection	• Subsidizing of and investing in environmental protection • Reinvesting environmental cost in capital maintenance	• Rules and regulations for environmental protection • Setting of discount rates

Market instruments are somewhere between soft and hard tools of environmental–economic policy making. They are based on the rules of law but leave considerable leeway for households and enterprises to adapt demand and supply or to avoid governmental intervention altogether. They are the classic tools of economics for dealing with externalities and restoring optimality in market behavior. The assumption is that governmental (dis)incentives aim at improving the efficiency of the economy. They would also correct the self-centered behavior of economic agents.

The objective is to prompt economic agents into accounting for their environmental and other social impacts. The tool of integrated environmental–economic accounting (cf. section 4.2.2) could provide the information for budgeting the necessary costs by enterprises and households. A recent survey of statistical offices, ministries and experts found, however, that "there is very little use of natural capital accounts for public policy decisions" (Recuero Virto et al. 2018, p. 251). The problems appear to be a lack of awareness of the relatively new accounting tools and a lack of power to combine or at least coordinate different ministerial agendas.

192 What should we do about it?

Market instruments tend to aim at enterprises, rather than consumers, as enterprises usually have better knowledge of their impacts and of the techniques and costs to avoid or reduce them. Environmental charges, taxes and subsidies, and the creation of markets for pollution permits are the main tools. In case of uncertain impacts, refundable deposits could be charged to those suspected or expected to cause the impacts.

Charges and taxes create funds, which policy makers could use for environmental action. There is no compelling reason, though, why these funds should be restricted to environmental objectives. In principle, damage costing should already have internalized the damage cost into the overall price and value system of the economy. In practice, market instruments may cover only selected or partial damage costs and further environmental protection might be warranted. Still, letting actual or fictitious markets decide about the environmental cost frees the assessment of environmental impacts from top-down normative standards and thresholds. Individual preferences revealed by supply and demand will come into the picture of bottom-up – more democratic – decision making.

Box 12.1 describes the problems of dealing with a surrogate for environmental decline, climate change. The purpose of choosing a surrogate is to facilitate data collection, aggregation and policy evaluation. Even then, different concepts and definitions of the damage and mitigation costs and benefits of climate change require different assumptions. Also, focusing on one particular concern might not permit an unambiguous assessment of its importance in a broader context. The reason is the need to assume perfect or otherwise specified market conditions for the whole economy and the difficulty of comparing the significance of the cost and policy of climate change with other social costs and benefits (Bartelmus 2015).

Beyond measurement, integrative modeling could be a powerful tool of integrated policy planning. Modeling assumptions reflect, however, hidden and open expectations and priorities, which may go beyond economic concerns. Chapter 5

BOX 12.1 COSTING CLIMATE CHANGE

Physical indicators of climate change are difficult, if not impossible, to combine in an overall measure of environmental impact. But the use of a monetary unit of measurement does not fare much better due to a host of different valuation concepts and techniques.

For example, average carbon price estimates range between 12\$/ton CO_2eq (IPCC 2007) and 85\$/ton CO_2eq (Stern 2006), with World Bank (2010) calculations somewhere in between. Assessments of abatement costs for CO_2 stabilization at 550 ppm amount to an average of 35\$/ton CO_2 by the end of the century in IPCC (2007) estimates; they are modeled to increase from 7.4\$/ton to 55\$/ton by 2100 when looking for an optimal carbon price (Nordhaus 2008).

Strategies, policies, politics **193**

examined the pros and cons of extending current economic behavior into business-as-usual and optimal models. No clear conclusions could be drawn from the large variety of models. A relatively new approach of "ecological macroeconomics" (Rezai and Stagl 2016; Hardt and O'Neill 2017) points to a similar variety of "post-growth" models and corresponding policies. Their policy themes look therefore more like a wish list for post-growth strategies than a way of combining policies in an integrative model.[7]

The environmental Kuznets curve hypothesis claims that economic growth will provide an automatic improvement of environmental quality. Its predictions are not confirmed though by the available data (section 5.1.1). This applies also to the steady-state theorem, which calls for a constant material throughput of matter and energy to generate ecological sustainability and a better quality of life (Daly 1996, pp. 31–3; Dietz and O'Neill 2013, p. 45). In particular there is no clear specification of the necessary limits to economic growth, which would indicate the level of reducing material throughput and thus the corresponding decoupling of economic activity from economic growth. Technological innovation plays an important role in all models, but its assumptions differ widely (cf. section 5.2.2).

Some authors take the problem of predicting the future as an incentive for offering scenarios under different assumptions. They believe that such scenarios may still help policy making by providing policy options in different situations. Kubiszewski et al. (2017) thus advance "plausible" policy scenarios that cover the gamut from liberal and exploitative business to policy reform and ultimately a society that exercises sufficiency and equity in the distribution of its natural resources. However, their scenarios aggregate different impacts on ecosystems by pricing their services, even if most of these services provide "benefits" that are not created in markets.[8] The resulting estimates are therefore more in the nature of an "encouragement" for future policy directions than actual recommendations for integrative policy. Mentioning sustainable wellbeing looks more like an afterthought than a unifying paradigm.

The interaction between environment and economy can be measured and modeled more realistically than the effects of "immaterial" development concerns of distributional equity, security and other influences on human welfare. "Rather than filtering data through abstract models, policy makers might be better advised by a direct supply of comparable biophysical and economic data in the systemic format of the (extended) national accounts" (Bartelmus 2015, p. 61). Integrated environmental–economic accounting appears to be the best bet for integrative analysis and policy. Other hardly quantifiable features of development will have to be dealt with by political negotiation to obtain some agreement on policies.

Democratic policies will tend to minimize intrusion into individual plans and budgets; more autocratic governments will tend to rule by command and control. The latter might be more effective and integrative, but might also be more normative and will come with a loss of freedom of choice and adaptation to environmental impacts.

194 What should we do about it?

12.4 Global governance

12.4.1 Sustainability in a globalizing world

The focus has been mostly on national strategies and policies, even if they were couched in regional terms. The reason is that the sovereign nation-state still has the greatest power to decide on the fate of its citizens. At the same time the economic, social, cultural and environmental interaction of nations has sped up and intensified. New information and transportation technologies, trade liberalization and economic migration encouraged the integration of lifestyles, production and markets across national boundaries. Globalization may now have reached a peak with protectionist movements in the USA and Europe. The purpose of reversing globalization is to regain the powers given up to transnational institutions and conventions, but now also to prevent further acts of terrorism.

Globalization could indeed be reversible. Environmentalists alert to the negative effects of globalization, brought about by a power shift from governments to transnational corporations and institutions (Daly 1996; Mander 2001). Economists, on the other hand, argue "in defense" of international corporations (Bhagwati 2002) since globalization has improved standards of living and environmental protection. Table 12.4 lists perceived drawbacks and benefits of globalization. The polarization of environmentalists and economists is obviously also at work at the international level.

The pros and cons of Table 12.4 make it difficult to come to a conclusion about whether globalization is good for us or not. On the benefits side, mainstream economists argue that trade-triggered economic growth facilitates environmental protection, poverty mitigation and innovation. Moreover, trade liberalization and a resulting increase in competition creates greater efficiency in the use of natural resources and could remove mismanagement and corruption by spreading environmental and social standards. Environmental and other anti-globalization groups dispute these effects. They point to wasteful Western consumption and the influence of dominant profit-oriented corporations in dumping environmental and social standards. Unfortunately the paucity of data does not permit an authoritative assessment of the net benefits or damage of globalization.

Even in theory it is not clear whether the net effects in any of the different assessments of globalization help or hinder the attainment of economic, ecological or developmental sustainability. Enhancing economic growth is the main objective of international trade liberalization. It is based on the Ricardian (Ricardo 1817) theorem of comparative advantage; the theorem is believed to ensure the efficient use of the different know-how and resource endowment of countries by specialization in production and trade. The result has been unprecedented economic growth and interdependence of countries after World War II. If such growth succeeds in maintaining the produced and natural capital base of the economy it could achieve at least economic sustainability.

Environmentalists warn, however, that the unfettered pursuit of profit by transnational corporations prevents attempts at looking beyond produced capital. If at

Strategies, policies, politics **195**

TABLE 12.4 Globalization effects

Benefits	*Drawbacks*
Economy	
• Economic growth: comparative advantage of trade liberalization	• Job losses from outsourcing
• Removal of mismanagement and corruption by competition	• Market dominance by transnational corporations
• Technological development: innovation in larger markets	• Volatile international capital flows
Environment	
• Natural resource saving from competition	• Natural resource depletion by transnational corporation: tragedy of the commons[a]
• Sustainability transfer: spread of environmental awareness and innovation, removal of damaging subsidies	• Spread of wasteful consumption
	• Environmental burden shifting: relocation of business to pollution havens, import of natural resources
	• Environmental dumping: competitive race to the bottom
Social values	
• Trickle-down effects of economic growth	• Marginalization of poor countries: domination of transnational corporations, asymmetric mobility of production factors
• Removal of corruption by competition	
• Transfer of social standards: labor standards, minimum wages	• Disembedding of economic activity: abandoning social and cultural standards under competitive pressures (race to the bottom)
• Promotion of social values by inter-governmental organizations and global civil society such as the United Nations, Red Cross etc.	• Cultural homogenization: McDonaldization, fordism
• Information exchange: spread of epistemic culture	

Source: Bartelmus (2008, Table 14.1, modified), with permission by Springer Nature.

Note
a Loss of "open-access" resources, triggered by ignoring the risk of depletion.

all, claims of corporate – social and environmental – responsibility works only in good times when such responsibility has been touted as goodwill, enhancing the image of a corporation. In bad times, national achievements of social security, environmental quality and cultural heritage could be lost in a competitive race to the bottom. Once "stuck to the bottom" (Porter 1999) any revival of social and environmental values is unlikely because of continuing competitive pressures. There is also the temptation of shifting environmentally and socially harmful production from dominant international corporations in rich countries to enterprises in weak developing nations (cf. section 4.3).

196 What should we do about it?

It might not be possible therefore to make a conclusive evaluation of the sustainability effects of globalization and to formulate corresponding international policies. One attempt at linking globalization to sustainable development seeks to find correlations between a globalization index and different sustainability indices (Martens and Raza 2010). They show some connections of socioeconomic, cultural, technological and environmental globalization "domains" with the HDI, an Environmental Performance Index and a Responsible Competitiveness Index, but stress uncertainties about measurement and prediction. The final ranking of countries by globalization levels does not generate great surprises, placing the integrated economies of the European Union at the top and leaving poor and more or less isolated countries either out of the picture (notably African nations) or at the bottom (Figge and Martens 2014). Apart from the problems of measuring a phenomenon, whose future looks uncertain, the critique of sustainable development discredits the evaluation of the relationship of globalization and the development paradigm.

12.4.2 Institutions and conventions

Section 11.3 could not come up with an unequivocal conclusion about whether globalization helps or hinders sustainable development. Nonetheless, international organizations set their hope on international conventions and support to tackle interconnected international and global problems that cannot be solved by single responses (Zollinger 2007; Martens and Raza 2010). International institutions and conventions abound. There are over 200 fragmented and overlapping multilateral environmental agreements, but there are no institutions with similar enforcement power as the national government. We have a "world of states" (Messner and Nuscheler 2000, p. 171) rather than a world state.

The difficulty of reaching consensus on philosophical questions is the reason why the United Nations Conference on Environment and Development abandoned the idea of creating an Earth Charter in favor of a weaker, human-needs oriented Rio Declaration (United Nations 1994). Non-governmental organizations continue to promote an Earth Charter Initiative (2012–2016), whose principles include caring for all forms of life, the environment, sustainable development and peace. In the end, the Earth Charter Initiative looks for help from the United Nations, hoping that implementation will be achieved "with an international legally binding instrument on environment and development." Such a policy tool would indeed be more effective than generic admonitions.

The international community promoted the paradigm of sustainable development through a number of Earth Summits (Box 12.2). Their recommendations are not legally binding, unless adopted by governments, and include long lists of policies in different social, economic and environmental areas. The latest 2012 Rio Summit showed some commitment to a multitude of conventions, regimes and agendas for international organizations. The MDG and SDG (cf. section 10.2.2) seek to implement the Summit's recommendations by coordinating and supporting

BOX 12.2 EARTH SUMMITS

The environmental movement and its dire predictions triggered the first United Nations Conference on the Human Environment (1972) in Stockholm. The following Earth Summits kept alive the debate of environment and development and their sustainability. Responding to persistent policy failure in implementing environment and development, the 1992 Conference on Environment and Development in Rio de Janeiro (United Nations 1994) adopted sustainable development and translated the paradigm into an international action program, the Agenda 21, a Rio Declaration and conventions including the Framework Convention on Climate Change (UNFCCC 2014). A 2002 World Summit on Sustainable Development in Johannesburg (United Nations 2003) attempted to break the lethargic response to the Agenda 21 by "public–private partnership" of government and civil society. The latest 2012 Rio+20 Summit (United Nations, no date-a) focused on greening the economy in the "context of sustainable development." Sustainable Development Goals are now to promote and help implementing the strategies of the latest Earth Summit by 2030 (United Nations, no date-b).

national policy initiatives where single responses cannot solve interconnected international and global problems. A "high-level political forum on sustainable development" will follow up. It held a meeting on "eradication of poverty and promoting prosperity in a changing world" in July 2017 (United Nations Sustainable Development Knowledge Platform, no date-a).

Environmentalists and economists continue to disagree on the benefits of global arrangements. The former call for curbing economic growth and reversing globalization, held responsible for serious environmental impacts. A grassroots movement of "localization" might be needed (Mander 2001) to overcome globalization. On the other hand, Rodrik (1997) weighs pros and cons of globalization, suggesting to "unleash the creative energies of private entrepreneurship without eroding the social basis of cooperation" (ibid., p. 85). The worst symptoms of globalization would have to be treated by particular responsive action. This seems to be a rational way of controlling the undesirable social and environmental effects of globalization without relying on proclamations about "change in people's heads and hearts" (Meadows et al. 2004, p. 240; Adams 2006, p. 14).[9] However, tackling particular problems is not a holistic approach to implementing a vision. Rather, it caters to ad-hoc responses and corresponding piecemeal solutions, indicating a return to muddling-through approaches at the international level.

198 What should we do about it?

Notes

1 The United Nations promote corporate social responsibility as part of public–private partnership (United Nations 2003) and of a Global Compact (United Nations Procurement Division 2004).
2 Some industrial ecologists contest, though, the no-waste-in-nature argument (Ehrenfeld and Chertow 2002).
3 The setting of development goals is added in Table 12.1 as a further policy instrument.
4 Pareto optimality in perfectly competitive markets generates prices that are equal to marginal production cost and consumption benefits (utility). Textbooks of economics try to maintain the assumption of perfect markets, treating environmental issues as "externalities" that should be fully internalized into the budgets of economic agents. The purpose is to regain optimality at micro- and macro-levels.
5 Ecological economists may not shun market incentives and disincentives if they help change lifestyles and production patterns. But they consider the marginal costing and pricing of such incentives at best a supplementary tool. At worst, they see it as little more than a game of "puzzle solving" (Funtowicz and Ravetz 1991).
6 Chapter 13 will explain ways to overcome this polarization between environmentalists and economists.
7 The policy proposals include the reduction of environmental impacts and inequality, reform of the monetary system, change of lifestyles and work patterns, corporate responsibility, strengthening local initiatives, stabilizing population growth and the development of new indicators.
8 Kubiszewski et al. (2017) estimate that the worst policy of "barbarization" (socio-economic and moral deterioration) would lead to a decline of the global value of ecosystems by US$51 trillion/year, whereas the "great transition" to visionary solutions would increase their value by US$30 trillion/year, by the year 2050.
9 Meadows et al. (2004, p. 271) argue that insufficient knowledge about the tools of attaining sustainability requires complementing current knowledge with softer tools of "visioning, networking, truth-telling, learning, and loving."

References

Adams, W.M. (2006). *The Future of Sustainability: Re-thinking Environment and Development in the Twenty-first Century*, IUCN Report. Online: http://cmsdata.iucn.org/downloads/iucn_future_of_sustainability.pdf (accessed 4 June 2017).
Bartelmus, P. (2008). *Quantitative Eco-nomics: How Sustainable are Our Economies?* Dordrecht: Springer.
Bartelmus, P. (2015). How bad is climate change? *Environmental Development* 14: 53–62.
Bénabou, R. and Tirole, J. (2016). Mindful economics: the production, consumption, and value of beliefs, *Journal of Economic Perspectives* 30 (3): 141–64.
Bhagwati, J. (2002). Coping with antiglobalization, *Foreign Affairs* 81: 2–7.
Biomimicry Institute (2017). What is biomimicry? Online: https://biomimicry.org/what-is-biomimicry/ (accessed 13 February 2017).
Braungart, M., McDonough, W. and Bollinger, A. (2007). Cradle-to-cradle design: creating healthy emissions – a strategy for eco-effective product and system design, *Journal of Cleaner Production* 15 (13–14): 1337–48.
Crook, C. (2005). The good company, a survey of corporate social responsibility, *The Economist*, 22 January.
Daly, H.E. (1996). *Beyond Growth*, Boston, MA: Beacon Press.
Dietz, R. and O'Neill, D. (2013). *Enough is Enough*, San Francisco, CA: Berrett-Koehler Publishers.

Earth Charter Initiative (2012–2016). The Earth Charter. Online: www.earthcharterin action.org/content/pages/Read-the-Charter.html (accessed 1 August 2017).

Ehrenfeld, J.R. and Chertow, M.R. (2002). Industrial symbiosis: the legacy of Kalundborg, in R.U. Ayres and L.W. Ayres (eds.), *A Handbook of Industrial Ecology*, Cheltenham, UK: Edward Elgar: 334–48.

Elliot, R. (2001). Ethics and value, in M.K. Tolba (ed.), *Our Fragile World: Challenges and Opportunities for Sustainable Development*, Oxford: Eolss Publishers: 973–82.

Figge, L. and Martens, P. (2014). Globalization continues: the Maastricht globalization index revisited and updated, *Globalizations* 11 (6): 875–93. Online: http://pimmartens.info/ wp-content/uploads/2013/05/Figge-and-Martens_2014_Globalisation-continues.pdf (accessed 12 February 2017).

Frank, R.H. (1999). *Luxury Fever: Why Money Fails to Satisfy in an Era of Excess*, New York: Free Press.

Funtowicz, S.O. and Ravetz, J.R. (1991). A new scientific methodology for global environmental issues, in R. Costanza (ed.), *Ecological Economics: The Science and Management of Sustainability*, New York: Columbia University Press: 137–52.

Gray, R. and Bebbington, J. (2007). Corporate sustainability: accountability or impossible dream, in G. Atkinson, S. Dietz and E. Neumayer (eds.), *Handbook of Sustainable Development*, Cheltenham, UK: Edward Elgar: 376–95.

Hardt, L. and O'Neill, D.W. (2017). Ecological macroeconomic models: assessing current developments, *Ecological Economics* 134: 198–211.

Helliwell, J.F., Huang, H. and Wang, S. (2017). Social foundations of world happiness, in J.F. Helliwell, R. Layard and J.D. Sachs (eds.), *World Happiness Report 2017*, New York: Sustainable Development Solutions Network. Online: http://worldhappiness.report/ wp-content/uploads/sites/2/2017/03/HR17.pdf (accessed 13 September 2017).

Huber, J. (2004). *New Technologies and Environmental Innovation*, Cheltenham, UK: Edward Elgar.

Intergovernmental Panel on Climate Change (IPCC) (2007). *Climate Change 2007: Synthesis Report*. Geneva: IPCC. Online: www.ipcc.ch/pdf/assessment-report/ar4/syr/ar4_syr_ full_report.pdf (accessed 22 July 2017).

Intergovernmental Panel on Climate Change (IPCC) (2014). Climate change 2014: mitigation of climate change. Online: www.ipcc.ch/report/ar5/wg3 (accessed 6 October 2017).

Kates, R.W., Clark, W.C., Corell, R., Hall, J.M., Jaeger, C.C., Lowe, I., McCarthy, J.J., Schellnhuber, H.J., Bolin, B., Dickson, N.M., Faucheux, S., Gallopin, G.C., Grübler, A., Huntley, B., Jäger, J., Jodha, N.S., Kasperson, R.E., Mabogunje, A., Matson, P., Mooney, H., Moore III, B., O'Riordan, T. and Svedin, U. (2001). Sustainability science, *Science* 292 (5517): 641–2. Online: www.albany.edu/gogreen/files/documents/ faculty%20forum/Kates.pdf (accessed 3 January 2017).

Kirchner, J.W. (2002). The Gaia hypothesis: facts, theory and wishful thinking, *Climatic Change* 52: 391–408. Online: http://seismo.berkeley.edu/~kirchner/reprints/2002_55_ Kirchner_gaia.pdf (accessed 29 October 2017).

Kubiszewski, I., Costanza, R., Anderson, S. and Sutton, P. (2017). The future value of ecosystem services: global scenarios and national implications, *Ecosystem Services* 26: 289–301.

Lambin, E.F. and Meyfroidt, P. (2011). Global land use change, economic globalization, and the looming land scarcity, *Proceedings of the National Academy of Sciences of the United States of America* 108 (9): 3465–72. Online: www.pnas.org/content/108/9/3465/T1. expansion.html (accessed 26 February 2017).

Lovelock, J.E. (2009). *The Vanishing Face of Gaia: A Final Warning*, New York: Basic Books.

200 What should we do about it?

Mander, J. (2001). Introduction: facing the rising tide, in E. Goldsmith and J. Mander (eds.), *The Case Against the Global Economy and for a Turn Towards Localization*, London: Earthscan: 3–19.

Martens, P. and Raza, M. (2010). Is globalization sustainable? *Sustainability* 2: 280–93. Online: www.neweconomictheory.org/files/Is%20Globalisation%20Sustainable.pdf (accessed 20 November 2017).

Meadows, D., Randers, J. and Meadows, D. (2004). *Limits to Growth: The 30-years Update*, White River Junction, VT: Chelsea Green Publishing.

Messner, D. and Nuscheler, F. (2000). Politik in der Global Governance Architektur [Policy in the global governance architecture], in R. Kreibich and U.E. Simonis (eds.), *Globaler Wandel, Ursachenkomplexe und Lösungsansätze* [Global Change, Causal Complexities and Solutions], Berlin: Berlin Verlag, Arno Spitz: 171–88.

Nordhaus, W.D. (2008). *A Question of Balance: Weighing the Options on Global Warming Policies*, New Haven, CT: Yale University Press.

O'Donnel, G. and Oswald, A.J. (2015). National well-being policy and a weighted approach to human feelings, *Ecological Economics* 120: 59–70.

Organisation for Economic Co-operation and Development (OECD) (2015). *Material Resources, Productivity and the Environment*. Online: www.oecd.org/environment/waste/material-resources-productivity-and-the-environment-9789264190504-en.htm (accessed 7 October 2017).

Organisation for Economic Co-operation and Development (OECD) (2016). Net official development assistance from DAC and other donors. Online: www.oecd.org/dac/stats/ODA-2015-complete-data-tables.pdf (accessed 7 October 2017).

Porter, G. (1999). Trade competition and pollution standards: "Race to the bottom" or "stuck to the bottom"? *Journal of Environment and Development* 8 (2): 133–51.

Pressman, S. and Scott III, R.H. (2017). Thomas Piketty, growth, distribution and the Environment, in P.A. Victor and B. Dolter (eds.), *Handbook on Growth and Sustainability*, Cheltenham, UK and Northampton, MA: Edward Elgar: 356–71.

Recuero Virto, L., Weber. J-L. and Jeantil, M. (2018). Natural capital accounts and public decision: findings from a survey, *Ecological Economics* 144: 244–59.

Rezai, A. and Stagl, S. (2016). Ecological macroeconomics: introduction and review, *Ecological Economics* 121: 181–5.

Ricardo, D. (1817, 1963 ed.). *The Principles of Political Economy and Taxation*, Homewood, IL: Irwin.

Rodrik, D. (1997). *Has Globalization Gone Too Far?* Washington, DC: Institute for International Economics.

Røpke, I. (2005). Trends in the development of ecological economics from the late 1980s to the early 2000s, *Ecological Economics* 55: 262–90.

Sachs, W. (1995). From efficiency to sufficiency, *Resurgence* 171: 6–8.

Sachs, W. (2015). Suffizienz: Umrisse einer Ökonomie des Genug [Sufficiency: sketch of an economy of enough], *Umweltwirtschaftsforum* 23 (1–2): 3–9. Online: www.researchgate.net/publication/276129777_Suffizienz_Umrisse_einer_Okonomie_des_Genug (accessed 1 October 2017).

Sala, S., Ciuffo, B. and Nijkamp, B. (2015). A systemic framework for sustainability assessment, *Ecological Economics* 119: 314–25.

Segal, J.M. (1999). *Graceful Simplicity: Towards a Philosophy and Politics of Simple Living*, New York: Holt.

Stern, N. (2006). The economics of climate change: the Stern review, commissioned by the UK Treasury. Online: http://mudancasclimaticas.cptec.inpe.br/~rmclima/pdfs/destaques/sternreview_report_complete.pdf (accessed 22 July 2017).

Sustainable Development Solutions Network (2015). Getting started with the sustainable development goals. Online: http://unsdsn.org/wp-content/uploads/2015/12/151211-getting-started-guide-FINAL-PDF-.pdf (accessed 7 October 2017).

Tamanini, J. and Valenciano, J. (2016). *The Global Green Economy Index, GGEI 2016*. Online: http://dualcitizeninc.com/GGEI-2016.pdf (accessed 4 October 2017).

Thaler, R.H. and Sunstein, C.R. (2008, 2009). *Nudge: Improving Decisions about Health, Wealth, and Happiness*, New York: Penguin Group.

Tolba, M.K. (ed.) (2001). *Our Fragile World: Challenges and Opportunities for Sustainable Development*, Oxford: Eolss Publishers.

United Nations (1994). *Earth Summit, Agenda 21: The United Nations Programme of Action from Rio*, New York: United Nations.

United Nations (2003). *Johannesburg Declaration on Sustainable Development and Plan of Implementation of the World Summit on Sustainable Development*, New York: United Nations.

United Nations (2013). *Inequality Matters: Report of the World Social Situation 2013*, New York: United Nations. Online: www.un.org/esa/socdev/documents/reports/Inequality Matters.pdf (accessed 1 October 2017).

United Nations (no date-a). Sustainable development: future we want – outcome document. Online: https://sustainabledevelopment.un.org/futurewewant.html https://sustainable development.un.org/rio20/futurewewant (accessed 29 October 2017).

United Nations (no date-b). Sustainable development goals. Online: www.un.org/sustainable development/sustainable-development-goals/ (accessed 27 August 2017).

United Nations Conference on the Human Environment (1972). *Development and Environment*, report and working papers of a panel of experts, Mouton: United Nations and École Pratique des Hautes Études.

United Nations Environment Programme (UNEP) (2011). *Decoupling Natural Resource Use and Environmental Impacts from Economic Growth*, A Report of the Working Group on Decoupling to the International Resource Panel. Online www.gci.org.uk/Documents/Decoupling_Report_English.pdf (accessed 14 February 2017).

United Nations Framework Convention on Climate Change (UNFCCC) (2014). The Paris Agreement. Online: http://unfccc.int/paris_agreement/items/9485.php (accessed 16 January 2017).

United Nations Procurement Division (2004). The Global Compact. Online: www.un.org/Depts/ptd/about-us/un-global-compact (accessed on 29 October 2017).

United Nations Sustainable Development Knowledge Platform (no date-a). High-level political forum on sustainable development. Online: https://sustainabledevelopment.un.org/hlpf (accessed 1 October 2017).

United Nations Sustainable Development Knowledge Platform (no date-b). Multi-stakeholder partnership. Online: https://sustainabledevelopment.un.org/sdinaction (accessed 29 October 2017).

Van den Bergh, J.C.J.M. and Grazi, F. (2013). Ecological Footprint policy? Land use as an environmental indicator, Yale University, research and analysis. Online: www.cei-bois.org/files/03_van_de_Berg_et_al_2013.pdf (accessed 26 February 2017).

Veblen, T. (1967, 1899 ed.). *The Theory of the Leisure Class*, New York: Macmillan.

von Weizsäcker, E.U., Lovins, A. and Lovins, H. (1997). *Factor Four: Doubling Wealth, Halving Resource Use*, London: Earthscan.

Wiedmann, T.O., Schandl, H., Lenzen, M., Moran, D., Suh, S., West, J. and Kanemoto, K. (2015). The material footprint of nations, *Proceedings of the National Academy of Sciences* 112 (20), 6271–6. Online: www.pnas.org/content/112/20/6271.full.pdf?with-ds=yes (accessed 15 August 2017).

202 What should we do about it?

World Bank (2010). *World Development Indicators 2010*, Washington, DC: World Bank. Online: https://openknowledge.worldbank.org/handle/10986/4373 (accessed 3 August 2017).

World Business Council for Sustainable Development (WBCSD) (no date). Online: www.devex.com/organizations/world-business-council-for-sustainable-development-wbcsd-50289 (accessed 19 November 2017).

World Commission on Environment and Development (WCED) (1987). *Our Common Future*, Oxford: Oxford University Press.

Zero Emissions Research and Initiative (ZERI) (2013). What is ZERI? Online: www.zeri.org/ZERI/About_ZERI.html (accessed 29 October 2017).

Zollinger, U. (2007). The effects of globalization on sustainable development and the challenges to global governance. Online: www.kingzollinger.ch/pdf/uz_referat_e.pdf (accessed 19 June 2017).

13

BRIDGING THE ENVIRONMENTAL–ECONOMIC POLARIZATION

Whether it is our vision, measures or policies, in all cases we face considerable differences in concepts and methods. The annex presents a historical polarization of representatives of the ecological and economic sciences. They seem now to have coalesced around ecological and environmental economics with mainstream economists largely ignoring this polarization.[1] Ecological economics seeks to link environment and economy by means of biophysical concepts and measures. In contrast environmental economics uses the help of monetary (economic) values to compare the role of the economy and the environment in furthering social progress. Sustainable development, on the other hand, has run its course and seems to be unable to integrate its dimensions in a practical framework (sections 10.3 and 11.2.2).

The question is how to overcome the environmental–economic polarization. Section 13.1 examines first the polarizing differences. Section 13.2 then makes suggestions for tackling these differences.

13.1 The nature of polarization

Figure 13.1 visualizes the main features of the polarization. It uses a simple sequence translating human values into sustainability concepts, their measurement and policy. The figure compares thus the main features of environmental and economic thought as treated by ecological and environmental economics.

Basic views about the environment and the economy were expressed as a matter of nature's intrinsic values or as human preferences for nature's services. Nature's own valuation may differ radically from human bias about the value of nature's "services" (section 6.1.1). Of course, both valuations are by humans. Ecological economics uses "social values and ethical norms" (Faucheux 2001, p. 1863) to describe the role of the natural environment in human and non-human life. In contrast, environmental economics looks for prosperity and wellbeing from using

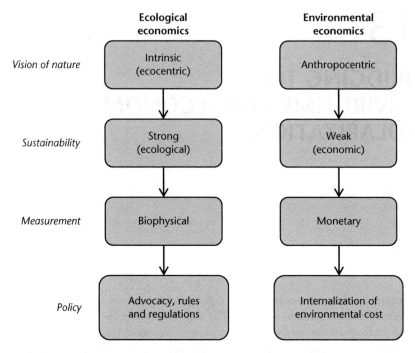

FIGURE 13.1 Environmental–economic polarization. The polarization of environmental and ecological economists shows up in the visions, concepts and measurement of sustainability and policy making. The use of physical indicators vs. monetary values is a characteristic distinction of the two camps

nature by economic activities of production, accumulation of capital and final consumption.

Different strengths of sustainability capture this disparity in more operational and forward-looking terms. Ecological economists call for strong sustainability as a way of staying within the limits of nature's carrying capacities. Environmental economists claim on the other hand that weak sustainability of maintaining the value of produced and natural capital – which allows for substitution among different production factors – can balance environmental costs and benefits with economic ones. The next section will examine if measurement and policy analysis can overcome these differences in defining sustainability from an ecocentric or anthropocentric point of view.

Basically environmentalists (and ecological economists) prefer to focus on non-monetary environmental impact data. Environmental economists explore possibilities to expand monetary market valuation into the environmental field. The differences in these valuations and evaluations are indeed the most glaring manifestations of the polarization. The weight of biophysical material inputs and outputs into and from the national economy paints a very different picture of environmental impact and sustainability compared to the monetary values of environmental benefits, cost and damages.

Irreversible physical environmental impacts could lead to disaster, which would make current human preferences for particular uses of the environment quite irrelevant. However, such disaster is difficult to predict and evaluate, especially if it happens in the far-away future. Human preferences for the present would tend to discount the willingness to pay for preventive environmental protection. Opposing views about trends towards disaster, sudden disastrous events and preventive or responsive actions translate into different environmental and economic policies. Chapter 12 described these policies. Of course, a sudden and unexpected "collapse" (Meadows et al. 2004, pp. xxi, 174) would render futile any risk assessments based on expected trends.

Environmental activists are typically in a weak position to enforce curbing or at least radically changing economic activity. While still calling for hard restrictions, they resort, at least as a first step, to soft instruments of advocacy and education that might help change "our hearts and intuitions" (ibid., p. 263). What they seem to be really after is tackling at least the worst environmental impacts by standards, rules and regulations. Clearly such action of tackling particular impacts has to be piecemeal in the absence of a consistent framework that could assess overall physical impact.

Governments may let market forces decide – possibly with some fiscal encouragement to take environmental concerns into account when budgeting the costs of production. Governments do not shy away from rules and regulations, if public environmental pressure is mounting. Administrations may change, though, and populist pressure, as in the USA, might lead to abandoning established environmental standards. It comes as no surprise that governments tend to maintain their policies of established environmental protection, providing limited (dis)incentives and thus avoiding any radical changes. Environmentalists dismiss these half-hearted efforts of applying hardly effective market instruments and insufficient regulation, considering established conventional policies as inadequate for tackling current and expected environmental decline.

13.2 Overcoming the polarization

Figure 13.2 attempts to bridge the economic–environmental polarization. Its center column confronts the polarizing sequence of Figure 13.1 with compromises in tackling this sequence. This could provide a framework for opening a dialogue between environmentalists and economists. Such a framework could be strongest (unbroken vertical connection) between hybrid measurement/accounting and policy analysis. It could be weakened, however, by the risk of sudden environmental disasters that would break any connection between the evaluation of environmental impacts in physical terms and their valuation in monetary ones.

To harmonize philosophical visions is not easy as it entails a change of basic values in opposing views. Perhaps the solution lies in agreeing – in a more or less democratic way – on the goals of the broadest approach to socioeconomic progress, i.e., sustainable development. Such agreement could also be a conceptual save for a

206 What should we do about it?

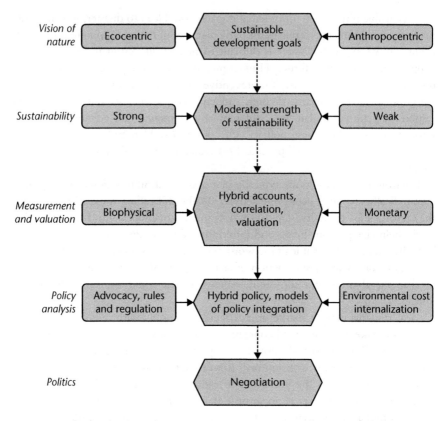

FIGURE 13.2 Bridging the polarization. Common goals, measures and models can overcome or at least weaken the polarization of Figure 12.1. If these tools do not work out, one would have to resort to political negotiation to find a compromise in addressing the polarization

paradigm that lost its relevance for practical policy making. In this case one would have to resort to political negotiation for agreed policy making.

Consensus seems to have emerged in Sustainable Development Goals (SDG) that are mostly anthropocentric in nature. Almost all governments (and perhaps even the people they more or less represent) adopted the SDG at the United Nations Sustainable Development Summit in 2015. For the natural environment they agreed on non-binding goals of using freshwater, the oceans, energy, terrestrial ecosystems and combatting climate change (cf. Table 9.1, environmental sustainability). However, this consensus remains doubtful when it comes to implementation as evidenced for example by the recent anti-environment actions of the most powerful nation. Still the SDG adoption indicates that the anthropocentric view dominates the international discussion of the environment in the context of sustainable development. It remains to be seen if the SDG will serve as a fig leaf of good intentions, mentioned in section 10.3, or as a – negotiated – tool of overcoming the polarization.

The compromise between strong and weak sustainability might be to clearly identify renewable and exhaustible resources and possibilities of replacing the latter by renewable or reproducible materials in production and consumption. The problem is to determine the time of exhaustion of non-renewables and the need for their actual use or replacement in the future. Here the assessments become vague since they would have to cover changing consumption and production patterns brought about by changes in relative prices. It is easy to call for a "moderate" or "partial" strength of sustainability, but near impossible to specify where and when this compromise may hold.

Polarization is most conspicuous when it comes to the actual measurement of nature's role in the activities and wellbeing of people. "Pricing the priceless" describes the difficulty of evaluating changes in the availability of natural assets and their services in "natural" units of weight, joule or volume or in economic values of prices. Three approaches can be distinguished to link biophysical measures to monetary values:

- *Hybrid accounts* place non-monetary environmental effects next to the monetary benefits or cost they may cause, without expressing them in a common unit of measurement; they leave the choice between environmental and economic effects to the decision maker.
- *Correlation* of physical growth and its environmental impacts with economic growth could assess the environmental impacts resulting from economic activities or changes in economic activity by environmental impacts.
- *Valuation* of physical impacts by integrated ("greened") environmental–economic accounts or eco-prices would reveal the economic significance of environmental impacts or reflect intrinsic values of ecosystems.

A companion volume of the System of integrated Environmental and Economic Accounting (SEEA) 2012 on "applications and extensions" (UNCEEA, no date) presents a hybrid input–output table. Such a table could link environmental effects to economic processes of production, consumption and investment. Table 4.3 is a simplified version, showing physical material flows of natural resource use and emissions of residuals next to monetary flows. The table could be used as a starting point for the monetary valuation of material flows and for supporting mixed or integrated environmental and economic policies.

Before venturing into monetary valuation of physical impacts one could compare physical and monetary flows over time or across regions. Correlational analyses focus on time series of material flows and economic growth for "decoupling" environmental pressure from economic activity. As mentioned in section 12.2 this approach does not generate clear results. It faces difficulties in measuring the correlational strength between environmental impacts and economic performance, expressed in disparate units of measurement.

A truly integrative accounting system such as the original SEEA (section 4.2.2) would make physical environmental and monetary economic data comparable at least in terms of human preferences for environmental and economic goods and services. Monetizing the stocks and flows of the biosphere would provide a tool of communicating the value of nature in the commonly understood language of money. However, it would lean towards weak sustainability and corresponding economic analysis, which apply common monetary valuation such as maintenance (replacement) cost to hitherto unpriced environmental assets and services. Consequently, it might be difficult to obtain the approval of this valuation by environmental activists and even ecological economists, who suspect that some assets cannot be replaced by other (reproducible) materials.

Some agreement between the two camps could be found by manipulating the discount rate for valuing natural assets: lower "social" discount rates would preserve nature for future generations; high economic discounting would assume a rapidly declining economic value of nature, freeing funds for new investment. A compromise between low (or even zero) social discount rates and high economic ones might "reduce the tension" between economists and environmentalists (Hepburn 2007, p. 120).

Attempts at finding nature's "own" (intrinsic) values of its processes and commodities look for their "eco-prices" (cf. section 6.3.2). In general these attempts determine only relative prices of environmental assets and asset changes. Consequently one would obtain only a hypothetical monetary value for the inputs and outputs of nature. To obtain the absolute values one would have to set a standard price for a particular asset.[2] The valuation of nature's intrinsic – system-inherent – processes and quantities is intriguing. The methodological assumptions, problems of covering diverse ecological stocks and flows in an input–output system and difficulties of interpreting the resulting monetary values as nature's own prevented a widely accepted use of eco-pricing.

A review of the vast literature on the valuation of ecosystem services found a "literature blindspot" that either ignores the use of ecosystem valuation or reflects an actual lack of practical applications (Laurans et al. 2013). Some international organizations promote the valuation of ecosystems. The Economics of Ecosystems and Biodiversity (TEEB 2010) initiative calls for calculating the costs and benefits of ecosystem services and ecosystem conservation, and the Wealth Accounting and the Valuation of Ecosystem Services (WAVES) of the World Bank (no date) intends to make its findings part of ecosystem accounts.

A group of ecological economists tried to assess the benefits of the world's ecosystem services in a mix of valuation methods that include market values, welfare valuations, replacement and restoration costs for services lost, and shadow prices of optimizing models (Costanza et al. 1997). Their rather eclectic use of different valuation methods makes it difficult to interpret the results (see section 6.3.2) and its relevance for policy analysis. This applies also to a more recent attempt at valuing ecosystem services (de Groot et al. 2012). The need for monetary ecosystem accounts can be questioned, however (section 6.3.2), since the monetization of ecosystem functions would distort the aggregation of complex ecological processes within and between ecosystems (Bartelmus 2015).

Policy makers could use the information of hybrid accounts directly, according to their own priorities and preferences for formulating responses to a deteriorating physical environment. Alternatively the cost of their responses of environmental protection could be incorporated in models to assess their effects on the economic system. A potential policy revision could be the advice of the models.

Integrative models, which could help bridging the environmental–economic polarization, include:

- environmentally extended input–output analysis that assesses the direct and indirect physical environmental effects of changes in final demand on the costs and outputs of industries and household consumption (section 4.2.2);
- linear and dynamic non-linear programming models, which introduce produced and natural capital constraints into the input–output system; they could show the physical and monetary sustainability notions of ecological and environmental economics (section 5.2.1);
- computable general equilibrium (CGE) models, which introduce environmental protection expenditure or environmental (dis)incentives (taxes, charges, subsidies) and standards into competitive markets (FAO et al. 2014); they could assess the resulting environmental impacts as well as their monetary effects on economic variables;
- models of environmentally expanded economic growth, which stay in the monetary realm and focus on the medium and long term; they could incorporate environmental costs and benefits in a maximizing welfare function (section 5.2.2);
- simulation models like the limits-to-growth (LTG) model (section 5.1.2), which use the interactions of selected variables such as population, economic output and environmental impact; though differing in their assumptions, they look at overall welfare as the ultimate outcome, without attempts at optimizing model processes and results.

A number of drawbacks impair such policy analysis. Input–output analyses and CGE models are usually limited to the short term. Fixed input–output coefficients hold, if at all, only for short periods. Unrealistic measurement of micro-economic production and consumption functions and behavioral assumptions impair CGE modeling when looking beyond the short term. The problem of specifying environmental and other constraints in linear programming might be the reason why this approach has largely been ignored in nation-wide sustainability analysis and policy making. Optimal growth models face the challenge of determining an intertemporal welfare function that includes environmental damage. It remains to be seen if replacing optimality by sustainability standards can replace behavioral equations in these models (cf. section 5.2.2).

The LTG model is a brave attempt at predicting the world's development with the help of a few relationships between key social, economic and environmental factors. Unfortunately, the model has to cope with large data gaps. To make this picture more

210 What should we do about it?

realistic one could introduce key functions and data of extended accounting and input–output analysis. This could wake up antagonists, who criticized the first publication of the model (see section 5.1.2) but remained silent thereafter.

For going beyond the environmental–economic interaction, i.e., for assessing the influences of other social, institutional, cultural and political impacts, one would have to resort to political negotiation. This was the approach of obtaining agreement on the different dimensions and goals of sustainable development. Unavoidably subjective preferences and evaluations enter the picture, making any assessment and policy of social progress a matter of politics.

So far only the extended environmental–economic monetary accounting system can present a fairly objective picture of the environment–economy interface and its sustainability. The tentative conclusion about realistically and systematically bridging the gap between environmental and economic analysis is therefore to set out from greened national accounts to build a rational consensus on integrative environmental–economic policy.

Notes

1 The categorization into ecological and environmental economics is of course a simplification of overlapping and diverging approaches to dealing with the interaction of environment, economy and social networks; it is meant to identify typical features of the environmental–economic polarization.
2 Methods of calculating system-inherent prices and the absolute value of the biosphere include the dual of a physical input–output table or optimizing input–output interactions under restrictions by a linear programming model. See for example the discussion of these approaches by Patterson (2002).

References

Bartelmus, P. (2015). Do we need ecosystem accounts? *Ecological Economics* 118: 292–8.

Costanza, R., d'Arge, R., de Groot, R., Farber, S., Grasso, M., Hannon, B., Limburg, K., Naeem, S., O'Neill, R.V., Paruelo, J., Raskin, R.G., Sutton, P. and van den Belt, M. (1997). The value of the world's ecosystem services and natural capital, *Nature* 387: 253–60.

De Groot, R., Brander, L., van der Ploeg, S., Costanza, R., Bernard, F., Braat, L., Christie, M., Crossman, N., Ghermandi, A., Hein, L., Hussain, S., Kumar, P., McVittie, A., Portela, R., Rodriguez, L.C., ten Brink, P. and van Beukering, P. (2012). Global estimate of the value of ecosystems and their services in monetary units, *Ecosystem Services* 1: 50–61.

Faucheux, S. (2001). Summary principles for sustainable development, in M.K. Tolba (ed.), *Our Fragile World: Challenges and Opportunities for Sustainable Development*, Oxford: Eolss Publishers: 1761–78.

Food and Agriculture Organisation of the United Nations, European Commission, Organisation for Economic Co-operation and Development, United Nations and World Bank (2014). *System of Environmental–Economic Accounting 2012: Applications and Extensions* (white cover publication). Online: http://documents.worldbank.org/curated/en/8937 01468198001180/pdf/103742-WP-PUBLIC-applications-and-extensions.pdf (accessed 20 March 2017).

Hepburn, C. (2007). Valuing the far-off future: discounting and its alternatives, in G. Atkinson, S. Dietz and E. Neumayer (eds.), *Handbook of Sustainable Development*, Cheltenham, UK: Edward Elgar: 109–24.

Laurans, Y., Rankovic, A., Billé, R., Pirard, R. and Mermet, L. (2013). Use of ecosystem services economic valuation for decision making: questioning a literature blindspot, *Journal of Environmental Management* 119: 2081–9.

Meadows, D., Randers, J. and Meadows, D. (2004). *Limits to Growth: The 30-years Update*, White River Junction, VT: Chelsea Green Publishing.

Patterson, M.G. (2002). Ecological production based pricing of biosphere processes, *Ecological Economics* 41: 457–78.

The Economics of Ecosystems and Biodiversity (TEEB) (2010). *Mainstreaming the Economics of Nature: A Synthesis of the Approach, Conclusions and Recommendations of TEEB*. Online: http://doc.teebweb.org/wp-content/uploads/Study%20and%20Reports/Reports/Synthesis%20report/TEEB%20Synthesis%20Report%202010.pdf (accessed 29 October 2017).

United Nations Committee of Experts on Environmental-Economic Accounting UNCEEA) consultation draft (no date). System of Environmental-Economic Accounting (SEEA), SEEA applications and extensions. Online: https://unstats.un.org/unsd/nationalaccount/workshops/2013/Samoa/Apia-BG2.pdf (accessed 23 November 2017).

World Bank (no date). Wealth accounting and the valuation of ecosystem services (WAVES). Online: www.wavespartnership.org (accessed 4 August 2917).

14

CONCLUSIONS

After examining the concepts, measures and sustainability of prosperity, environmental quality and development, the suspicion that "we believe more than we believe" (section 11.2.3) can be confirmed. An overload of information hides significant information gaps and contradictory interpretations of data. Hopefully the evaluation of available indicators and indices in this book will help find out whether we really are and might be "better off," and what we could do about it. A previous publication (Bartelmus 2008) gave inconclusive answers. This book comes up with more conclusive conclusions. It pushes data analysis as far as rationally possible, avoiding questionable information that may support popular views.

Income and wealth measure personal prosperity and its distribution among the people of a country. Globally, per-capita wealth doubled since the beginning of the century, but is now slowing down. This does not mean that the inhabitants of poor countries attained a sufficient level of prosperity as they take off from relatively low levels of personal prosperity. Most African and Asian nations still remain in the lowest deciles of income and wealth. The USA, and to a lesser degree Europe, stand out with regard to the concentration of income and wealth in the hands of the rich. In contrast, Asia (without China which shows concentration of wealth in the upper deciles) and Latin America show a more equal distribution of prosperity. To evaluate the distributional inequality of people one would have to set standards that tell when inequality turns into "inequity." The broad paradigm of sustainable development includes distributional equity in its social dimension. Unfortunately measurement problems prevent a reliable assessment of the paradigm.

Policy recommendations of non-governmental organizations seek to improve the distribution of personal income and wealth. They rely on soft instruments of education, information and moral suasion. In particular, they call upon rich people and corporations to show sufficiency in consumption and social responsibility in production to support the poor. They promise wellbeing and personal gratification as rewards of leading a "good life" of frugality. But can we believe these promises when self-interest is deeply ingrained in the preferences of economic agents? Still, non-governmental prompting has brought about some consensus about tackling extreme poverty as an essential goal of international development strategies.

The macro-economic vision of prosperity looks for an increase in national wealth, product, income and welfare. Extended national accounts include, besides produced capital, the availability and consumption of natural capital. A first global study of these accounts indicates that adjusting gross domestic product (GDP) for produced and natural capital consumption might lower the indicator by 3–6 percent globally but would not change the rates of adjusted economic growth. Negative adjusted capital formation in African and Latin American countries point to non-sustainable economic growth, since these countries were not able to maintain their produced and natural capital base. Other measures of inclusive and comprehensive wealth and genuine progress are flawed as they are derived from hardly measurable social welfare.

Non-governmental calls for action use soft tools to prompt governments into attaining and maintaining macro-economic prosperity. The role of market incentives and hard instruments of command and control require, however, governmental power to launch and maintain them. They depend therefore on the priorities of governments and the underlying push by people's voting and lobbying – at least in democracies. The question is if this push can reach beyond economic preferences to make governments include at least environmental damage and extreme poverty in their policies. Taking climate change as *the* environmental concern, some implementation of climate and environmental policy took place after the Earth Summits. However, recent populist gains seem to halt or even reverse this process in several nations.

Environmental decline can also be seen as a stand-alone issue of changes in life support. However, the biophysical measures of environmental quality tell widely differing and hardly comparable stories. Failing to reduce the use of material inputs would increase pressure on the environment, but it is unclear what would be its ultimate effect on humans and non-human species. An unsustainable loss of environmental source and sink services is the message of the current ecological deficit, which might double by 2030. By that time we might also lose food security by a decrease of agricultural land; other predictions see an opposite increase of productive land. The surrogate measure of global warming for environmental decline finds that continuing global CO_2 emission – if no action is taken – might push global warming up to 5 °C by the end of the century. Disastrous consequences for the economy and social welfare would be the result.

Most measures point to significant environmental deterioration. There is no clear advice what action or bundle of actions could decrease or reverse environmental decline. Deep ecologists give priority to nature's own preference for its restoration or conservation as a matter of a new environmental ethics. Trust in the self-healing power of *gaia* could relinquish policy response. However, the prevailing anthropocentric view of ecological economists calls for regulatory restrictions

214 Conclusions

of production and consumption and for subsidizing environmental innovation. For now, governments appear to stay with economic policy, adjusted to address the worst actually observed environmental symptoms of economic activity. Different models of the effects of further policies do not give a clear answer about what is needed to attain a sustainable use of environmental services.

Unsurprisingly, the search for an all-encompassing measure supporting consistent policy intensified. This book argues that the paradigm of sustainable development, advanced to this end, is of little use. Such development uses an even greater variety of indicators than those needed for environmental purposes. It is near impossible to aggregate the indicators into an overall index of sustainable development. Still, selective sets of indicators can alert to the causes and trends of economic, environmental and social components of development.

Qualitative responses to surveys of happiness, wellbeing or life satisfaction cannot give a valid measure of social progress. At best, they provide a spurious indication of people's feelings about being better off. At worst, they distort any trends of increasing or declining wellbeing. Similarly data on the connection between globalization and sustainable development cannot conclusively demonstrate whether globalization helps or hinders the paradigm. The answer would lie in the connection of individual behavior and wellbeing and their link to macro-economic conditions and policies. No clear micro–macro link has been assessed in quantitative terms to this end.

All in all, the indicators indicate the obvious: poor countries appear to fare worse than rich ones in their current state of national prosperity. It is uncertain whether they might catch up with rich countries in their economic development. A rather subjective summary assessment of the effects of prosperity, environmental quality, development and welfare pushes the limits of valid assessment (Table 11.4); it paints a gloomy picture, except perhaps for Latin America and Europe. Africa is worst off, followed by the USA when non-economic indicators are taken into account. Only Latin America and Europe might at least have avoided a decline. The future is even less assured. GDP might be steadily growing till the end of the century but environmental quality and human wellbeing might diminish; it could be stuck at low levels, invoking a revival of the Easterlin paradox.

Questionable information and assumptive and differing models of the future raise the question of what could and should be done to improve or at least maintain our prosperity and wellbeing. Chapter 12 tries to bring some order into the abundance of policy recommendations. It distinguishes visionary rhetoric, practical ad-hoc responses to the worst impacts and attempts at policy integration.

Visionary recommendations are normative. They call for sufficiency in consumption and corporate social responsibility in production. Global development goals reflect some of these visions. Consensus by negotiating parties about long lists of goals hides a lack of real commitment to the goals. The reality of "muddling through" by tackling only the worst economic, social and environmental impacts reveals opportunistic attitudes of governments. Better progress could be made by expanding the economic accounts and policy tools to include environmental effects.

"Green growth" emerged in the latest Earth Summit with some reference to the "context" of sustainable development. Implementation of the green accounts might lend transparency to a potential international commitment to the greening of economic activity.

Not everyone agrees with the negotiated results. Those largely left out of governmental decision making, i.e., non-governmental organizations and academia, continue to propagate their views about what needs "really" to be done. This created a counter-productive polarization that threatens to seep into policy making.

Environmentalist and environment-oriented ecological economists claim that their analysis is based on (natural) science, which should guide human behavior, rather than economics, which caters to the greed of economic agents. Unfortunately, they fail to provide the evidence for this strategy since the wide variety of data advanced cannot be convincingly compared and aggregated. They address therefore particular symptoms of economic misbehavior or call generally for curbing economic activity.

Economists, on the other hand, seek to pacify "unruly" environmentalists. They have the advantage of using a limited approach that can apply a monetary value to the factors of *economic* wellbeing. They can therefore employ market instruments for internalizing environmental damage into the budgets of economic agents. In their view such disincentives could maintain economic growth and trigger environmentally sound production and consumption. Rules and regulations should apply only to imminent and irreversible hazardous impacts that cannot be mitigated by changing production and consumption patterns.

To overcome the economic–environmental polarization in assessment and policy analysis policy makers should focus on what can be assessed realistically: they could base their policies on integrated environmental and economic data compiled in "greened" national accounts. Other social, political or cultural concerns would have to be compared and assessed separately. Their management should be left to transparent political negotiation between society's share- and stakeholders.

Reference

Bartelmus, P. (2008). *Quantitative Eco-nomics: How Sustainable are Our Economies?* Dordrecht: Springer.

ANNEX

A brief history of sustainability science and thought

Figure A.1 gives a rough and necessarily incomplete picture of when and how economics and ecology sought to bridge the gap between the natural and social sciences. Their attempt narrowed, but at the same time solidified, a polarization between ecological and environmental economics, described in Chapter 13.[1]

Considering economics as the art of managing scarce resources and ecology as the "economics of nature" Haeckel (1898) gives a first indication of the potential relations between the two sciences. Haeckel (1866, Vol. II, p. 286) is also credited with the first definition of ecology as the "total science of relationships of the organism with its surrounding outer world."[2] When referred to human organisms this gives a generic definition of the human environment.

An early eighteenth-century forestry and mining official from Saxony in Germany was probably the first to coin the notion of sustainability. In his *Sylvicultura Oeconomica* von Carlowitz (1713) called on humans to "act with nature and not against it." Specifically he postulated that the "conservation and cultivation of timber should be conducted so as to provide a continuous, persistent and sustained utilization."[2] Eighteenth century physiocrat François Quesnay (1759) made the first systematic and quantitative attempt at linking the power (gr. *kratos*) of nature (gr. *physis*) with the management of the national "household." His famous *tableau économique* reflects ideas of sustainability in the relationships between society and economy and the process of their reproduction and maintenance.

Adam Smith (1776, p. 446) dismissed the physiocratic "political economy" as "that system which ... exists only in the speculation of a few men of great learning and ingenuity in France." His derisive critique and the success of industrialization sent Quesnay's *tableau*, and in fact environmental concerns in economics and accounting, into oblivion. In the wake of unprecedented economic growth in industrialized countries, classical and neoclassical economic theory could not be bothered by dire Malthusian (1798) warnings about population pressures on limited

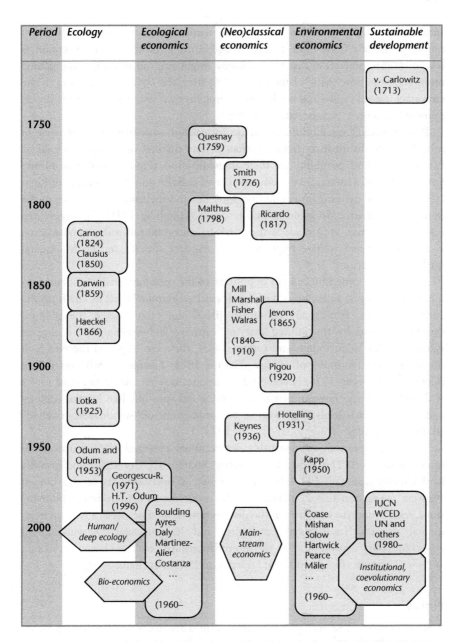

FIGURE A.1 Historical sketch of environmental–economic thought. Ecological science and economics converged towards polarized domains of ecological and environmental economics. Sustainable development goals reflect thought from ecological and environmental economics, but its implementation remains rhetoric

Source: Bartelmus (2008, Plate 2.1), with permission from Springer Nature.

218 Annex

agricultural land, diminishing returns from natural resources (Ricardo 1817) or minor deviations from perfect general equilibrium. One notable exception is Jevons' (1865) prediction that the economy might run out of coal, a key natural resource at the time. Much later Daly (1996) uses Mill's (1871) evaluation of the stationary state of capital and wealth for arguing his own vision of sustainable development based on a "steady-state economy."

Perfect market equilibrium could be formalized with mathematical rigor in models where disturbances from less-than-perfect markets or pollution would be externalized. The possibility of their internalization (Pigou 1920) was mostly ignored. It took a looming environmental crisis and the visionary intellect of Kapp (1950) to make mainstream economists look beyond the micro-economics of the optimal use of an exhaustible natural resource (Hotelling 1931). Environmental economists (Coase, etc.) made it their task to study the full micro- and macro-economic cost and welfare implications of resource scarcity and environmental quality deterioration.

At about the same time, and in opposition to the monetary analyses of environmental economists, a new branch of "ecological economics" took its cue from the natural sciences. Ecological economists (Boulding, etc.) studied the physical thresholds posed by the limited carrying capacity and resilience of ecological systems (Lotka 1925; Odum and Odum 1953); they also explored the effects of the dissipation (entropy) of energy (Carnot 1824; Clausius 1850) and matter (Georgescu-Roegen 1971). Ecological economics covers a wide range of topics with spillovers into environmental economics and spin-offs like human ecology and bioeconomics. It also claims to be the protagonist of "sustainability science" (Kates et al. 2001).

A broader approach to sustainable development emerged in particular at the international level. The World Conservation Strategy (IUCN 1980), the Brundtland Commission (WCED 1987) and ensuing World Summits of the United Nations (see section 12.4.2) include, besides economic and environmental dimensions, social concerns of equity in the distribution of income, wealth and environmental impacts. Institutional economics and its particular Darwin-inspired co-evolutionary version describe the interrelationships between changes in natural and social systems (Norgaard 1994; Söderbaum 1999; Faucheux 2001).

Notes

1 See Bartelmus and Seifert (2003) for a more detailed description of the polarizing history of environmental and economic measurement and thought.
2 Own translation from German of titles and citations of Haeckel and von Carlowitz.

References

Bartelmus, P. (2008). *Quantitative Eco-nomics: How Sustainable are Our Economies?* Dordrecht: Springer.
Bartelmus, P. and Seifert, E.K. (eds.) (2003). *Green Accounting*, Aldershot, UK: Ashgate.

Carnot, N.L.S. (1824). *Réflexions sur la puissance motrice du feu et sur les machines propres à développer cette puissance* [Reflections on the Motive Power of Fire and the Machines Appropriate for Developing this Power], reprint 1966, London: Dawson.

Clausius, R.J.E. (1850). Über die bewegende Kraft der Wärme [On the moving force of heat] Leipzig: Engelmann, *Annalen der Physik* 79, 368–97, 500–24.

Daly, H.E. (1996). *Beyond Growth*, Boston, MA: Beacon Press.

Darwin, C. (1859, 1951 ed.). *The Origin of Species*, New York: Dutton.

Faucheux, S. (2001). Summary principles for sustainable development, in M.K. Tolba (ed.), *Our Fragile World: Challenges and Opportunities for Sustainable Development*, Oxford: Eolss Publishers: 1761–78.

Georgescu-Roegen, N. (1971). *The Entropy Law and the Economic Process*, Cambridge, MA: Harvard University Press.

Haeckel, E. (1866). *Generelle Morphologie der Organismen* [General Morphology of Organisms], vol. 2, Berlin: Reimer.

Haeckel, E. (1898). *Natürliche Schöpfungsgeschichte* [History of the Natural Creation], Berlin: Reimer.

Hotelling, H. (1931). The economics of exhaustible resources, *Journal of Political Economy* 39: 137–75.

International Union for Conservation of Nature and Natural Resources (IUCN) (1980). *World Conservation Strategy*, IUCN-UNEP-WWF. Online: https://portals.iucn.org/library/efiles/documents/WCS-004.pdf (accessed 6 August 2017).

Jevons, W.S. (1865, 1965 ed.). *The Coal Question: An Inquiry Concerning the Progress of the Nation, and the Probable Exhaustion of Our Coal Mines*; reprint of the 3rd ed., New York: Augustus Kelly.

Kapp, K.W. (1950). *The Social Costs of Private Enterprise*, Boston, MA: Harvard University Press.

Kates, R.W., Clark, W.C., Corell, R., Hall, J.M., Jaeger, C.C., Lowe, I., McCarthy, J.J., Schellnhuber, H.J., Bolin, B., Dickson, N.M., Faucheux, S., Gallopin, G.C., Grübler, A., Huntley, B., Jäger, J., Jodha, N.S., Kasperson, R.E., Mabogunje, A., Matson, P., Mooney, H., Moore III, B., O'Riordan, T. and Svedin, U. (2001). Sustainability science, *Science* 292 (5517): 641–2. Online: www.albany.edu/gogreen/files/documents/faculty%20forum/Kates.pdf (accessed 3 January 2017).

Keynes, J.M. (1936, 1973 ed.). *The General Theory of Employment, Interest and Money*, London: Macmillan.

Lotka, A.J. (1925, 1956 ed.). *Elements of Physical Biology*, New York: Dover.

Malthus, T. (1798, 1963 ed.). *Principles of Population*, Homewood, IL: R.D. Irwin.

Mill, J.S. (1871). *Principles of Political Economy*, London: Longmans, Green, Reader and Dyer.

Norgaard, R.B. (1994). *Development Betrayed: The End of Progress and a Coevolutionary Revisioning of the Future*, London: Routledge.

Odum, E.P. and Odum, H.T. (1953, 1st ed.). *Fundamentals of Ecology*, 3rd ed., Philadelphia, PA: Saunders.

Odum, H.T. (1996). *Environmental Accounting, Emergy and Decision Making*, New York: Wiley.

Pigou, A.C. (1920, 1932 ed.). *The Economics of Welfare*, London: Macmillan.

Quesnay, F. (1759). The "Third Edition" of the *Tableau Économique*, in M. Kuczynski and R.L. Meek (eds.) (1972), *Quesnay's Tableau Économique* (facsimile reproduction and English translation), London: Macmillan; reprinted in P. Bartelmus and E.K. Seifert (eds.) (2003). *Green Accounting*, Aldershot, UK: Ashgate.

Ricardo, D. (1817, 1963 ed.). *The Principles of Political Economy and Taxation*, Homewood, IL: Irwin.

Smith, A. (1776, 1991 ed.). *Wealth of Nations*, Amherst, NY: Prometheus.

Söderbaum, P. (1999). Values, ideology and politics in ecological economics, *Ecological Economics* 28: 161–70.

von Carlowitz, H.C. (1713). *Sylvicultura Oeconomica* [Economic Forestry], Leipzig: Braun.

World Commission on Environment and Development (WCED) (1987). *Our Common Future*, Oxford: Oxford University Press.

INDEX

Adams, W.M. 182
Adjusted Net Saving 44
Ahlert, G. 163
Arrow, K.J. 61
assets *see* wealth
Ayres, R.U. 80

Bartelmus, P. 10, 42, 47, 175, 193
basic human needs 125, 142
Baumol, W.J. 62
Bebbington, J. 182
Better Life Index 119
biocapacity *see* Ecological Footprint; *see also* carrying capacity
Boulding K.E. 37
Brecht, B. 22
Brown, M.T. 68, 98
Bulte, E.H. 97
burden shifting 49, 77

Cantril ladder 115, 118
capital 23; critical 14, 103; financial 39; human 23; vs. labor 27–8, 160; natural 106–7; return 30–1; social 38; *see also* wealth
capital consumption 50n11, 60, 106; natural 42, 45, 104
capital formation 42; *see also* Environmentally adjusted net Capital Formation
capital maintenance *see* economic sustainability
carbon: account 87; damage 38, 74, 88–9;

emission 170; footprint 88, 107; price 192
carrying capacity 101–2, 182
climate change 88, 103, 170; *see also* carbon; cost 88–9, 103, 192; model 61, 103; strategies 103, 187; sustainability 99, 103
Cobb, C. 36, 164
Comprehensive Wealth Measure 37–40, 161–2, 165
corporate social responsibility 182–3

Daly, H.E. 4, 100, 182
Dasgupta, P. 12
Dasgupta, S. 55
decoupling *see* economic growth; dematerialization
deep ecology 13, 67
defensive expenditure 35, 165
degradation *see* environmental decline
dematerialization *see* economic growth, dematerialization
depletion *see* environmental decline
development 124, 125; goals *see* Millennium Development Goals and sustainable development goals; measures 128–35; strategies *see* International Development Strategies; sustainable *see* sustainable development
Duesenberry, J.S. 114

Earth Charter 196
Earth Summits 196–7

222 Index

Easterlin paradox 161, 174
eco-development *see* sustainable
development
eco-efficiency 183
ecological economics 14, 17n2, 95, 190
Ecological Footprint 57, 82–4, 177;
sustainability 96–7, 167
ecological sustainability 10, 11, 15, 95; *see
also* sustainability
economic growth 177, 194;
dematerialization 100–1, 187; green 153,
213, 215; models 38, 55, 60–1, 163;
physical 76–7; sustainable *see* economic
sustainability
economic sustainability 10–11, 16, 29, 163;
see also sustainability
eco-price 85–6, 208
ecosystems: services 84, 170; valuation 68
emergy 68, 71–2; sustainability 98–9
energy 68; balance 88
England, R.W. 61
environment-economy interaction 6,
210
environmental debt 39, 73
environmental decline 3; *see also*
environmental impact
environmental economics 13–14, 17n2,
68–9; strategies 190–2
environmental ethics 183
environmental impact 4, 54–5, 80–2,
166–7, 205; *see also* externalities
environmental Kuznets curve 26, 53–5
environmental movement 3–4
environmental pressure 75, 79; *see also*
material flow
environmental quality 213
environmental space *see* planetary
boundaries
environmental sustainability 17n1; *see also*
sustainability
environmental–economic accounting *see*
System of Environmental-Economic
Accounting
Environmentally adjusted net Capital
Formation 44, 47–8, 162
Environmentally adjusted net Domestic
Product 44, 165
equity 31–2; inter-generational 142
European Commission 10, 101
exergy 86–7, 89n1
externalities 41–2

feasibility space 59
Fischer-Kowalski, M. 75
food security 98, 167

Framework for the Development of
Environment Statistics 7
Funtowicz, S.O. 12

gaia hypothesis 13, 182
Gallup poll 115, 118
Genuine Progress Indicator 34–6, 161,
164–5
Global Competitive Index 132, 137
Global Green Economy Index 49
Global Sustainability Indicator 47
global warming *see* climate change
Global Wellbeing Index 118
globalization 194–6, 197
good life 182
Gray, R. 182
green accounting *see* System of
Environmental-Economic Accounting
green growth 215; measure 175
greenhouse gas emission 88, 103; *see also*
carbon, emission
Gross Domestic Product 36, 49n3, 164;
green 50n11; physical 80; *see also*
economic growth
Gross National Happiness Index 120
Gross National Income 135, 186

happiness 113–15; survey 115–18, 174–5
Helliwell, J. 145
Hepburn, C. 208
Hicks, J.R. 28, 29, 30
Human Development Index 128, 131–2,
147, 172; sustainability 147–8, 172–3
human welfare *see* wellbeing

Inclusive Wealth Index 38–40, 161–2,
165
income 21–2; distribution 26–8, 31, 160;
sustainability 28–9, 30, 160
indicators: aggregation 128, 136–7;
environmental 4–6; objective/subjective
119
inequality *see* wealth, distribution; income,
distribution
inequity *see* equity
information overload 4–6, 212
Intergovernmental Panel on Climate
Change (IPCC) 88, 170, 187
international development strategies 125,
154
international investment position 39
IPAT equation 4
Islam, S.M.N. 61

Koopmans, T.C. 61

labor *see* capital, human
land 69–70; cover 70; use 97–8, 167
Laurans, Y. 208
least developed countries 124
Legatum Prosperity Index 120, 132
life satisfaction *see* wellbeing
limits-to-growth model 55–7, 177
linear programming *see* feasibility space
localization 197
Lomborg 4
Lovelock, J.E. 13, 182

market instruments *see* policy, instruments
Marx, K. 27
material and energy balances 80
material consumption 77, 100, 171
material flows: accounts 47, 75–6, 90n9;
  factors 100, 101
material footprint *see* material
  consumption
Max-Neef, M. 163
Meadows, D.H. 55
Measure of Economic Welfare 34, 164
Meyer, B. 163
Millennium Development Goals 126–8,
  135, 148–52
Millennium Ecosystem Assessment 84–5
modelling 60–2, 100–1, 163, 209;
  sustainability 97
muddling through 188
Munasinghe, M. 61

Naess, A. 67
nature 12, 67–9; instrinsic value 183, 208
natural resources *see* capital, natural
Nordhaus, W.D. 12, 61

Organisation for Economic Co-operation
  and Development (OECD) 119–21

physical growth *see* economic growth,
  physical
physical input-output table 80
Piketty, T. 25–6, 27–8, 30–1
planetary boundaries 102
polarization: environmental-economic
  203–5; bridging 205–10; history 218
policy: failure 189; instruments 190–2, 213;
  integration 189
politics 210, 215
poverty 135–6, 143; alleviation 152, 186
pre-analytic vision 95
prosperity 21, 159, 214; USA 164; *see also*
  income; wealth
public-private partnership 184, 197

quality of life 114, 119

Ravetz, J.R. 12
relative income hypothesis 114
Ricardo, D. 194
Røpke, I. 95

Sachs, W. 182
Samuelson, P.A. 12
Sessions, G. 13
Social Progress Index 122n4
Solow, R. 12
steady-state economy 99–100
Stiglitz, J.E. 31, 61
Strassert, G. 80
sufficiency 182
Sunstein C.R. 184
sustainability xv, 10–12, 15–16, 17n1;
  history 216–18; science 183; weak/
  strong 13, 162, 207
sustainable development 12, 111, 126,
  141–2, 154; goals 126–8, 148, 206;
  measures 214; *see also* sustainability
Sustainable Development Index 132
System of Environmental-Economic
  Accounting 42–3, 45, 104; case study
  47–8, 105–6; ecosystem accounts 45, 86;
  hybrid accounts 45–7; physical accounts
  69–70
System of National Accounts 22, 29, 40–1;
  greened *see* System of Environmental-
  Economic Accounting

Talberth J. 35
Tamanini, J. 188–9
technological progress 61, 163
Thaler, R.H. 184

Ulgiati, S. 68, 98
United Nations 125–6; Statistics Division 4,
  7
United Nations Environment Programme
  (UNEP) 100–1, 187
USA 113, 114, 164–6

Valenciano, J. 188–9
valuation 68, 104–5, 171, 203
van Kooten, G.C. 97
von Weizsäcker, E.U. 100

wealth 21–3; distribution 23–5, 27, 28,
  160; financial 39; measures *see*
  Comprehensive Wealth Index *and*
  Inclusive Wealth Index; natural 106–7
Weisdorf, M. 35

welfare *see* wellbeing
Welfens, P.J.J. 47
wellbeing 36; measurability 119, 142; sustainability 153, 174
White, L. 3

World Bank 37–8, 135
World Commission on Environment and Development 126, 142
World Happiness Index 145
World Wide Fund for Nature 97

PGMO 05/21/2018